The Scottish Enlightenment

The Scottish Enlightenment

1730–1790

A HOTBED OF GENIUS

Edited by

David Daiches, Peter Jones
and Jean Jones

SCOTLAND
ALBA

SALTIRE
SOCIETY

First published in 1986
as *A Hotbed of Genius: The Scottish Enlightenment, 1730–1790*
by The Institute for Advanced Studies in the Humanities,
University of Edinburgh

This paperback edition published 1996
by The Saltire Society, 9 Fountain Close,
22 High Street, Edinburgh EH1 1TF

The publisher acknowledges subsidy from the Scottish Arts Council
towards the publication of this volume.

A catalogue record for this book is available from the British Library.

ISBN 0 85411 069 0

1766 portrait of David Hume by Ramsay reproduced in front cover
design by permission of the Scottish National Portrait Gallery

Designed by Iain Love Graphics Ltd.

Printed and bound by Oriental Press, U.A.E.

Preface

NOT ONLY IN Edinburgh, as it is often wrongly claimed, but in Glasgow, Aberdeen, and to a lesser extent throughout Lowland Scotland, there were great intellectual, artistic and technical advances in the eighteenth century. This period, now generally referred to as 'The Scottish Enlightenment', was at its most remarkable between about 1730 and 1790 and made Scotland briefly the cultural leader of Europe. There are many scholarly studies of the period but this book is the first illustrated introduction. A wide-ranging first chapter is followed by essays on the men whose ideas carry most force in the modern world – the philosopher David Hume, the economist Adam Smith, Joseph Black the chemist and the geologist James Hutton. The final chapter deals briefly with the influence of the Scottish Enlightenment in America.

Since the book first appeared ten years ago there have been many calls for a reprint, particularly from the universities which intend to use it as a course textbook. Conceived and edited by the Institute for Advanced Studies in the Humanities in the University of Edinburgh and first published by the Edinburgh University Press, it is now reissued by the Saltire Society.

The decision to write the book grew out of the preparations for the exhibition, 'A Hotbed of Genius', which was organised by the Institute for Advanced Studies in 1986, thanks to the National Museums of Scotland who provided the location, and the sponsors, the Royal Bank of Scotland. Both the book and the exhibition were part of a larger project on the Scottish Enlightenment organised by the Institute. Subsequently, two volumes of essays were published: *Philosophy and Science in the Scottish Enlightenment*, ed. Peter Jones (John Donald, Edinburgh, 1988), and *The Science of Man in the Scottish Enlightenment*, ed. Peter Jones (Edinburgh University Press, 1989). Two further exhibitions were also mounted in the Royal Museum of Scotland: 'Revolutions in Science: 1789–1989' which traced scientific developments since the Scottish Enlightenment, and 'Morals, Motives & Markets:

Adam Smith 1723–1790' which celebrated Smith's bicentenary. In association with the project on Adam Smith, Edinburgh University Press published *Adam Smith Reviewed*, ed. Peter Jones and Andrew Skinner, 1992.

ACKNOWLEDGMENTS. It would not have been possible to illustrate this book without the help of the institutions and individuals whose names appear on the list below and, no less, of those who have chosen to remain anonymous. Some owners also generously waived reproduction fees. We acknowledge, too, the good offices of the galleries and libraries who worked patiently on our behalf. To all of them we extend our grateful thanks: British Museum, p.48; Duke of Atholl p. 63; Duke of Buccleuch and Queensberry (from the collection at Bowhill, Selkirk), p.73; Sir John Clerk of Penicuik, pp. 115, 127, 129, 130, 131, 132; Professor Gordon Craig, p. 119; Edinburgh University Library, pp. 26, 28, 103, 105, 108, 155; Faculty of Advocates, p. 7; Hunterian Art Gallery, pp. 56, 140; Hunterian Museum, p. 101; Kirk Session of Canongate Kirk, p. 14; Kirkcaldy Museum, pp. 72, 77; Musée Condé, Chantilly, p. 53; Musée du Louvre, p. 52; National Galleries of Scotland, pp. 2, 8, 12, 13, 30, 49, 57, 58, 60, 61, 65, 68, 82, 85, 122, 126, 128, 153; National Library of Scotland, pp. 16, 136; National Maritime Museum, p. 110; National Museums of Scotland, pp. 92, 110, 112, 113; National Portrait Gallery, London, p. 78; National Portrait Gallery, Washington, p. 50; National Trust for Scotland, pp. 11, 39; Prestonfield House Hotel Ltd, p. 122; Private Scottish collections, pp. 19, 42, 46, 84, 106; Joe Rock, Esq., pp. 66, 78, 91; Earl of Rosebery, p. 61; Royal College of Physicians of Edinburgh, p. 96; Royal College of Surgeons of Edinburgh, p. 27; Royal Infirmary, Edinburgh, p. 95; Royal Medical Society, p. 102; Mrs Maxwell Scott, Abbotsford, p. 96; Mrs Olive Smith, p. 15; Royal Scottish Academy, p. 27; University of Aberdeen, pp. 64, 138; University of Edinburgh, pp. 18, 31, 35, 145; University of Strathclyde, p. 104; Victoria and Albert Museum, pp. 44, 75; American Philosophical Society, p. 148; Historical Society of Pennsylvania, pp. 142, 149.

"Edinburgh is a hotbed of genius."
SMOLLETT, *Humphrey Clinker*

Contents

Illustrations

The Scottish Enlightenment

DAVID DAICHES

THE SCOTTISH ENLIGHTENMENT is a relatively recent term for the extraordinary outburst of intellectual activity that took place in Scotland in the eighteenth century. Some historians apply the term to the whole course of Scottish culture between the Union of 1707, when Scotland lost its separate political identity by joining with England in a common British state, and the death of Sir Walter Scott in 1832, but this century and a quarter covers too much change and diversity to be usefully considered as defining a single cultural movement. The latter half of the eighteenth century, perhaps a period as limited as 1760 to 1790, is more easily defensible as the true Golden Age. It was right in the middle of that period that the printer, antiquary and biographer William Smellie recorded an observation made by 'Mr Amyat, King's Chemist, a most sensible and agreeable English gentleman' who spent a couple of years in Edinburgh: 'Here I stand at what is called the *Cross of Edinburgh*, and can, in a few minutes, take fifty men of genius and learning by the hand'.[1] Fifty men of genius, and that only in Edinburgh! Other Scottish cities, especially Glasgow and Aberdeen, produced their own geniuses, but, although the Scottish Enlightenment can be said to have begun in Glasgow with the publication of Francis Hutcheson's *Inquiry into the Originals of our Ideas of Beauty and Virtue* as early as 1724, the movement in its heyday was centred in Edinburgh.

Who were these 'men of genius and learning'? What kind of social and intellectual climate nourished them? What were their objectives? How can we account for the fact that the seed-bed of much of the later thought of the western world is to be found in this little northern country over such a short period of time? Consider just some of the names: David Hume, Britain's greatest philosopher and one of the greatest and most influential philosophers of the western world; Adam Smith, the founder of the modern science of economics and pioneer economic historian; Adam Ferguson, who is now considered to be the founder of sociology; William Robertson, who might be said to have founded modern historiography; James Hutton, the founder of modern geology; Joseph Black, the great chemist who discovered carbon dioxide and the phenomenon of latent heat; William Cullen, the great and influential teacher of clinical medicine; John Millar, whose studies in the relations between law, social structure, history and philosophy were strikingly in advance of his time; Hugh Blair, whose analysis of rhetoric and of literary language had enormous influence, especially in America, in the succeeding century; Henry Home, Lord Kames, who combined legal, philosophical and literary inquiries with practical experiments in agricultural improvement; James Burnett, Lord Monboddo, lawyer, philosopher and pioneer cultural and linguistic anthropologist; Dugald Stewart, philosopher, economist and great teacher; Thomas Reid, the influential exponent of 'common sense' philosophy; and, to turn to more practical matters, James Watt, whose contribution to the development of the steam engine every schoolboy knows; Robert and James Adam, the architects of international fame; the road-makers, bridge-builders, town planners, creators of model villages, whose work is still visible throughout Scotland and admired throughout the world. Four of these men have been particularly influential in the development of modern thought and are therefore the subject of separate chapters in this book – Hume, Smith, Black and Hutton.

Edinburgh. The High Street, by David Allan (1744-96). Built on the crest of a ridge, the High Street was the centre of social and intellectual life until the late-18th C.

Let me now return to what is perhaps the easiest of the questions I have posed: what were their objectives? In very general terms, these could be defined as improvement of man's understanding of himself, both body and mind, both the individual and the social self; and improvement of his understanding of the natural world. (The understanding of man also included a visual exploration of the human physiognomy: this is the age of the great Scottish portrait painters, including Allan Ramsay and Sir Henry Raeburn.) There was also general interest in communication, both physical (roads, bridges, canals), and intellectual and social (conversation, written essays, clubs and societies). And everywhere was the aim of improvement, not only of human knowledge but also of the environment in which men lived and worked and of the processes by which men produced what they needed. A concept of improvement meant an interest in history and change, and this interest was directed not only at history and society and to such subjects as the rise and progress of language and of the arts but also to the physical world, where change was involved at every stage, whether in the processes defined by chemistry and physics or the much slower processes studied by geology. Francis Bacon in an earlier age had defined the aim of knowledge as 'the relief of man's estate', and this well defines the aims of the men of the Scottish Enlightenment, who in addition to (and often in conjunction with) their interest in what Hume called 'the science of man', were also interested in the improvement of man's environment.

There were some paradoxes inherent in this pattern of aims and beliefs, such as the belief held by some (though far from all) of them in the value of the primitive held together with a belief in progress. And there were of course differences in emphasis to be found among different thinkers, some more interested in the physical sciences than

Perth. Smeaton's bridge (1765-72) across the Tay. Bridge-building was encouraged by government policies to improve transport and trade in the more populous parts of the Highlands.

Thurso. Over 100 planned towns and villages were built in Scotland during the later 18th and early 19th centuries. Sir John Sinclair's plan for Thurso was particularly ambitious.

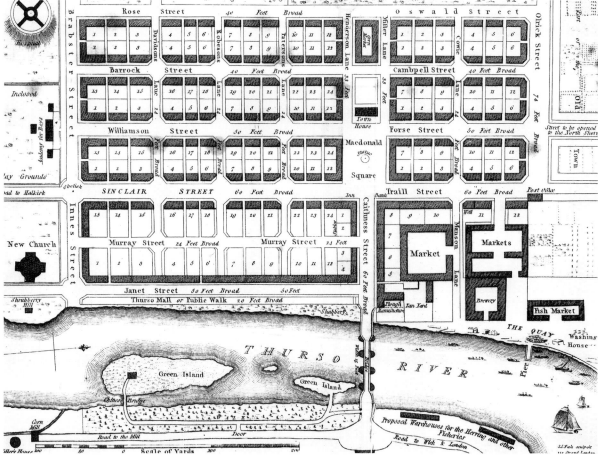

Encyclopaedia Britannica, *frontispiece to 3rd ed., 1788. The engraving exemplifies the ideals and inspiration of the Scottish Enlightenment, with arts, science and technology, shown in a classical setting.*

others, some more interested in the lessons of the past, some more sympathetic than others to religion (of the 'moderate' variety). But most of the men of the Scottish Enlightenment shared a common optimism about the ability of eighteenth-century man to bring new and helpful insights into all aspects of the human condition. Most of them knew each other; many were close friends; some were related by marriage. All were stimulated by enormous *curiosity* and a determination to find new answers to old questions. How did this all happen?

One explanation of the Scottish Enlightenment sees it as a belated consequence of the Union of 1707, and this explanation itself has been put forward in different ways. It has been said that frustrated national pride, denied adequate political expression now that Scotland was part of Great Britain, eventually manifested itself in a determination that North Britain (as many unionists called Scotland) should show the world that it was in the van of intellectual and technological progress. It has been argued that the liberalising of religious attitudes resulting from the establishment of the Church of Scotland at the Glorious Revolution of 1689 made for freer development of ideas. Correlations have been made between economic progress and intellectual advance (but which came first has been argued about). One recent scholar has argued at length that the thought of some of the leading figures of the Scottish Enlightenment can be explained by the way in which their social experiences moved them from the 'Calvinist dependency and particularism' which they imbibed in the early part of their lives to 'a commitment to independence and universalism'. But the trend of most recent scholarship is to look further back, into the seventeenth century, to see the roots of the movement and to see the Scottish Enlightenment as a natural development of an earlier phase of Scottish culture.

Precursors

Mathematics, medicine and law are three areas in which we find remarkable Scottish activity in the latter part of the seventeenth century. Continuity between this activity and the Scottish Enlightenment of the next century can be seen in a variety of ways. For example, the book by William Smellie which is quoted at the beginning of this essay was entitled *Literary and Characteristic Lives of Gregory, Kames, Hume and Smith*. The Gregory here was Dr John Gregory, Professor of the Practice of Physic at Edinburgh from 1766 until his death in 1773 and a member of one of the most remarkable academic

families of Scotland. His grandfather was James Gregory (1638-1675), friend of Newton and inventor of the reflecting telescope, first Professor of Mathematics at Edinburgh University. His father Dr James Gregory was Professor of Medicine at King's College, Aberdeen, and was succeeded in that position first by his older brother and then by John himself. John was in turn succeeded in his medical chair at Edinburgh by his son James. John's grandfather's brother David (1661–1708), also a friend and a protégé of Newton, was a distinguished astronomer who from 1683 to 1691 was Professor of Mathematics at Edinburgh, where he introduced Newton's theories long before they were taught in England, before becoming Savilian Professor of Astronomy at Oxford. Other members of this extraordinary family include David Gregory, Professor of Mathematics at St Andrews, whose death in 1765 produced one of the first Scots poems by Robert Fergusson, then a student there. Fergusson, in the half-comic tone traditional in this type of Scottish elegy (or mock-elegy), paid tribute to the professor's knowledge of Newton's theory of fluxions (defined by the mathematician Charles Hutton as 'the rate or proportion at which a flowing or varying quantity increases its magnitude').

> He could, by Euclid, prove lang sine
> A ganging point compos'd a line; . . .[2]

It was the Scottish mathematician Colin MacLaurin (1696–1746) who first sought to rebut objections to Newton's theory of fluxions by demonstrating that it could be deduced from the principles of the ancient geometricians (*A Treatise of Fluxions*, 1742); MacLaurin also wrote *An Account of Sir Isaac Newton's Philosophy* (1748).

The beginning of Edinburgh's pre-eminence in medicine can be traced to the work of Sir Robert Sibbald (1641–1722), who studied at Leyden and Paris and in 1662 took his doctorate of medicine at Angers. Sibbald was a polymath of great influence, who in 1667, together with Dr Andrew Balfour, founded the Edinburgh 'physic garden' which eventually became the Royal Botanic Garden, and was jointly responsible for the foundation of the Royal College of Physicians in Edinburgh in 1681. In 1685 Edinburgh Town Council appointed Sibbald Professor of Physic at the University (or the Town's College, as it was then more commonly called) and shortly afterwards appointed two other fellows of the Royal College of Physicians, James Halket and Archibald Pitcairne, to share the post of Professor of Medicine. Pitcairne (1652–1713) was, like Sibbald, a polymath and a most remarkable man. He wrote Latin poetry, including a famous

The North Front of the Royal Infirmary facing the City of Edinburgh

epitaph on Graham of Claverhouse after his death in the victory at the battle of Killiecrankie in 1689. Bred a Scottish Episcopalian with Jacobite leanings, Pitcairne became something very like a freethinker, attacking Presbyterian orthodoxy in the anonymous satirical comedy *The Assembly* (which is almost certainly his). As well as being a Latinist, a poet and one of the most famous physicians of his day, Pitcairne was also a mathematician, having studied mathematics at Edinburgh under David Gregory, and an eloquent proponent of scientific method. His kind of brilliance was able to flourish in the atmosphere encouraged by the foundation of the Royal Society at the Restoration, for Charles II's insistence on religious conformity, which resulted in the persecution of Covenanters, was not inconsistent with the free development of ideas where specific matters of church and state were not involved, and the atmosphere which followed the Glorious Revolution of 1689 did not threaten such development in spite of some unhappy examples of religious intolerance in the last years of the century. In any case, as we shall see, the Jacobite Episcopalian tradition to which Pitcairne belonged had its own sources of cultural strength.

Many of the literati (as they liked to call themselves) of the Scottish Enlightenment were lawyers or were trained in the law. The Union of 1707 left Scotland its own legal system, and henceforth the law in Scotland became identified with Scottish national feeling, as well as with culture and intellectual progress in the most general sense. The capacity of Scots law to sustain such a role was in considerable measure the consequence of the great advance made in the late seventeenth century in formulating its philosophy and principles. The setting of a study of the legal system of Scotland in a context of philosophical inquiry into the fundamental principles of law and their relation to morality, social structure and customs, politics and economics, first achieved by Viscount Stair's *Institutions of the Law of Scotland*, published in 1681 and in an improved edition in 1689, proved an important intellectual force in the Scottish Enlightenment right through the next century. Sir George Mackenzie's work with the same title as Stair's, published in 1684, and later works by Lord Bankton (1751–53), John Erskine (1754), Lord Kames (1760) and Baron David Hume (nephew of the philosopher and Professor of Scots Law at Edinburgh University) developed this tradition. The interaction between law, philosophy, political economy and history stimulated not only whole areas of Enlightenment thought but also helped to develop the historical novel. Walter Scott recalled how Baron Hume's lectures had stimulated his ideas on the relationship between law, history and society:

> I copied over his lectures twice with my own hand, from notes taken in the class, and when I have occasion to consult them, I can never sufficiently admire the penetration and clearness of conception which were necessary to the arrangement of the fabric of law, formed originally under the strictest influence of feudal principles, and innovated, altered, and broken in upon by the changes of times, of habits, and of manners, until it resembles some ancient castle, partly entire, partly ruinous, partly delapidated, patched and altered by a thousand additions and combinations, yet still exhibiting, with the marks of its antiquity, symptoms of the skill and wisdom of its founders, and capable of being analyzed and made the subject of a methodical plan by an architect who can understand the various styles of the different ages in which it was subjected to alteration. Such an architect has Mr Hume been to the law of Scotland, neither wandering into fanciful and abstruse disquisitions, which are the more proper subject of the antiquary, nor satisfied with presenting to his pupils a dry, undigested detail of the laws in their present state, but combining the past state of our legal enactments with the present, and tracing clearly and judiciously the changes which took place, and the causes which led to them.[3]

'The changes which took place, and the causes which led to them': this identifies an important theme in the Waverley Novels, especially those set in Scotland in the generations immediately preced-

ing Scott's own. It is interesting that this theme should be associated with Scottish law studies as they developed from the 1680s. The movement from Stair's *Institutions* to Scott's novels runs right through the Scottish Enlightenment.

'The Historical Age'

We have mentioned change and history as being important preoccupations of the eighteenth-century Scottish literati. An important reason for this is the events in Scottish history from at least 1603 to 1707 that forced so many Scotsmen to ponder on the changes in which they had become involved. When James VI of Scotland inherited the throne of England in 1603 to become also James I of England, Scotland lost its Court (the centre of cultural patronage) and lost also its significance as a prime centre of her King's attention; for after 1603 the King was more concerned with his larger and richer southern kingdom than with his poorer and smaller northern one. The political and religious turmoil of the seventeenth century raised all sorts of questions about Scotland's position, identity, culture and (most of all) religion, as well as about Scotland's relation to England. Under Cromwell, Scotland was forced into a Commonwealth which included the whole of the British Isles, but recovered her status as an independent kingdom at the Restoration of 1660. However, there remained the paradox, inheritance of the Union of the Crowns in 1603, of

two countries with a single King. Charles II and his brother James VII governed Scotland in their own interests through Royal Commissioners. The Scots Parliament had its agenda and many of its decisions arranged in advance by a committee known as the Lords of the Articles. Yet in the last years of its life, before the Scots Parliament voted for its own abolition to produce the Union of 1707, the Lords of the Articles were removed and Parliament exhibited a vigour and independence it had not done for a long time. The Union went through, however, under all kinds of pressure from English interests, which looked on a separate Scottish political entity as a threat to English security – especially after the Glorious Revolution of 1689, with the banishment of James VII and the recurring possibility that Scottish national feeling might join with French military force (and France was then at war with England) to restore the exiled Stuarts and threaten England through her 'back door' in Scotland.

There were Scottish supporters of the Union, too, who looked forward to peaceful economic progress in co-operation with England and to a Britain in which not only the old feuds between England and

Scotland would be abolished but even the old names of 'England' and 'Scotland' would give way to 'Britain', with Scotland becoming North Britain and England South Britain. In the century and more after 1707 many Scotsmen did indeed call Scotland North Britain, and though for a short time a few Englishmen did sometimes use the term South Britain, the term did not catch on and was soon dropped. But Britain remained an ideal in the mind and imagination of many progressive Scotsmen of the eighteenth century; it was a Scotsman, the poet James Thomson, who wrote 'Rule, Britannia!' and another Scotsman, William Smellie, who founded the *Encyclopaedia Britannica*.

All this meant that Scots in the eighteenth century were forced by events to consider what history had done to them. 'This is the historical age and we are the historical people'.[4] David Hume exclaimed proudly. The literati talked, wrote and argued continually about the meanings of their national history. Was Mary Queen of Scots good or bad? Was the Union of 1707 good or bad? What was the meaning of the Jacobite rising of 1745? What was the nature of the Highland culture to their north

Sir John Clerk's journal (1724) contains the best contemporary sketch sections of Hadrian's Wall, Ditch, and Vallum (detail).

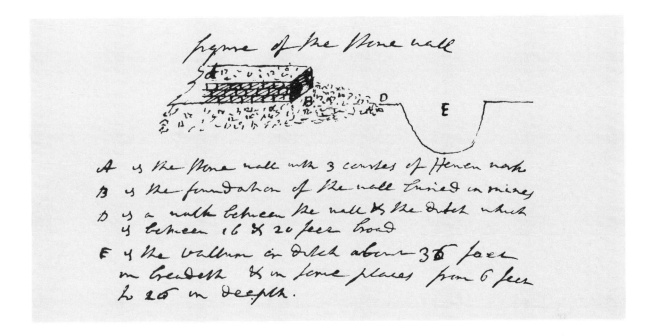

and how did this relate to their own? Was the alleged epic poetry of Ossian, the old Gaelic bard that James Macpherson claimed to have translated, genuine, and if so what did it tell us of an earlier stage of Scottish culture and society? What was the nature of the language we now know as Scots or Lowland Scots, and how did it relate to the standard English of the time? What language should Scotsmen use *now*? Above all, what had *change* effected in Scottish life and society and how might it be expected to operate in the future? These questions forced their way into philosophical, historical, sociological and legal discussions. 'The institutions of men are . . . likely to have their end as well as their beginning: but their duration is not fixed to any limited period', wrote Adam Ferguson in the last section of the *Essay on the History of Civil Society* (significantly entitled 'Progress and Termination of Despotism').

Rise, progress, development, change – these represent concepts found again and again in the writers of the Scottish Enlightenment. Eighteenth-century Scotland was in fact obsessed by history. Beside the achievement in mathematics and medicine of the Gregory family we might set the historical achievements of the Tytler family: William Tytler, who defended Queen Mary and discovered *The King's Quair* by James I; his son, Alexander Fraser Tytler, Lord Woodhouselee, Professor of Universal History (no less) at Edinburgh University and author of *Elements of General History* and other historical works; and *his* son, Patrick Fraser

Tytler, friend of Sir Walter Scott, whose many historical works include his *History of Scotland*. And of course there were the influential historical works of David Hume, William Robertson and many others of the period.

As well as the study of modern history the study of antiquities was pursued with increasing earnestness. It began in the late seventeenth century with Sibbald, whose reputation as an antiquary and as a geographer was as great as his reputation as a physician. Roman antiquities were particularly a focus of attention since most Scottish gentlemen had some form of classical education and their attitude to Roman remains was consequently one of veneration and passionate curiosity.

The most prominent antiquary of the first half of the century was Sir John Clerk of Penicuik, and in the second David Stewart Erskine, 11th Earl of Buchan. Their work is difficult to illustrate because in both cases their influence as patrons, advisers and connoisseurs was much greater than their personal achievements. Clerk, besides being a Baron of the Exchequer and a knowledgeable patron of both the arts and sciences, amassed a great deal of information about archaeological and historical sites in Scotland and stressed the need for conservation and the need for material to be available to scholars. Buchan founded the Society of Antiquaries of Scotland, on the model of the Society of Antiquaries in London, and this society still flourishes today. A prolific writer and an authority who maintained a fruitful correspondence with the

> *St. Andrews Day, Sir, is a Day propitious to the hardy Scot, and if the Flower of this Country is to be tarnished by a Senatus Academicus on such a Day, I shall renounce it as my Country & plead the Proverb that being born in a Stable does not make a man a Horse. And certainly Sir, if I were a Horse I would not consent to be governed by a Mule.*
>
> *I now dismiss the Foolish Principal of the University of Edinburgh, Historiographer Royal, Minister of the Gray Friars & Chaplain to the best of Princes.*

leading antiquaries in England, Buchan's eccentricities obscured his merits in his own day and have tended to do so ever since.

The enthusiasm which sustained the study of Roman antiquities at home also carried men away on the Grand Tour, with Rome as the ultimate goal. A journey which usually involved a visit to the major cities on the Continent and an extended stay in Italy, the Grand Tour often occupied a couple of years or more and was an eighteenth-century phenomenon. Young English aristocrats set off in search of culture and polish, armed with introductions to the best families and often accompanied by a suitably staid and scholarly tutor. The Scots responded to this English innovation with fervour. Though in the first half of the century it was largely only the aristocrats who could afford to undertake the journey, later on the professional and middle classes set out in increasing numbers. Expatriate Scots in Rome and to a lesser extent in other parts of Italy, set themselves up as lecturers and guides, and as dealers in paintings and antiquities. The adulation of Rome had a profound effect on architecture and the decorative arts, and the neoclassical style came to dominate building in Britain and the Continent and was even found as far away as America. Scots architects had enormous success in England as well as at home. In the first half of the century the most imitated house was

Colin Campbell's Palladian mansion at Wanstead. In the second half of the century Robert Adam, fresh from four years' study in Italy, became the most celebrated architect in Britain. With the help of his brother John, he produced more comprehensive designs than any other architect before him, lavishing as much care on the interior as the exerior. The classical and renaissance motifs that he adapted as decorative themes on ceilings, panelled walls, carpets and other furnishings have had an even more enduring influence than his architectural designs and are not without their imitators today.

The work of Adam and his fellow architects in the neoclassical style is so much the most conspicuous surviving feature of the Scottish Enlightenment – particularly in Edinburgh where the New Town is a lasting memorial – that it is often the only aspect of the period that people know about. Much has been written on the subject and further description here is unnecessary. Less heralded, perhaps, are the buildings Adam designed at the end of his life when he turned away from the order and clarity of classical forms to romantic castellated exteriors. Nearly all his buildings in this style are in Scotland rather than England, the most magnificent being Culzean.

As in architecture, the Scottish Enlightenment was the great age of painting, particularly portrait

Culzean Castle, Ayrshire, allowed Robert Adam, in the 1780s, to 'indulge to the utmost his romantic and fruitful genius' (Clerk of Eldin).

''Sightseers passing Vesuvius'' from Sir Wm. Hamilton's Campi Phlegraei (1776). Natural phenomena, too, excited enthusiasm on the Grand Tour.

"Agrippina landing with the ashes of Germanicus", by Alexander Runciman (1736-85), illustrates the interest in history and classical subjects reflected in the art of the period.

painting which emphasised naturalness, liveliness, individuality and a humane engagement with personality. Allan Ramsay the Younger (son of Allan Ramsay the poet) is now recognised as the greatest Scottish portrait painter of the century. Ramsay was a founder of the Select Society and painted many of its members, including David Hume. At the end of the century Sir Henry Raeburn developed Ramsay's natural and unidealised method of portrait painting. Ramsay's contemporary Gavin Hamilton spent much of his life in Rome, where he developed an epic style based on his conception of Homer's *Iliad*, thus introducing into Scottish painting a literary element that was to be developed later.

Alexander Runciman and David Allan worked for a while with Hamilton in Rome. Runciman applied Hamilton's concept of epic painting to Ossianic themes, introducing Scottish landscapes as a lyrical background to his characters. Runciman's pupils David More and Alexander Nasmyth developed his concept of Scottish landscape, Nasmyth bring-

ing new romantic and historical feeling into his landscapes, seen in his illustrations to Sir Walter Scott's *Border Antiquities* and in his views of Scottish country seats. Nasmyth thus bridges the Enlightenment and the Romantic Movement.

Moderatism

Before the various currents of ideas and interests that have been outlined could flow into the movement we now call the Scottish Enlightenment, there had to be a moderating of the fierce theological controversies which had for so long characterised so much of Scottish thought. This did not happen quickly or easily. The Act of Union of 1707 left Scotland its own established Presbyterian Church, but the strains of representing a nation ecclesiastically proved sometimes too great, as the numerous splits in the Church through the century indicate. Yet a movement towards a more humane and tolerant religious attitude is clearly discernible, at least from the time of the appointment of William Carstares (King William's chief adviser on Scottish

"A sleepy congregation", by John Kay. The Kirk nevertheless exercised significant control over the lives of its members.

THE SCOTTISH ENLIGHTENMENT · 13

affairs) as Principal of Edinburgh University in 1703, when he became also leader of the Church of Scotland. A subtle politician, Carstares both bowed to popular extremist opinion and found many indirect ways of guiding it. Without yielding an inch in his stern religious convictions, he was able to ensure that the Scottish Church, as it moved from the period of the Glorious Revolution to that of the Union, contained within itself the possibility of adapting to new circumstances.

A much bigger step in the direction of moderating extremist opinion and intolerance in the Church of Scotland was marked by the appointment of the humane moralist, William Leechman, to the Chair of Divinity at Glasgow in 1743, and unsuccessful attempts to prosecute him for his views on prayer. But the process is most of all evident in the careers of the two William Wisharts, father and son, both of whom held office as Principal of Edinburgh University. The elder Wishart was five times Moderator of the General Assembly, and gave offence to the unco guid by his genial humanity, while the younger was in the habit of using the prayer: 'Lord rebuke and bear down a spirit of imposition and persecution, not only in Papists, but in Christians of whatever denomination'.

As the eighteenth century progressed, the emergence of Moderatism as a religious position became more marked: there was no general agreement among those who considered themselves Moderates on detailed theological matters – they left these things to the 'High Flyers', or committed Calvinists – and they tended to emphasise benevolence and morality rather than discuss election and predestination and other Calvinist doctrines. Sometimes they spoke like Deists rather than Christians, though they certainly considered themselves Christians. Hugh Blair, literary critic as well as writer of sermons, who became the first Professor of Rhetoric and Belles Lettres at Edinburgh University in 1762, was a minister of the Church of Scotland and officiated at the High Kirk of St Giles; Adam Ferguson, philosopher, historian and sociologist, was also a Church of Scotland minister and served as chaplain of the Black Watch before turning to the academic profession; William Robertson, another Church of Scotland minister and leader of the Moderates, had a career in the Church before he turned to historiography and became Principal of Edinburgh University. These and many others, who were both clergymen and 'literati', were on familiar terms with non-religious thinkers and sceptics such as Hume and Adam Smith and formed part of a close-knit circle of philosophers, historians, moralists and scientists. What Richard

Sher has called 'the Moderate literati of Edinburgh' also had close links of kinship with each other, their careers illustrating, in Sher's words, 'the role of kinship and connection in Scottish ecclesiastical and academic politics during the age of the Scottish Enlightenment'.[5]

Hugh Blair's volumes of sermons were enormously popular, and they spoke for a humane Christianity with emphasis on the good heart and good works in a way that appealed to those philosophers of the Enlightenment who derived their moral ideas in the first instance from Francis Hutcheson's *Inquiry into the Original of our Ideas of Beauty and Virtue*, with its emphasis on man's innate Moral Sense which led to the instinctive approval of benevolence and disapproval of its opposite. Blair associated such a sense with God's character and God's purpose, as the philosophers as a rule did not, but the moral implications were the same. 'For what purpose,' asked Blair in one of his sermons, 'did God place thee in this world, in the midst of human society, but that as a man among men thou mightest cultivate humanity; that each in his place might contribute to the general welfare; that as a spouse, a brother, a son, or a friend, thou mightest act thy part with an upright and a tender heart; and thus aspire to resemble Him who ever consults the good of his creatures,

Hugh Blair (1718-1800) by Raeburn. Blair's Edinburgh Chair of Rhetoric and Belles Lettres was the first university chair of modern literature in the English-speaking world.

and whose *tender mercies are over all his works.*'[6] Hume would not have accepted this view of God's role, but he would have thoroughly agreed with its practical consequences.

Blair's sermons also show a belief in order and social hierarchy that he shared with most of the literati, who, for all their belief in progress and 'improvement', were on the whole politically conservative. 'True religion,' wrote Blair, 'introduced the idea of regular subjection, by accustoming mankind to the awe of superiour power in the Deity, joined with the veneration of superiour wisdom and goodness. . . . The doctrine of Christianity is most adverse to all tyranny and oppression, but highly favourable to the interests of good government among men. It represses the spirit of licentiousness and sedition. It inculcates the duty of subordination to lawful superiours.'[7] It is one of the paradoxes of eighteenth-century Scottish thought that humane, enlightened and progressive thinkers tended to be politically conservative while the opposing Calvinists, with their hell-fire sermons and stern belief in election and predestination, were socially much more radical. If the emergence of Moderatism helped to produce an intellectual climate in which the Scottish Enlightenment could flourish, it also, by its emphasis on order and social hierarchy (so clearly seen in the great controversy about church patronage – whether ministers should be appointed by lay 'superiors' or by the free choice of the congregation concerned – which eventually split the Church of Scotland into two), brought about its eventual decline. For Moderatism had nothing to offer in an age threatened by the French Revolution but what Lord Cockburn was to call 'a passive devotion to the gentry'. The great age of the Scottish Enlightenment could not cope with the new social and political ideas that emerged at the end of the century. Its optimistic belief in human benevolence and in the calm progress of an ordered society seemed to many to be irrelevant after 1789.

Scottish or British?

Whatever happened to Moderatism by the end of the eighteenth century, there can be no doubt that its earlier emergence helped to make the Scottish Enlightenment possible or that many of the Moderates were themselves active in the movement. That Scottish intellectual culture would move in this direction after the achievements of the late seventeenth century in medicine, mathematics and law, aided by the rise of Moderatism in religion, may seem a natural expectation to us looking back now, but in fact there were other directions in which at one time it seemed it might go. One was in the direction of a native Scottish humanism, a direction indicated by the life and work of Thomas Ruddiman.

Ruddiman was born in Aberdeenshire in 1674 and as a young man was discovered by Dr Archibald Pitcairne who encouraged him to settle in Edinburgh. Aberdeen and the north-east of Scotland in general were a centre of Episcopalian and Jacobite feeling, seeing the former as providing continuity with the traditions of an earlier Scotland which Calvinism broke with so abruptly and the latter as embodying a form of Scottish cultural nationalism. In reaction to the Union of 1707, the kind of nationalism represented by Ruddiman looked to the international language of Latin as Scotland's means of making its culture known throughout Europe and to the Scots language as a means of asserting Scotland's identity. Ruddiman worked with the printer and bookseller Robert Freebairn, and with another patriotic Edinburgh printer James Watson, in his career as editor and publisher of books calculated to restore Scotland's pride in her native traditions. He was also a Latin scholar, whose *Rudiments of the Latin Tongue* (1714) remained a standard work for generations and whose edition (published by Freebairn) of Gavin Douglas's translation of the *Aeneid*, that classic of

Gavin Douglas' translation of Virgil's Aeneid; *title-page of Thomas Ruddiman's edition of 1710.*

Fergusson, Poems. *Title-page of Ruddiman's edition of 1773. Edinburgh, Thistle Court, in the vernacular classical tradition.*

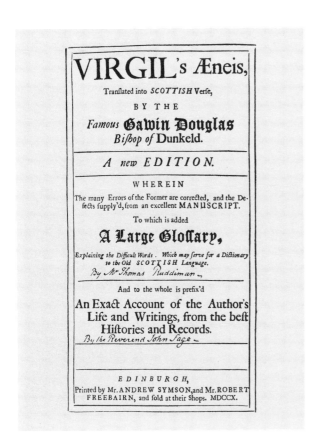

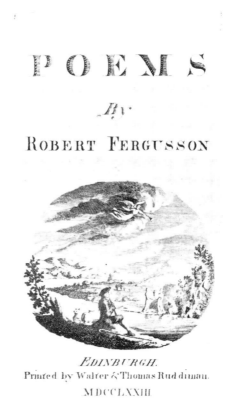

late Middle Scots poetry, is a remarkable piece of editing, with a glossary of Scots words that laid the foundation for Scots lexicography. Ruddiman also edited for Freebairn the *Opera Omnia* of the great sixteenth-century Scots humanist poet and scholar George Buchanan (1715), produced a collection of *Epistolae Regum Scotorum* (1722) and edited, again for Freebairn, selected Latin poems of Pitcairne. Ruddiman preceded David Hume as Keeper of the Advocates' Library, founded by Sir George Mac-Kenzie in 1689 (and whose great collections were the nucleus round which the National Library of Scotland was later built). He inspired a movement of Scottish patriotic publishing which at one time looked as though it would represent a major re-action to the Union. Ruddiman's vernacular humanism, as it may be called, was however not really a serious option for Scotland: it was alto-gether too late in the day for a Scoto-Latin culture. But its influence can be seen, however indirectly, in the Scots poetry of Robert Fergusson (1750–74) and perhaps in the vernacular classical architecture of some Edinburgh building of the 1760s (George Square, for example) as compared with the more international classical style of Edinburgh's New Town, so much, as we shall see, a symbol of the ideals of the Scottish Enlightenment.

The men of the Scottish Enlightenment did not operate in Scots or in Latin, but in English. Some of the literati praised the 'richness, energy and har-mony' of vernacular Scots which, like Sir John Clerk of Penicuik, they saw as 'genuine Saxon'; some, like Hugh Blair and Henry Mackenzie, wel-

Mrs Siddons (1755-1831) in 'Douglas', 1785. ''The rage for seeing her was so great that one day there were 2577 applications for 630 places.''

John Home, Douglas. *An Edinburgh playbill of 1756.*

comed its use in pastoral poetry only, and some, like the Aberdeen poet and philosopher James Beattie, praised local vernacular poetry (Alexander Ross's *Helenore*). But even though Beattie wrote a vernacular poem in praise of *Helenore* he also published a list of *Scotticisms* to be avoided by educated Scots in their prose writing. In general, the literati strove hard to eliminate Scots from their own written work. 'Is it not strange,' wrote David Hume to Gilbert Elliot of Minto on 2 July 1757, 'that, at a time when we have lost our Princes, our Parliaments, our independent Government, even the presence of our chief Nobility, are unhappy, in our accent & Pronunciation, speak a very corrupt Dialect of the Tongue which we make use of; is it not strange, I say, that, in these Circumstances, we shou'd really be the People most distinguish'd for Literature in Europe?'[8] Ruddiman would have known better than to stigmatise Scots as 'a very corrupt dialect' of English. Yet Hume would not have yielded to Ruddiman in proud Scottish patriotism. Even though Hume strove hard to eliminate from his written work those 'Scotticisms' which he used readily in speech, even though he accepted the Union and saw Scotland as part of a united Britain, he was jealous of Scotland's reputation and did all he could to promote such indifferent Scottish poets as Professor William Wilkie, whom he hailed as the Scottish Homer.

Hume's over-valuation of Wilkie as a poet, like the over-valuation by the literati of John Home's play *Douglas* (the Scottish Shakespeare) shows the failure of the Scottish Enlightenment to cope adequately with works of the poetic imagination. Philosophy, history, law, the sciences, did not involve, as ideally poetry does, intimate engagement with a language in which passion and reason work together in subtle interplay and the spontaneous language of daily speech interacts with more formal elements to produce an idiom in which the whole man – 'the whole passionate, reasoning self' as Yeats was to call it – can speak. The Scottish poets who did achieve this in the eighteenth century were few and far between; the greatest, Robert Burns, walked a tightrope between the genteel world of the Edinburgh literati and the realistic vitality of peasant life and sometimes played up almost cynically to the expectations which the theorists of the Edinburgh Enlightenment had of a peasant poet (or, as Henry Mackenzie called him, a 'heaven-taught ploughman'). But the reception of Burns by the literati, like their enthusiasm for Macpherson's *Ossian*, is a matter worthy of separate treatment (see p.20 below).

The relation between the British and the Scottish

SECOND NIGHT.

THEATRE CANONGATE,

THIS EVENING,

Being 15th DECEMBER 1756,

A CONCERT OF MUSIC.

After which will be presented (*gratis*)

The NEW TRAGEDY

DOUGLAS.

Taken from an Ancient *SCOTS STORY*,

A N D

Writ by a GENTLEMAN of SCOTLAND.

The Principal PARTS to be performed

By Mr. D I G G E S;

Mr. L O V E.

Mr H E Y M A N,

Mr Y O U N G E R,

Mrs. H O P K I N S,

And Mrs. W A R D.

With New *DRESSES* and *DECORATIONS.*

A PROLOGUE to be spoke

By Mr. D I G G E S,

And an EPILOGUE to be spoke

By Mrs. H O P K I N S.

Between the ACTS will be performed Select Pieces of

OLD *SCOTS* M U S I C K.

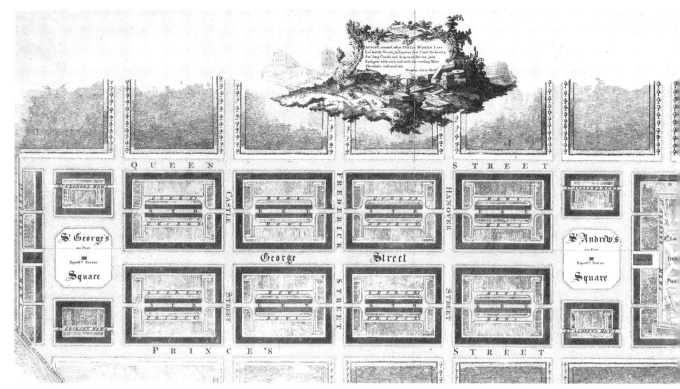

dimensions in the Scottish Enlightenment is not always easy to define, because of the combination of pride in the Scottish achievement and defensiveness about the Scots language that is so well illustrated in Hume's case. The interests of the literati were international and they saw their achievements as simultaneously helping their country (in material matters such as economic development and better communications as well as in more profound knowledge about man and nature) and assisting human progress. The New Town of Edinburgh, planned to achieve in architecture and in the use of space the ideals of order, elegance, rationality, progress and proper social relationships represented by the Scottish Enlightenment, was built in what might be called an international classical style. At the same time its aim was both Scottish and British. When James Craig won the gold medal presented in 1767 by the Town Council of Edinburgh 'as a reward for his merit for having designed the best plan of the New Town', he put at the head of his plan some lines from a poem by his uncle, James Thomson, which conclude a section of Thomson's poem *Liberty*:

August, around, what Public Works I see!
Lo! stately Street, lo! Squares that court the breeze!
See long Canals and deepened Rivers join
Each part with each, and with the circling Main
The whole enlivened Isle.

These lines are spoken, in Thomson's poem, by the Goddess of Liberty, who, in the words of the poet's own synopsis, 'points out the chief virtues which are necessary to maintain her establishment there [i.e. in Great Britain]. Recommends as its last ornament and finishing, Sciences, Fine Arts, and Public Works. . . . The whole concludes with a Prospect of Future Times, given by the Goddess of Liberty: this described by the Author, as it passes in vision before him.' It is from this final vision that the lines quoted by Craig are taken. They sum up very effectively the practical implications of the Scottish Enlightenment: human progress was to be encouraged by an appropriate environment, human ingenuity was to be called upon to build that environment, communication was to put everyone in touch with every one else, and liveliness of mind was an essential condition for all this.

Sense and Sensibility

It is characteristic of an important aspect of the Scottish Enlightenment that its greatest philosopher and perhaps the key figure in the whole movement, David Hume, was at the same time 'le bon David', a kindly, sociable man who loved good conversation and the atmosphere of clubs and parties, and a rigorous thinker who propounded startling new ideas. These ideas (like those of our other three principal characters, Smith, Black and Hutton) are discussed in a separate chapter. Here it is necessary only to outline them in order to set them in the general context of the Scottish Enlightenment. Hume's dual interest in human nature and in our knowledge of the external world was really a single interest in the way the human mind forms judgements and acquires knowledge. A philosopher who bases so much on his analysis of human nature, and whose epistemology is based on what he called the passions ('reason is, and ought only to be, the slave of the passions', he wrote with deliberate paradox) is bound to be interested in how human beings have actually behaved, and Hume's turn to the writing of history seems a natural development from his philosophical ideas. History provides indispensable data for the student of the 'science of man'. Such history should be balanced and impartial, not written in the partisan spirit in which so much history had been written, and Hume is indeed a pioneer in the writing of balanced history which tries to explain developments without taking a stand on party issues. Moral philosophy and history are both products of an interest in the science of man.

The moral philosophy of the men of the Scottish Enlightenment, from Hutcheson to Adam Smith, took on the whole an optimistic view of human nature and placed great emphasis on man's innate quality of sympathy and benevolence. 'All mankind,' wrote Hume in his *Enquiry concerning the Principles of Morals* (1751), 'so far resemble the good principle that, where interest or revenge or envy perverts not our disposition, we are always inclined, from our natural philanthropy, to give the preference to the happiness of society, and consequently to virtue above its opposite. Absolute, unprovoked, disinterested malice has never perhaps place in any human breast.'[9] Adam Smith, whose *Theory of Moral Sentiments* appeared in 1759, agreed with both Hutcheson (whose pupil he had been in Glasgow) and Hume in basing his moral philosophy on the idea of sympathy: his opening sentence proclaims this: 'How selfish soever man may be supposed, there are evidently some principles in his nature, which interest him in the fortune of others, and render their happiness necessary to him though he derives nothing from it except the pleasure of seeing it.' Hume developed Hutcheson's theory of the 'moral sense' by distinguishing natural virtue (such as benevolence) from artificial virtue (such as justice) and bringing in the concept of utility. Smith, building on Hume as well as Hutcheson, adds his own concept of the imagined

impartial spectator acting in the role traditionally ascribed to conscience. Subsequent chapters render further details here unnecessary. Suffice it to say that for both Hume and Smith the principles of moral philosophy could be worked out by self-knowledge, by an understanding of the human 'passions', and by seeing individual man and social man as bound up in continuous mutual interrelation.

Like so many writers of the Scottish Enlightenment, Adam Smith was interested in history, in how things changed, in how things came about, and much of his argument in *The Wealth of Nations*, that classic pioneer work of political economy, is drawn from history. Among the lectures he gave at Edinburgh between 1748 and 1751 were a set on Rhetoric and Belles Lettres and these included a discussion 'of the origin and progress of language' which illustrates very well the mode of historical writing which Dugald Stewart called 'conjectural history', a mode much practised by the Scottish writers of that time. 'Two savages who met together and took up their dwelling in the same place would very soon endeavour to get signs to denote these objects which most frequently occurred and with which they were most concerned. The cave they lodged in, the tree from whence they got their food, or the fountain from whence they drank would all soon be distinguished by particular names, as they would have frequent occasion to make their thoughts about them known to one another, and would by mutual consent agree on

Dugald Stewart (1753-1828) and family, by Alexander Nasmyth.

certain signs whereby this might be accomplished. Afterwards when they met with other trees, caves, and fountains, concerning which they would have occasion to converse, they would naturally give the same name to them as they had before given to other objects of the same kind.'[10] Smith later expanded this lecture in the appendix to the third edition of his *Theory of Moral Sentiments* (1767) under the title *Considerations concerning the First Formation of Languages*.

James Burnett, Lord Monboddo, the Kincardine-shire-born Lord of Session known for his liveliness and eccentricity, his 'learned suppers', his veneration of the ancient Greeks, his support of the theatre, and in general for the part he played in the social and intellectual life of the literati, published his massive six-volume work *Of the Origin and Progress of Language* between 1773 and 1792. Monboddo argues that language is not natural to man but is the result of acquired habit. There are not only 'solitary savages' but also 'whole nations' who 'have been found without the use of speech'.[11]

He discusses the emergence of the political state, which 'is not natural to man any more than language, to which it gave birth'[12] and pays great attention to the relation between the animal and the human world, which he sees as more closely linked than any other thinkers of the time. His view that men originally had tails and that the oran-outang was originally a variety of the human species aroused considerable mirth among his contemporaries, but today it can be seen as anticipating later evolutionary theories. Yet in some ways Monboddo was the most backward-looking of all the thinkers of the Scottish Enlightenment. He adored the ancient Greeks and considered the moderns much their inferior. His *Antient Metaphysics* (1779–99), also in six volumes, attacks modern empiricism from Locke to Hume and uses arguments drawn from both Plato and Aristotle to develop a metaphysic which saw the universal mover in the universe as Mind. In spite of his deep disagreement with his contemporary philosophers Monboddo was a friendly and sociable man who

Lord Monboddo (1714-99) by John Kay.

Oran-outang from the Encyclopaedia Britannica *(1788-97).*
In 1748 Linnaeus had classified it as Homo, *not* Simia.

expressed his differences forcefully but without quarrelling; he was also one of the most learned men of this time.

Ossian

'Rise and progress', 'origin and progress' – such phrases abound in the writers of the Scottish Enlightenment, and can be found among literary critics as well as among philosophers and historians. 'When we attend to the order in which words are arranged in a sentence,' wrote Hugh Blair in his *Lectures on Rhetoric and Belles Lettres* (1783), originally delivered at the University of Edinburgh, 'we find a very remarkable difference between the ancient and the modern tongues. The consideration of this will serve to unfold farther the genius of language, and to show the causes of these alterations which it has undergone in the progress of society.'[13] The study of poetry in particular was bound up with the study of the relation between primitive and sophisticated society. Although the modern age showed all the improvements of elegance and refinement that such teachers as Hugh Blair were at pains to point out, the same teachers also admitted that 'no principle of the human mind is, in its operations, more fluctuating and capricious than taste',[14] and that the Ancients provided some excellent models of taste. The interest, almost the

obsession, with a theoretical primitive state of society in which poetry was the natural speech, co-existed with a passionate belief in 'improvement'. Nowhere is this more clearly evident than in the reception of James Macpherson's *Fragments of Ancient Poetry, collected in the Highlands of Scotland, and translated from the Gaelic or Erse Language* which appeared in 1762 with a preface by Hugh Blair, and in Blair's *Dissertation concerning the Æra of Ossian*, 'collected and translated by James Macpherson'. We now know that, while Macpherson did make use of a number of genuine Gaelic ballads, his whole conception of Ossian as a great epic poet and the high rhetorical-sentimental language of the rhythmic prose in which he 'translated' that alleged epic, were confidence tricks. But Blair, with his breezy use of 'conjectural history', had no difficulty in persuading himself and many of his readers how such a barbarous age as that in which it was believed Ossian flourished could 'produce poems abounding with the disinterested and generous sentiments so conspicuous in the poems of Ossian'. The bards, Blair assures us, 'assumed sentiments that are rarely to be met with in an age of barbarism' because they had 'had their minds opened, and their ideas enlarged, by being initiated in the learning of that celebrated order [of the Druids]'. Each prince tried to emulate the flattering

portrait painted by the generous bards. 'This
emulation continuing, formed at last the general
character of the nation, happily compounded of
what is noble in barbarity, and virtuous and
generous in a polished people.' The question of the
genuineness of Macpherson's *Ossian* was thus
bound up with theories about the nature and
function of early poetry and with ideas about the
proper balance between the primitive and the
polished which were very much in the air at the
time.

Lord Kames, in an argument as 'conjectural' as that
of Blair and rather more circular, also proved to his
own satisfaction that Macpherson's poems were
the genuine works of an ancient bard. No modern
writer, he argued, could have imagined primitive
society to be as Ossian depicts it; therefore, it must
really have been like that, and Macpherson's *Ossian*
must be genuine. 'Genuine manners never were
represented more to the life by a Tacitus nor a
Shakespeare. Such painting is above the reach of
pure invention: it must be the work of knowledge
and feeling.'[15] Such arguments were bound up
with the *a priori* anthropology of the period and the
associated theory of language and of the origin of
poetry. 'During the infancy of taste,' wrote Kames
in his *Sketches of the History of Man* (1774), 'imagination is suffered to roam, as in sleep, without control.
Wonder is the passion of savages and of rustics; to
raise which, nothing is necessary but to invent
giants and magicians, fairy-land and inchant-
ment.'[16] Hugh Blair, in his *Lectures,* made an effort
to ground such theories in known facts: 'It is chiefly
in America,' he wrote, 'that we have had the opportunity of being made acquainted with men in their
savage state. We learn from the particular and con-
curring accounts of travellers, that, among all the
nations of that vast continent, . . . music and song
are, at all their meetings, carried on with an incred-
ible degree of enthusiasm; that the chiefs of the
tribe are those who signalize themselves most on
such occasions; that it is in songs they celebrate
calamities, the death of friends, or the loss of
warriors; express their joy on their victories; celebrate the great actions of their nation, and their
heroes; excite each other to perform great exploits
in war, or to suffer death and torments with un-
shaken constancy. Here then we see the first
beginnings of poetic composition, in those rude
effusions, which the enthusiasm of fancy or passion
suggested to untaught men, when roused by
interesting events, and by their meeting together
in public assemblies.'[17] The Hebrew poetry of the
Bible, the alleged folk literature of North American
Indians and Peruvians, Homer, Norse sagas, medi-

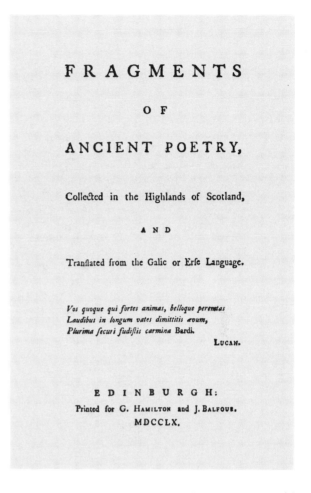

aeval romance, ballads, even Shakespeare, could
be lumped together as illustrations of 'primitive'
poetry. This line of thought, strong among a certain
section of the Scottish literati (though not among
all of them – David Hume, for example, had no use
for this kind of primitivism) was also to be found in
England, where literary historians, antiquarians
and poets (Thomas Warton, Bishop Percy, Thomas
Gray) looked to Scotland for help in illustrating
their views on these matters.

Taste, Morality and Sentiment

For all his interest in the primitive, Blair agreed
with most of the thinkers of the Scottish Enlightenment in his belief in the basic uniformity of human
nature. 'Taste is far from being an arbitrary principle, which is subject to the fancy of every individual, . . . Its foundation is the same in all human
minds. It is built upon sentiments and perceptions
which belong to our nature; and which, in general,
operate with the same uniformity as our other
intellectual principles.'[18] At the same time he

believed that taste had recently been improved. 'The public ear is become refined. It will not easily bear what is slovenly and incorrect.'[19] In his belief in the importance of rhetoric, Blair showed himself in the Ciceronian tradition of associating it with civic virtue. (Plato attacked rhetoric for its ability to 'make the worse appear the better reason'; Aristotle considered it as neutral, the art of persuasion, capable of being put to good or bad use; Cicero saw it as a force for good in the citizen's conduct of affairs.) 'Without possessing the virtuous affections in a strong degree, no man can attain eminence in the sublime part of eloquence. He must feel what a good man feels, if he expects greatly to move, or to interest mankind.'[20] It is this aspect of Blair that made him so influential in America, where his *Lectures* were studied right through the nineteenth century and played a significant part in the development of American political rhetoric.

It was partly the genial elegance of Blair's style that helped to make him the most popular and the most influential writer on rhetoric produced by the Scottish Enlightenment. But his exact contemporary, George Campbell, of Marischal College, Aberdeen (he was first Professor, then Principal there) was in some ways a more profound and sophisticated student of the subject. Like Blair, Campbell was a minister of the Church of Scotland, one of the Moderates, and like his fellow-Aberdonian James Beattie he was much concerned to vindicate Christianity against Humean scepticism. His *Dissertation on Miracles* (1763) is an ingenious defence of the historicity of the Gospel miracles against Hume. Campbell also produced many other theological works, including *A New Translation of the Gospels*. But for us his most significant work is *The Philosophy of Rhetoric* (1776), perhaps the most important product of the Scottish Enlightenment's interest in the relationship between the structure of the human mind and the effects of certain uses of language on human emotions. Campbell is both psychologically and philosophically subtler than Blair, but his flintier style and his greater interest in investigation than in presentation (unusual in the literati) limited his influence.

One of the most representative men of the Scottish Enlightenment is Henry Home, Lord Kames, who, according to his much younger contemporary John Ramsay of Ochtertyre, 'did more to promote the interests of philosophy and *belles lettres* in Scotland than all the men of law had done for a century before'. Raised to the Bench in 1752, he proceeded to combine legal, philosophical, literary, historical and agricultural activities. His interest in agricultural improvement, so characteristic of the age,

manifested itself first in his work on his estate at Kames, then, after his wife succeeded to the estate of Blair Drummond, on his lands there. 'Farming,' wrote Ramsay of Ochtertyre, 'was one of the sciences in which he wished to be thought as learned as in jurisprudence or ethics. He deserves great praise for the part which he had in introducing English husbandry into Scotland.'[21] In addition to six books on legal subjects, Kames wrote *Essays on the Principles of Morality and Natural Religion* (1751), *Elements of Criticism* (2 volumes, 1762), *Sketches of the History of Man* (3 volumes 1774), *Loose Hints upon Education, Chiefly Concerning the Culture of the Heart* (1781), and a number of books on agriculture including his practical manual, *The Gentleman Farmer* (1776). His written prose was smooth and elegant neo-classic English, but he spoke a forceful Scots, even on the Bench; this contrast between his spoken and written language was, as we have seen, characteristic of the literati. In Kames's case it was more exaggerated than in some others. Ramsay referred to his occasional 'levity or prurience of speech' on social occasions, while at the same time paying tribute to the liveliness and fascination of his table-talk and the popularity of his 'Edinburgh suppers'.

Kames's legal writings, considerably influenced by Montesquieu's *l'Esprit des Lois*, are important for his insistence on the historical approach to the study of law. Laws are human institutions evolving in response to changing human situations. Law, he argued, 'becomes only a rational study, when it is traced historically, from its first rudiments among savages, through successive changes, to its highest improvements in a civilized society'.[22] He saw the progress of society and the development of law as closely inter-related. 'When we enter upon the municipal law of any country in its present state, we resemble a traveller, who crossing the Delta, (of the Nile), loses his way among the numberless branches of the Egyptian river. But when we begin at the source and follow the current of law . . . all its relations and dependencies are traced with no greater difficulty, than are the many streams into which that magnificent river is divided before it is lost in the sea.'[23]

Kames was not a profound thinker, but he was a representative one. In moral philosophy, he was a somewhat naïve believer in the 'moral sense'. 'The sense by which we perceive right and wrong in actions, is termed the *moral sense*: the sense by which we perceive beauty and deformity in objects, is termed *taste*. Perfection in the moral sense consists in perceiving the minutest differences between right and wrong: perfection in taste consists in perceiving the minutest differences between beauty and deformity; and such perfection, is termed *delicacy of taste*.'[24] Kames was as interested as most of the philosophers of his day in what was

often called 'the knowledge of the human heart' (but which Hume called 'the science of man') and took a somewhat sentimental view of the matter: 'Good passions and impressions are flowers which ought carefully to be cultivated: bad passions and impressions are weeds which ought to be suppressed, if they cannot be totally rooted out. Such moral culture is not slight art: it requires a complete knowledge of the human heart, and of all its biasses.'[25] His literary criticism, like much of Blair's, is largely the study of rhetoric in the sense that he is concerned to analyse the ways in which different uses of language arouse different kinds of 'emotions and passions'.

Adam Ferguson (1723–1816) is one of the more flamboyant members of the *literati* – clubable, political, choleric, and with 'a boundless vein of humour', 'the manners of a man of the world, and the demeanour of a high bred gentleman'. In his youth he spent nine years as chaplain to the Black Watch, seeing active service against the French. Thereafter he succeeded Hume as Keeper of the Advocates' Library in 1757 and two years later was appointed Professor of Natural Philosophy at Edinburgh University, transferring to the Chair of Moral Philosophy in 1764, a post he held for more than twenty years. Though he was the only Gaelic speaker among his peers Ferguson had no truck with the Jacobite cause, publishing in 1746 'A Sermon preached in the Erse language', described as 'a vigorous denunciation of the Pretender, of popery and of France'. One can nevertheless trace in his most important work his deep sense of the contrast between the 'primitive' highland societies and the 'polished' society with all its moral dangers.

Ferguson wrote several pamphlets, all on political subjects, and three books, far the most influential being *An Essay on the History of Civil Society* (1767). This is a pioneer work of sociology which shows a new kind of sophistication in discussing different kinds of social order: it does not propound a simple view either of progress or decline but investigates the various ways in which human moral and intellectual qualities operate either as causes or effects in human social organisation. 'Mankind are to be taken in groups, as they have always subsisted', he asserts in his opening chapter, and he makes clear that his observations and inferences are based on observed and recorded facts about the behaviour of the human species. Ferguson dismisses those who separate the 'natural' from the 'unnatural' in human behaviour, 'for all the actions of men are equally the result of their nature', and he derives his sociological principles from the verifiable facts of human nature. He is even-handed in his distribution of praise and blame among different kinds of society, and without any romantic idealisation of the 'noble savage' he appreciates the virtues of those 'rude nations' unacquainted with property, even though 'property is a matter of progress'. Ferguson had strong moral principles and he constantly examines the different kinds of virtues and vices associated with different kinds of political organisation (none having a monopoly of either). He examines changes among nations, explores the causes of their rise and decline, assesses the good and bad effects of such passions as ambition and pride, deplores 'sordid habits and mercenary dispositions', investigates the nature and ambiguities of liberty, exposes the dangers of too great a separation of functions among citizens (so that, for example, citizens who do not take part in the defence of their country but leave it to mercenaries corrupt both themselves and the mercenaries – an interesting reflection of his passion about the militia question), and examines possible relationships between citizen, statesman and soldier with the social and moral implications of each. The whole work is illuminated with flashes of high moral feeling which reveal Ferguson's deep concern with the nature of the good society, the meaning of true progress, the moral as well as the other causes of 'rise and progress' and 'decline and fall'. *An Essay on the History of Civil Society* is still a relevant, stimulating and provocative work which sheds unexpected light even on aspects of our own capitalist industrial society.

There was a strain of sentimentality in much Scottish writing of the time, and even the rigorous and sceptical David Hume could, in discussing literary matters, take up a somewhat sentimental position. The arch-priest of Scottish sentimentalism was Henry Mackenzie, whose novel *The Man of Feeling* (1771) marked a high point in the sentimental movement in Europe. It was partly the insistence by the critics on the function of the arts in arousing emotion that explains this, although this does not itself explain why so many Scottish writers of this period took this view: it had something to do with the split between spoken and written language which help to encourage a split between emotion and intellect. Critics looked for such qualities as 'tenderness and warmth' in a play or novel; they admired 'generous and noble sentiments' and 'warm and genuine representations of human nature' while deploring 'cold and artificial performances' (Hugh Blair). They saw it as a sign of excellence in a play that 'the ladies in the audience were distinguished by their virtuous distress' (Mackenzie). They tended to read Robert Burns in this light, and to admire his more sentimental and rhetorical performances while undervaluing his satiric and celebratory poems which we today regard as among his greatest. Burns himself was much influenced by Mackenzie (he esteemed *The Man of Feeling*, he said, 'next to the Bible') and there was conflict within him between the claims of irony, passion and anti-gentility on the one hand and genteel sentimentality on the other. The Edinburgh literati tried to encourage him in the latter direction, but on the whole he was aware enough of the true nature of his genius to resist.

Science and Industry

Interest in man as a moral and social being, bound up with an interest in philosophy, psychology, sociology and history, was accompanied during the period of the Scottish Enlightenment with an equal interest in his physical make-up. We have already noted pioneer work in medicine done in Edinburgh in the late seventeenth century: by the latter part of the following century Edinburgh was in a position to vie with Salerno, Padua and Leyden as one of the great medical centres of the Western world. The first Alexander Monro, after studying

Sentimentality. Thomson's Seasons, *illustrated by Bartolozzi, after Hamilton, 1797; Ramsay's* Gentle Shepherd, *illustrated by David Allan, 1788; Mackenzie's* Man of Feeling, *illustrated by Bewick, 1808.*

University of Edinburgh, 1785. Class card admitting a student to Alexander Monro's lectures in medicine.

Herman Boerhaave (1668-1738), by Cornelis Troost, 1735.

in London, Paris and (under the great Boerhaave) at Leyden, began to lecture on anatomy and surgery at Edinburgh in 1719 at the age of twenty-three and went on to become the first Professor of Anatomy at Edinburgh University; his even more distinguished son, Alexander Monro *secundus*, anatomist, surgeon and medical researcher distinguished for his work in nervous physiology, assisted his father while still a student before succeeding him in 1758; while *his* son, Alexander Monro *tertius*, became joint professor with his father in 1798 before succeeding to the Chair in 1808. This remarkable dynasty, comparable to the Gregory dynasty of an earlier generation, helped to establish Edinburgh's reputation in medicine, although Monro *tertius* had not the originality or teaching ability of his father and grandfather.

The story of the development of medicine in Edinburgh is partly the story of the activity of George Drummond, six times Lord Provost of the city, who saw the building of a distinguished medical school as part of his ambitions for the development of Edinburgh and who engineered the appointment to Edinburgh University of many distinguished medical researchers including that of the

first Alexander Monro as Professor of Anatomy as well as inspiring the building of the Royal Infirmary. An even more influential medical figure than any of the Monros, and the one most responsible for establishing a tradition of research in Scottish chemistry, is William Cullen, a Glaswegian who began his academic career by lecturing on medicine at the University of Glasgow before moving on to teach chemistry, without dropping his medical teaching for he insisted on the close relationship between the two. In 1756 Cullen moved to Edinburgh where he became Professor of Chemistry while at the same time lecturing on clinical medicine at the Royal Infirmary. In 1766 he became Professor of the Theory of Physic and from 1773 to 1775 was President of the Edinburgh College of Physicians. Cullen was a great teacher as well as a researcher, who explored the relationship between medicine and the physical sciences and aroused enormous enthusiasm among his students. A student petition to Edinburgh Town Council in 1766 talked of the great debt the medical students of the city owed to Cullen, his success in diffusing 'an ardour for improvement and spirit of liberal inquiry in Medicine' and his re-modelling of the study of chem-

Charles O'Brien, the Irish Giant (by John Kay) was nearly 8 ft tall, and attracted much medical as well as popular attention. Edinburgh, Surgeons' Hall, c.1790.

Edinburgh, Royal Medical Society. The foundation stone was laid by Cullen in 1775.

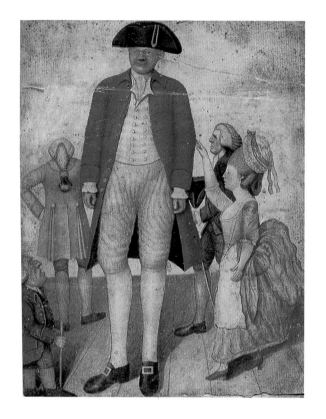

SACRED to *MEDICINE*
FOUNDED April 21st 1775
BY THOS McINNES *MASON*

istry, 'formerly little studied here' to raise it 'to the highest reputation'.[26] Cullen was a sociable man and a friend of David Hume, Adam Smith, Adam Ferguson and others, part of what Jupiter Carlyle called 'the whole circle of learned and ingenious men who had sprung up together at this time'. One of his students was the American Benjamin Rush, who on his return to America to practise as a doctor paid tribute to all that he owed to Cullen: Rush's name is perpetuated in the Rush Medical College of Philadelphia.

Perhaps Cullen's greatest pupil was Joseph Black, who first came in contact with him when Cullen was lecturing in chemistry at Glasgow. Black moved to Edinburgh in 1752 to complete his medical education and write the important thesis 'De humore acido a cibis orto, et magnesia alba', which announced the discovery of carbon dioxide (which Black termed 'fixed air') and laid the foundations of

Edinburgh, Royal Infirmary. Part of the first list of patients, 1729.

Patients Names.	From what Parish.	When taken in.	Diseases.	When recovered, cured, dismissed or dead.
Elizabeth Sinclair,	Caithness,	1729 August 6	Chlorosis,	1729 November 19. recovered
Barbara Haltic,	Lady Testers Edinburgh,	7	Pain in the Thigh and Loosenes,	August 19. dismissed.
Hew Richmond,	Ochiltry,	11	Cancer in the Face,	August 19. dismissed.
Isabel Brown,	Dunbar,	22	Inflamation of the Eyes,	September 20. cured.
Farquhar Mackinnan Soldier,		25	Pain of the Liver with hectick Fever,	September 6. cured.
John Simson,	West-Kirk,	25	Scorbutick painful Tumor of the Knee,	September 28. cured.
Helen Allan,	Edinburgh,	September 12	Hysterick Disorders,	September 23. dismissed.
Mary Dickson,	Canongate,	12	Bloody Flux,	October 31. cured.
Hector Morison,	Isle of Mull,	23	Consumption,	September 30 dismissed
James Short,	Edinburgh,	October 1	Beginning Consumption,	October 9. cured.
Katharine Macfarline,	Edinburgh,	4	Obstructions,	November 4. cured.
Jean Cuningham,	West-Kirk,	15	Cancer of the Breast,	November 30. cured.
Mary Walker,	Congalton,	31	Tertian Ague and sore Eyes,	November 17. cured.
Robert Brown Dragoon,		November 18	Quartan Ague,	1730 January 8. cured.
Alexander Lamb,		18	Flux,	1729 November 25. cured.

Cured. — 19

Recovered so as to go about their ordinary Affairs and requiring only some Time to confirm their Health, and to restore their Strength fully. — 05

Dismissed either as incurable or for Irregularities. — 05

Dead — 01

In the Infirmary. — 05

Total this first Year — 35

N. B. Besides these Patients in the above List (who were all maintained in Bed, Board, and Medicines in the Hospital) several Out-Patients were attended by the Physicians and Surgeons, who also gave Advice daily to all Sick that came to the Infirmary at the Hours of visiting.

quantitative chemical analysis. He then returned to Glasgow as Professor of Chemistry and also to practise as a physician, while pursuing his studies of the phenomena of freezing, melting and boiling which resulted in his development of the theory of latent heat. In 1766 Black moved to the Chair of Chemistry in Edinburgh; here he showed his brilliance as a teacher as well as his versatility as chemist, physician, and researcher into many practical applications of chemistry in agriculture and the textile industry. Like Cullen, Black was a friend of David Hume, Adam Smith and other leading literati, and in particular he was a friend of the great pioneer geologist James Hutton.

A native of Edinburgh, Hutton qualified as a doctor at Leyden, farmed in Berwickshire for 14 years, returned to his native city, and subsequently wrote books and papers on chemistry, physics, agriculture, meteorology, and philosophy as well as geology. As a result of lengthy and accurate observations, Hutton suggested that the surface of the earth is continually being destroyed and recreated and that the time necessary for these operations is almost infinite. His best known work is the *Theory of the Earth: with proofs and illustrations* (1795); this laid the foundations of modern geology with its careful inferences about the formation of the earth's crust and the enormous periods of time involved.

Agriculture. Agricultural improvement is perhaps the best known of all the economic developments sponsored by the literati. Historians now trace the beginnings of the agricultural revolution in Scotland well back into the seventeenth century. The abolition of the old runrig method and the general enclosing and blocking out of the farms into the kind of units we see today, together with improvements in draining, liming, ploughing and in the rotation of crops, went on apace throughout the eighteenth century. Landowners such as Andrew Fletcher of Saltoun, John Cockburn of Ormiston, John, Earl of Stair, Lord Deskford, Sir Archibald Grant of Monymusk, as well as the land surveyor James Donaldson and the jurist and philosopher Lord Kames, thought about, wrote about, and experimented with agricultural improvement. It was a national passion in the age of the Scottish Enlightenment.

Industry. By the middle of the century, textiles dominated Scottish industry. The Board of Commissioners for Improving Fisheries and Manufactures in Scotland, set up by the Government in 1727, devoted itself energetically to the development of the Scottish linen industry, the encouragement of new standards of weaving and of new techniques of manufacture. The Convention of Royal Burghs also interested itself in promoting trade and manufacture, and made special efforts to help both the linen industry and herring fishing. The result of the Jacobite rising of 1745–46 also involved Scottish industry and manufactures. In an attempt to ensure that Jacobitism would never raise its head again, the Government determined to bring the Highlands into line with the peaceful movement of progress in the south of the country

Farming before enclosure and improvement: Lowland farm-stead, c.1690; Haddington, showing open fields and run rigs.

Killin, Perthshire, c.1776, showing a former barren landscape transformed by forestry.

Lowland farmstead (High Cross Farm), c.1770.
Niddry House, near Edinburgh, by Alexander Runciman. The
scene shows the 'improved' state of agriculture.

A gentleman laird. Robert Trotter of the Bush (1750-1807), by David Martin, 1782.

by promoting 'the Protestant religion, good Government, Industry and Manufactures and the Principles of Duty and Loyalty to His Majesty, his heirs and Successors'.[27] It was for this purpose that an act was passed in 1752 annexing thirteen of the forfeited estates of Jacobite landowners 'unalienably' to the Crown. In 1753 Parliament granted from the proceeds of these estates an annual sum of £3,000 for nine years to help the linen industry in the Highlands, but in general the Forfeited Estates Commissioners, in spite of inquiries, surveys and much talk of development on Lowland lines, did little to effect radical change in the economy of the Highlands. In 1754 there was founded the Edinburgh Society for Encouraging Arts, Sciences, Manufactures, and Agriculture, which not only discussed Scotland's economic problems but also offered prizes for conspicuous agricultural and industrial achievement.

In all these activities the literati of the Scottish Enlightenment played a significant part. Cullen had begun experiments with bleaching when he was Professor of Anatomy at the University of Glasgow and in 1755, the year in which he was appointed Professor of Chemistry at the University of Edinburgh, the Board of Commissioners presented him with a gift of table linen for 'his in-

genious experiments in the art of bleaching'. Black, Cullen's successor at Glasgow, carried Cullen's experiments further at the Board's request.

The men of the Scottish Enlightenment also took an active part in the switch from linen to cotton pioneered in Glasgow in the later years of the century, continuing Cullen's and Black's researches in bleaching, dyeing and fabric printing. The inventor and chemist Dr John Roebuck established a factory in Prestonpans in 1749 to manufacture sulphuric acid, whose bleaching properties were finally demonstrated by Dr Francis Home, Professor of Materia Medica in Edinburgh, in 1756. This reduced the bleaching period of textiles from eight to four months. Then followed the discovery in 1774 by the Swedish Carl Scheele of the use of chlorine as a bleaching agent and its successful employment in France ten years later by Claude Louis Barthollet whom James Watt met in Paris and from whom he learned the method. By the end of the century further experiments by Professor Patrick Copland of Aberdeen and Charles Tennent of St Rollox had led to the perfection of the chlorine method with the introduction of 'bleaching powder' (chloride of lime) which reduced the whole bleaching process to a few hours, when it had originally taken months.

*Fishing Station, Torridon, and Cromarty harbour, both late
18th C., built with funds from the Boards of Trustees for
Fisheries and Manufactures.*

Banking. The relationship between intellectual,
industrial and commercial activities during the
period of the Scottish Enlightenment went much
further than the enlistment of men of science in the
service of agricultural improvement and of better
methods of bleaching, dyeing, coal-mining and
iron production. Eighteenth-century Scotland
pioneered in the development of banking services,
and in doing so provided a financial basis for intellectual as well as other activities of the century. It
was eighteenth-century Scotland that introduced
banking on the limited liability principle as well as
the circulation of notes to the point of the virtual
disappearance of gold and silver. The Bank of Scotland was founded as early as 1695, the Royal Bank
of Scotland in 1727 and the British Linen Company
(which was in fact a bank) in 1746. It was the Royal
Bank of Scotland that invented the cash credit
system, forerunner of the overdraft, in 1728. It was
the Scottish banks that developed the system of
local branches, that introduced the practice of holding each other's notes in difficult times, and that
adapted the joint-stock principle to banking.

'These initiatives,' in the words of the historian of
Scottish banking, S. G. Checkland, 'accompanied

by a strong sense of practicality and creditworthi-
ness, placed the banks of a tiny country in the
forefront of Europe and the world. They were the
product of Scotland's situation and culture: a liter-
ate population though initially poor and remote
from the commercial heartland of Europe, could,
through its ethos and education, thus generate a
remarkable system.'[28]

Scottish banking thus provided a mobility of
finance that enabled activities as different as town-
planning and publishing, bridge-building and
medical research, improvement in communications and development of education, in short both
doing and *thinking*, to be carried on with a confidence and a flexibility otherwise impossible in a
country with such limited resources.

Clubs and Societies

The literati of the Enlightenment believed profoundly in human contact, by means both of personal engagement and of published discourse.
How far was their ideal of social communication
confined to the professional and upper classes?
The traditional view that as a result of the Union of
1707 the Scottish landed aristocracy tended to

John Coutts (1699-1751) by a follower of Allan Ramsay. Coutts, an Edinburgh money-broker whose sons founded the banking house of Coutts and Co., was Lord Provost, 1742-44.

"Pursuit on the North Bridge", by John Kay.

migrate to London leaving the city under the social and intellectual leadership of a professional middle class consisting of lawyers, ministers, professors and doctors has recently been challenged by N.T. Phillipson, who has pointed out that far from all of the aristocracy left the city after the Union and 'it was not until the last quarter of the century that the aristocratic foundations of Edinburgh began to crumble as men of rank and property began to abandon Edinburgh in favour of London'.[29] Nevertheless, in spite of the fact that Scotland was 'managed' by approved members of the Scottish landed aristocracy for most of the eighteenth century, and also of the fact that members of the professional classes intermarried with the landed gentry and were sometimes themselves members of that class, the men of the Scottish Enlightenment could for the most part be called members of a professional middle class. It is difficult to consider this question in modern terms, for in spite of the social hierarchy of the time and of the social and political importance of the land-owning classes, there was a certain freedom of association in eighteenth-century Edinburgh and Glasgow society that belied the importance attached to what John Millar, in the title of a notable book published in 1771, called 'distinction of ranks'.[30] This is to be seen in the extraordinary number of clubs and societies that flourished.

One of the most ambitious of these clubs was the Select Society founded in 1754 by Allan Ramsay the painter (son of Allan Ramsay the poet, a self-made man). Alexander Carlyle, popularly known as 'Jupiter' Carlyle, one of the Moderate literati of Edinburgh and minister of Inveresk, Midlothian, gives in his illuminating *Autobiography* an interesting account of this society which provides an indication of its social range.

> Of the first [members] were Lord Dalmeny, the elder brother of the present Lord Rosebery, who was a man of letters and an amateur, and, though he did not speak himself, generally carried home six or eight of those who did to sup with him. There was also Peter Duff, a writer to the signet, who was a shrewd, sensible fellow, and pretending to be unlearned, surprised us with his observations in strong Buchan [i.e. in the accent of Buchan, a district in Aberdeenshire]. The Duke of Hamilton of that period, a man of letters, could he have kept himself sober, was also a member, and spoke there one night. . . . Mr. Robert Alexander, a wine merchant, a very worthy man, but a bad speaker, entertained us all with warm suppers and excellent claret, as a recompense for the patient hearing of his ineffectual attempts, when I have often thought he would have beat out his brains on account of their constipation. The conversation at these convivial meetings frequently improved the members more by free conversation than the speeches in the Society. It was those meetings in particular that rubbed off all corners, as we call it, by collision, and made the literati of Edinburgh less captious and pedantic than they were elsewhere.[31]

Carlyle supplied a list of members of the Select Society of October 1759 to Dugald Stewart, who printed it in an appendix to his *Account of the Life and Writings of William Robertson* (1801). The list includes Adam Smith, David Hume, John Home, Sir David Dalrymple (later Lord Hailes), Hugh Blair, John and James Adam, Robert Dundas (later President of the Court of Session), Dr William Cullen, Adam Ferguson, the Earls of Lauderdale, Errol, Aboyne, Selkirk, Roseberry and Cassils, the great Edinburgh Lord Provost George Drummond, who did so much for medicine at Edinburgh University and envisaged the New Town of Edinburgh, Henry Home Lord Kames, numerous advocates, ministers and medical men, seven merchants, and four military men.

Another influential Edinburgh society was originally founded ostensibly to further the cause of establishing a Scottish militia (considered to be a democratic national force conducive to Scotland's dignity as a nation and denied to Scotland by the Militia Act of 1757, which applied only to England) but ranging much further in its interests. Jupiter Carlyle again gives an account of it:

> In the beginning of 1762 was instituted the famous club called 'The Poker', which lasted in great vigour down to the year 1784. About the third or fourth meeting, we thought of giving it a name that would be of uncertain meaning, and not be so directly offensive as that of Militia Club to the enemies of that institution. Adam Smith fell luckily on the name of 'Poker', which we perfectly understood, and was at that time considered an enigma to the public. [The poker would *stir up* the militia question.] This club consisted of all the literati of Edinburgh and its neighbourhood, most of whom had been members of the Select Society, except very few indeed who adhered to the enemies of militia, together with a great many country gentlemen, who, though not always resident in town, yet were zealous friends to a Scotch militia, and warm in their resentment on its being refused to us, and an invidious line drawn between Scotland and England. The establishment was frugal and moderate, as that of all clubs for a public purpose ought to be. We met at our old landlord's of the Diversorium, now near the Cross, the dinner on the table soon after two o'clock, at one shilling a-head, the wine to be confined to sherry and claret, and the reckoning to be called at six o'clock. After the first fifteen, who were chosen by nomination, the members were to be chosen by ballot, two black balls to exclude the candidate. There was to be a new preses [chairman] chosen at every meeting. William Johnstone, Esq., now Sir William Pulteney, was chosen secretary of the club, with a charge of all publications that might be thought necessary by him, and two other members with whom he was to consult. In a laughing humour, Andrew Crosbie was chosen Assassin, in case any officer of that sort should be

needed; but David Hume was added as his Assessor, without whose assent nothing should be done, so that betwen *plus* and *minus* there was likely to be no bloodshed.[32]

This gives something of the flavour of some at least of the clubs of the period. But there were many different kinds. Robert Fergusson, the brilliant young Edinburgh poet who died at the age of twenty-four in the city's public Bedlam, belonged to the Cape Club, formally constituted in 1764 having existed less formally since 1733. This was one of the most socially mixed of the Edinburgh clubs of the time. The antiquary and collector of old Scots songs and ballads David Herd was a prominent member, and he prefaced the *sederunt* book of the Club with this account of it:

> The Knights Companions of the Cape began to call themselves by that name about the year 1764. The original constituents of the order occasionally admitted by a prescribed form such other members as they found agreeable. The purpose and intention of the Society was: after the business of the day was over to pass the evening socially with a set of select companions in an agreeable and at the same time a rational and frugal manner; for this purpose beer and porter were their liquors, from fourpence to sixpence each the extent of their usual expence, conversation and a song

William Smellie (1740-95), editor of the first edition of the
Encyclopaedia Britannica, *produced "by a Society of
Gentlemen in Scotland".*

THE SCOTTISH ENLIGHTENMENT · 37

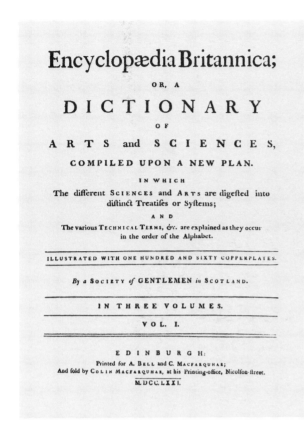

their amusement, gaming generally prohibited, and a
freedom for each to come and to depart at their pleasure was always considered as essential to the constitution of the Society. – Upon these principles, with
some few variations in different periods of time, incident to every association of mankind, they have gradually increased.[33]

The original members of the Cape Club were
twenty-five in number (they 'precede all others,
but have no precedency among themselves'),
including David Herd, Alexander Runciman the
painter, James Cummyng, lyon clerk, heraldic
painter and later secretary of the Antiquarian
Society, and John Wotherspoon, Herd's colla-
borator and printer. Other members covered a wide
social spectrum, from shoemakers and tailors to
doctors and naval officers.

If Robert Fergusson was a member of the varied
and democratic Cape Club, his successor as a Scots
poet, Robert Burns, was introduced by his printer
William Smellie to a club Smellie had founded
known as the Crochallan Fencibles when Burns
was in Edinburgh in 1786–87 arranging for the
publication of the second edition of his poems. The
German scholar Hans Hecht has linked the Crochallan Fencibles with the Poker Club as 'socially

homogenous' and 'aristocratic' as contrasted with
the socially varied Cape,[34] but the accounts that
have come down to us of scenes of 'rough banter'
and horse-play, together with the fact that Burns
assembled his collection of bawdy songs entitled
The Merry Muses of Caledonia for his fellow members
of the Crochallan Fencibles, suggest that its members were not known for their elegance and gentility. Not that Burns would have been out of place in
an elegant and genteel forum for discussion: he
was master of a poised neo-classic English speech
(as can be seen in his letters) and could beat the
literati at their own game when he wanted. What
he resented when he was trotted around Edinburgh drawing-rooms to be exhibited as a 'heaven-
taught ploughman', was the assumption that he
should defer to people of lesser intelligence than he
because they had rank or money or both. At the
Crochallan Fencibles he was able to relax, away
from the patronising gentility he so often encountered in the city, and this fact suggests some degree
of social inclusiveness among the membership.

Eighteenth-century Edinburgh had numerous
other clubs and societies meeting in taverns, oyster
cellars and 'laigh shops', and most seem to have
had remarkably democratic rules of membership.

Robert Burns, The Ploo'man, *from the* Merry Muses of Caledonia.

An Edinburgh tavern, much frequented by the local vernacular writers, in the mid-18th C.

THE PLOO'MAN.

THE ploughman he's a bonny lad,
  His mind is ever true, jo,
His garters knit below his knee,
  His bonnet it is blue, jo.

    Then up wi't a', my ploughman lad,
    And hey my merry ploughman,
    Of a' the trades that I do ken,
    Commend me to the ploughman.

As walking forth upon a day,
  I met a jolly ploughman,
I told him I had lands to plough,
  If that he would prove true, man.

He says, my dear, take ye na fear,
  I'll fit you to a hair, jo,
I'll cleave it up, and hit it down,
  And water furrow't fair, jo.

I hae three owsen in my plough,
  Three better ne'er plough'd ground, jo ;
The foremost ox is lang and sma',
  And twa are plump and round, jo.

Then he wi' speed did yoke his plough,
  Which by a gaud was driven, jo,
And when he was between the stilts,
  I thought I was in heaven, jo.

JOHNIE DOWIE'S TAVERN.

English visitors marvelled at ladies of rank attending parties at oyster cellars which were frequented by almost all ranks of society. Schetky the musician founded the Boar Club which met in a tavern in Shakespeare Square; all members were officially *boars*, the room they met in was a *sty*, their talk was *grunting*, and so on. There was the Pious Club, which met to eat pies, a club of porter drinkers, a Dirty Club, at which members were not allowed to appear in clean linen, and many other similar groups. What all this adds up to is that, however conscious of rank and social hierarchy in their normal behaviour, in the club life of eighteenth-century citizens there could be found varieties of social freedom not to be found in formal dinner parties. How relevant this is to the understanding of the Scottish Enlightenment cannot be easily determined; but it does suggest that social conversation (and, it will be remembered, David Hume expressed a wish that philosophy should be conducted as conversation) was an Enlightenment ideal and that it cut across class barriers.

Music

Many of the literati of the Scottish Enlightenment showed a lively interest in classical music. The Musical Society of Edinburgh was established in 1728 for the purpose of holding weekly concerts and in 1762 its members built St Cecilia's Hall (a small-scale version of the Opera House at Parma) where regular concerts were held which, in the words of a contemporary, 'formed one of the most liberal and attractive amusements that any city in Europe could boast of'.[35] Works by Corelli, Handel, Johann Stamnitz, Geminiani and Haydn were regularly performed, and Scotland was in touch with musical currents on the Continent to a degree it has not been since. Other cities than Edinburgh showed their enthusiasm for music, and musical societies were formed in many centres: the Aberdeen Musical Society was especially notable for its enthusiasm for recent music: in 1760 its library consisted largely of musical works published in the preceding fifteen years.

Scotland also had its own composers during this period, both native and immigrant. Francesco Barsanti, an Italian who settled in Edinburgh in 1735, published there his innovative, imaginative and complex concertos in 1742 (opus 3). The sixth Earl of Kelly, a key figure in the building of St Cecilia's

Edinburgh. The late-18th C. dining-room of the Georgian House, Charlotte Square.

THE SCOTTISH ENLIGHTENMENT · 39

Hall, was Scotland's greatest symphonic composer, whose six *Overtures* (Opus 1, 1761) were the first orchestral works in the new Mannheim orchestral style to be printed in Britain. Somewhat earlier, the violinist and composer William McGibbon developed the seventeenth-century Italian tradition, notably in his *La Folia* variations. The German-born Johann Schetky settled in Edinburgh in 1772 and played a prominent part in the musical life of the city as well as publishing string trios, cello sonatas and duets, and string quartets.

An interest in folk-music existed side by side with a taste for classical music and some composers were involved in both. McGibbon, in addition to his highly esteemed classical compositions, was deeply involved in Scottish fiddle music and published numerous folk-tune settings which combined a Scottish folk with an Italian baroque idiom. The invasion of native Scottish folk-music by Italian styles was denounced by the poet Robert Fergusson in his 'Elegy on the Death of Scots Music', but in fact, in McGibbon's case if not invariably, the Scots and Italian were combined without losing the qualities of either.

James Oswald was another Scottish composer who combined Scottish and Italian elements, in his sonatas for flute or violin continuo (*Airs for the Four Seasons*). Even Neil Gow, the great virtuoso Scottish folk fiddler, was an admirer of Corelli whose sonatas he enjoyed playing.

Side by side with all this, Scottish folk-songs were being collected, imitated, re-created and published, words alone, music alone, or words and music together. The violinist Adam Craig published his *Collection of Scots Tunes* as early as 1730; the most impressive of such collections of tunes alone was Oswald's *Caledonian Pocket Companion*, of which the first of many volumes appeared in 1740. The most comprehensive of the collections of songs with both words and music was James Johnson's *Scots Musical Museum*, to whose later volumes Burns contributed so much. But the literati of the Enlightenment, for all their interest in 'primitive' poetry and for all their enjoyment of the singing of Scots songs on social occasions, did not set great store by the native Scots folk-song tradition as it existed in their own time, and Burns's great work in restoring and in virtually re-creating the whole

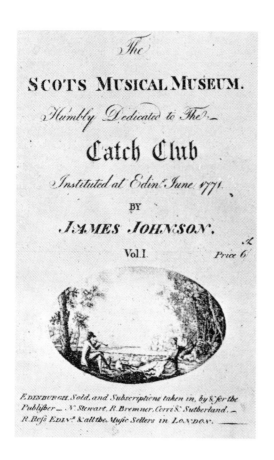

corpus of Scottish folk-song was not an aspect of his genius that appealed to them.

Conclusion

In a sense it can be said that the seeds of the Romantic Movement lay within the Scottish Enlightenment, with its emphasis on the passions in both moral philosophy and literary criticism. But Romanticism was a complex phenomenon with many different varieties and the modern cultural historian is cautious in using the term at all. There is little doubt, however, that with the coming of the French Revolution (which has its own connections with Romanticism) the world of the Scottish Enlightenment disintegrated. When the mists clear after the Napoleonic Wars we find ourselves in the world of Sir Walter Scott and Lord Cockburn and the *Edinburgh Review,* a world which owed much to the literati of the late eighteenth century, and a world of great literary and critical distinction, yet one lacking the great integrating ideals of understanding and improvement which united so many different kinds of thinkers in the earlier period. The Scottish Enlightenment remains a unique movement in the history of Scottish culture and one that still has not been wholly explained.

References

1. William Smellie, *Literary and Characteristic Lives of Gregory, Kames, Hume, and Smith* (Edinburgh, 1800), pp.161-2.
2. *The Poems of Robert Fergusson*, edited by M. P. McDiarmid, 2 (Edinburgh and London, 1956), p.1.
3. J. G. Lockhart, *Memoirs of the Life of Sir Walter Scott, Bart.*, 1 (Edinburgh, 1837), pp.58-9.
4. *Letters of David Hume*, edited by J. Y. T. Grieg (Oxford, 1932), 2, p.230.
5. Richard B. Sher, *Church and University in the Scottish Enlightenment* (Princeton, 1985), pp.27-8.
6. Hugh Blair, *Sermons*, 1 (Edinburgh, 1777), pp.15-16.
7. *Ibid.*, 2 (London, 1780), pp.450-1.
8. *Letters of David Hume*, edited by J. Y. T. Grieg (Oxford, 1932), 1, p.255.
9. David Hume, *Enquiries concerning the Human Understanding and concerning the Principles of Morals*, edited by L. A. Selby-Bigge (Oxford, 1902), p.227.
10. Adam Smith, *Lectures on Rhetoric and Belles Lettres*, edited by John M. Lothian (Edinburgh, 1963), p.7.
11. William Knight, *Lord Monboddo and some of His Contemporaries* (London, 1900), p.31.
12. *Ibid.*
13. Hugh Blair, *Lectures on Rhetoric and Belles Lettres*, 1 (Edinburgh, 1813), p.135.
14. *Ibid.*, p.29.
15. Henry Home, Lord Kames, *Sketches of the History of Man*, 1 (Edinburgh, 1813), p.83.
16. *Ibid.*, p.155.
17. Hugh Blair, *Lectures on Rhetoric and Belles Lettres*, 3 (Edinburgh, 1813), p.83.
18. *Ibid.*, 1, p.39.
19. *Ibid.*, 1, p.8.
20. *Ibid.*, 1, p.15.
21. *Scotland and Scotsmen in the Eighteenth Century from the MSS. of John Ramsay Esq. of Ochtertyre*, edited by Alexander Allardyce, 1 (Edinburgh and London, 1888), p.207.
22. Henry Home, Lord Kames, *Historical Law Tracts* (Edinburgh, 1758), 5.
23. *Ibid.*, 9-10.
24. Henry Home, Lord Kames, *Sketches of the History of Man*, 1 (Edinburgh, 1813), pp.153-4.
25. Henry Home, Lord Kames, *Loose Hints upon Education, chiefly concerning the Culture of the Heart* (Edinburgh, 1781), pp.1-2.
26. John Thomson, *An Account of the Life, Letters and Writings of William Cullen, M.D.*, 1 (Edinburgh, 1832), p.155.
27. Bruce Lenman, *Integration, Enlightenment and Industrialisation: Scotland 1746-1832* (London, 1981) (quotes the Act of 1752).
28. *A Companion to Scottish Culture*, edited by David Daiches (London, 1981), p.28 (article on 'Banking').
29. *A Companion to Scottish Culture*, edited by David Daiches (London, 1981), p.341 (article on 'Scottish Enlightenment').
30. John Millar, *The Origin of the Distinction of Ranks* (London, 1771).
31. *The Autobiography of Dr. Alexander Carlyle of Inveresk*, edited by John Hill Burton (London and Edinburgh, 1910), p.312.
32. *Ibid.*, pp.439-41.
33. *Songs from David Herd's Manuscripts*, edited with introduction and notes by Hans Hecht (Edinburgh, 1904), pp.36-7.
34. *Ibid.*, p.37.
35. Robert Chambers, *Traditions of Edinburgh* (Edinburgh, 1847), p.239 (quoting – anonymously – George Thomson).

Select Bibliography

The most important books written in the Scottish Enlightenment have been mentioned in the text. I give here a select list of modern studies of various aspects of the period.

Gladys Bryson (1945) *Man and Society: the Scottish Inquiry of the Eighteenth Century* (Princeton).
Charles Camic (1983) *Experience and Enlightenment* (Edinburgh).
R. H. Campbell and A. S. Skinner, eds (1982) *The Origins and Nature of the Scottish Enlightenment* (Edinburgh).
Anand C. Chitnis (1976) *The Scottish Enlightenment, a Social History* (London).
A. L. Donovan (1975) *Philosophical Chemistry in the Scottish Enlightenment* (Edinburgh).
Istvan Hont and Michael Ignatieff, eds (1983) *Wealth and Virtue: the Shaping of Political Economy in the Scottish Enlightenment* (Cambridge).
Neil McCallum (1983) *A Small Country, Scotland 1700-1930* (Edinburgh).
Davis D. McElroy (1969) *Scotland's Age of Improvement: A Survey of Eighteenth Century Literary Clubs and Societies* (Pullman, Washington).
John MacQueen (1982) *Progress and Poetry: The Enlightenment and Scottish Literature* (Edinburgh).
Thomas A. Markus, ed. (1982) *Order in Space and Society: Architectural Form and its Context in the Scottish Enlightenment* (Edinburgh).
Rosalind K. Marshall (1979) *Women in Scotland 1660-1780* (Edinburgh).
Nicholas T. Phillipson and Rosalind Mitchison, eds (1970) *Scotland in the Age of Improvement* (Edinburgh).
Roy Porter and Mikùlas Teich, eds (1981) *The Enlightenment in National Context* (Cambridge).
I. S. Ross (1972) *Lord Kames and the Scotland of his day* (Oxford).
Richard B. Sher (1985) *Church and University in the Scottish Enlightenment* (Princeton).
T. C. Smout (1972) *A History of the Scottish People 1560-1830*, paperback ed. (London).
R. E. Wright-Sinclair (1964) *Doctors Monro* (London).

David Hume

PETER JONES

DAVID HUME is regarded by many people as the greatest philosopher to write in English. The range of his work is wide, but he is perhaps best known for his views on causation, and on the nature of morality. He agreed with his predecessors that the only way to explain the past and plan for the future, is to understand how and why things change; only a knowledge of causes can help to dispel our most natural fears. He believed, however, that many had misunderstood the precise nature of that knowledge, and had thus failed to benefit from it. He also held that it was not enough to examine the natural world; it was man himself, as the investigator, who set out to know, but often in ignorance of his own contributions to the task. Philosophy should begin, therefore, with an investigation into the nature of man, for this would also enable us to understand the nature and limits of his knowledge. It will be discovered that man is governed much less by reason than has often been claimed, and is motivated essentially by his passions. Moreover, in everyday life he must learn to live with probabilities rather than certainties. Hume held that the public, and intensely practical, benefits which could result from such an understanding are profound.

Life

David Hume was born in Edinburgh in 1711. His father, who had studied at the Universities of Edinburgh and Utrecht, died in 1713 leaving his widow to look after their three children at Ninewells, their small farm in the Scottish Borders, near Chirnside. At the age of ten, David joined his elder brother at Edinburgh University, and studied there for three, or possibly four, years. As was usual at the time, he left without graduating, and began to

follow the family tradition of studying law. He soon found these studies uncongenial and embarked, instead, on a long and private study of philosophy, temporarily ruining his health in the process. His acquaintance with legal writings nevertheless stood him in good stead in later years: first, he was able to define his own moral and political views in relation to those of the legal philosophers whom he had studied, such as Grotius and Pufendorf; and secondly, as late as 1746, he secured a post as Judge-Advocate to a military expedition which unexpectedly launched him into a public career which he enjoyed immensely. Meanwhile, in 1734, he was advised to take a post as clerk in the thriving port of Bristol, in order to regain his balance, but the experience was brief and humiliating: he was sacked for attempting to correct the English grammar of his boss. Almost immediately he decided to leave for France.

Hume finally settled at La Flèche, on the Loire, where the Jesuit college was still the centre for disciples of Descartes and Malebranche, as it had been since they themselves studied there in the previous century. Although the official 'Auld Alliance' ended with the Reformation, Scots felt a special affinity with the French, and on several occasions throughout his life Hume thought seriously of settling permanently in France. During his first spell of three years there, 1734–37, Hume composed the philosophical work for which he is nowadays most famous: *A Treatise of Human Nature*. This long work, the first part of which reveals considerable French influence, was published anonymously in London in 1739 and 1740. In the Introduction Hume declares that he is proposing 'a complete system of the sciences built on a foundation almost entirely new': first, 'that all the

Hume, A Treatise of Human Nature, *1739; first page of Contents.*

Hume, A Letter from a Gentleman . . ., *1745; title-page.*

A bust of Cicero. On publishing the Treatise, *Hume told Hutcheson that he had Cicero's* De officiis (On Duty) *"in my eye during all my reasonings".*

THE

CONTENTS.

INTRODUCTION.

BOOK I.

Of the UNDERSTANDING.

PART I.

Of ideas, their origin, compofition, abftraction, connexion, &c.

SECT.
I. OF the origin of our ideas.
II. Divifion of the fubject.
III. Of the ideas of the memory and imagination.
IV. Of the connexion or affociation of ideas.
V. Of relation.
VI. Of modes and fubftances.
VII. Of abftract ideas.

VOL. I.   a   PART

A

LETTER

FROM A

GENTLEMAN

TO

His FRIEND in *Edinburgh:*

CONTAINING

Some OBSERVATIONS

ON

A Specimen of the Principles concerning RELIGION and MORALITY, *faid to be* maintain'd in a Book lately publifh'd, intituled, *A Treatife of Human Nature,* &c.

EDINBURGH,
Pinted in the Year M.DCC.XLV.

sciences have a relation, greater or less, to human nature'; secondly, that 'as the science of man is the only solid foundation for the other sciences, so the only foundation we can give to this science must be laid on experience and observation'. In 1740, disappointed by slow sales and generally unfavourable reviews in the few journals which noticed his work, Hume hit upon a bold idea. He published an anonymous summary of the main theses of the book, designed to boost sales. Several copies of this exciting sixpenny pamphlet, now simply called the *Abstract*, have come to light since J. M. Keynes first identified one in 1938. The document is important not only because it lets us see which tenets Hume wanted, or felt it prudent, to emphasise a few months after publication of the *Treatise*, but because it laid down, with exceptional clarity, the structure he later followed in re-writing parts of that work.

In 1741 and 1742 Hume published two more volumes, under the title *Essays, Moral, Political, and Literary*. Addressed to readers who admired the literary elegance of Addison and the political

Sir John Pringle, whose resignation in 1745 from the Edinburgh Chair of Philosophy encouraged Hume's hopes of academic advancement. Pringle later became the founder of military medicine.

DAVID HUME · 45

moderation of Bolingbroke, the essays make clear Hume's general debt to antiquity, and most particularly to Cicero. He takes over Cicero's many sided notion of moderation and underpins it with some assumptions from physics of a vaguely Newtonian nature, but he quite consciously omits the abstruse or contentious metaphysical reflections of the *Treatise*. One consequence is that philosophical allusions in the *Essays* are vaguer than they need have been although, with the hindsight denied to contemporary readers of these anonymous works, we can see the *Essays* as illustrating and exemplifying in a political context the abstract principles expounded earlier. Many of the observations on society, or religion, for example, re-appear in later writings.

Hume always counted moderate clergy and politicians among his friends, and in 1745 the Provost of the city proposed him for the chair of Moral Philosophy at Edinburgh University. The Principal, who may have had an interest in the post himself, went to considerable lengths to block any such appointment, and succeeded. In self-defence against allegations circulated by the Principal, Hume published another anonymous pamphlet (so much for anonymity), *A Letter from a Gentleman to his friend in Edinburgh*, a copy of which was found in 1967. In this *Letter* he tried to rebut the charges of scepticism and irreligion which were to dog him for the rest of his life, and the document enables us to see, once again, how Hume was being read, and what he was able to clarify. During this affair, Hume had become private tutor to the Marquess of Annandale. Unfortunately, he soon found the Marquess to be insane; to make matters worse, it was many years before he was fully paid for his efforts.

By chance, in May 1746, Hume met a distant relative, General James St Clair, and was invited to join him on a military expedition against the French in Canada. The whole episode marked a turning point for Hume, who was now thirty-five, who had spent the best part of twenty years in private study and writing, and who had been dismissed after only a few months from the only two jobs he had secured. The expedition introduced him to the realities of politics, and secured him enough money to make a public literary career possible. As it happened, the weather was too bad to set sail for Canada, but the Government, intent on sending somebody somewhere, anywhere, ordered St Clair to lead his party to France. They set off for Plymouth. Hume reports:

> They there found positive orders to sail immediately, with the first fair wind, to the coast of France, and make an attempt on L'Orient, or Rochefort, or Roch-

elle, or sail up the river of Bordeaux; or, if they judged any of these enterprises impracticable, to sail to whatever other place on the western coast they should think proper. Such unbounded discretionary powers could not but be agreeable to the commanders, had it been accompanied with better, or indeed with any intelligence.

They lacked not only 'intelligence' and guides, however. The General 'had no single map of any part of France on board with him'; and should he need money to buy information, or even to pay his men, 'except a few chests of Mexican dollars, consigned to other uses', he carried none. Hume reports the General's own response to the Duke of Newcastle:

> On the whole, he engaged for nothing but obedience; he promised no success; he professed absolute ignorance with regard to every circumstance of the undertaking; he even could not fix on any particular undertaking; and yet he lay under positive orders to sail with the first fair wind, to approach the unknown coast, march through the unknown country, and attack the unknown cities of the most potent nation of the universe.

General St Clair, by Allan Ramsay. The Hon. James St Clair served as a Scottish MP, and also, from 1722 to 1762, as an officer in the Royal Scots.

Frankfurt-am-Main, mid-18th C., by C. G. Schütz.

After confused delays the General was once more ordered 'to land any where he pleased in France', although he was still 'without any map of the country to which he was bound, except a common map, on a small scale, of the kingdom of France, which his Aid-de-camp had been able to pick up in a shop at Plymouth'.[1] Accidents, incompetence and the weather combined to render the whole expedition a farce. The British guessed the wrong road to the town of L'Orient and lost many deserters on the way who, nevertheless, terrified the citizens of the town with predictions of an impending massacre. The British, however, mounted an artillery barrage of such ineptitude that cannon-balls bounced obliquely onto their own troops; drenched and dispirited they withdrew, only to encounter further storms on the way home. Meanwhile, the French had prepared themselves for surrender and emerged from the town in all due subservience: but the attackers had gone.

Nothing daunted by his experiences, Hume agreed to accompany St Clair on secret missions to Vienna and Turin in 1748, and the letters to his brother which describe the journey through Europe reveal his taste in landscape and architecture. The Hague and Rotterdam impress him greatly: 'every person & every house has the Appearance of Plenty

Edinburgh. Riddle's Court, Lawnmarket, where Hume lived, 1752-53: "I (have) got a house of my own, and completed a regular family; viz., myself . . . a maid, and a cat".

and Sobriety, of Industry & Ease'. But the country-side is barely describable, especially after the melting of the snows: 'nothing can be more disagreeable than that heap of Dirt & Mud & Ditches & Reeds, which they here call a Country, except the silly Collection of Shells, & clipt Ever Greens which they call a Garden'. Their route took them via Breda, Nijmegen, Cologne, Bonn, Koblentz, Frankfurt, Wurzburg, Ratisbon to Vienna. Near Frankfurt he records that he 'never saw such rich soil, nor better cultivated; all in corn and sown Grass. For we have not met with any natural grass in Germany'. To a man from a Scottish border farm the sight was clearly amazing. Of the Bishop's palace at Wurzburg he remarks: ''Tis a prodigious magnificent Palace of the Bishop, who is the Sovereign'. He also comments on the 'great Magnificence of some Convents, particularly Moelk, where a set of lazy Rascals of Monks live in the most splendid Misery of the World'. Hume freely confesses that 'there are great Advantages, in travelling, & nothing serves more to remove Prejudices: For I confess I had entertain'd no such advantageous Idea of Germany'. In Vienna, the mother of Maria Theresa helpfully exempts Hume from the need to exit backwards, curtsying [sic]: 'We esteemd ourselves very much oblig'd to her for this Attention, especially my Companions, who were desperately afraid of my falling on them & crushing them'. Finally, the new palace at Schonbrunn is, 'indeed a handsome House; but not very great, nor richly furnish'd'.[2]

In 1748 Hume published yet another anonymous pamphlet, in defence of Archibald Stewart, who was tried and eventually acquitted for neglect of duty whilst Provost of Edinburgh during the rebel occupation of the city in 1745. The title of this fascinating document is *A True Account of the Behaviour and Conduct of Archibald Stewart, Esq; late Lord Provost of Edinburgh, In a Letter to a Friend.* For some time Hume had been re-writing parts of the first and third Books of the *Treatise,* and these appeared in 1748 and 1751: they are now known as the *Enquiry concerning Human Understanding,* and the *Enquiry concerning the Principles of Morals.* In 1752 he published a dozen essays on political and economic topics, under the title *Political Discourses,* and under his own name (which he had only acknowledged on his books in the previous year). This volume was immediately successful at home and abroad, and attracted long reviews. In the same year, 1752, he failed to gain the chair of Logic at Glasgow University, but within a few days was appointed Keeper of the Advocates' Library in Edinburgh. With access to their magnificent collec-

tion, he was able to bring out, between 1754 and 1762, the six volumes of his great *History of England,* having sketched out plans for the Stuart volumes (which he wrote first) around the time of the '45. The *History* at once established itself as a classic in the field, rivalled in English only by Clarendon's masterpiece which had appeared posthumously in 1702. Hume resigned as librarian in 1757 after a long and acrimonious battle with the Curators who censured his purchase in 1754 of three books, the *Contes* of La Fontaine, *L'Ecumoire* of Crébillon *fils,* and *L'Histoire amoureuse des Gaules* of Bussy-Rabutin. The charge that they were pornographic was, of course, preposterous, and Hume remarks archly in a letter: 'if every book not superior in merit to *La Fontaine* be expelled the Library, I shall engage to carry away all that remains in my pocket. I know not indeed if any will remain except our fifty pound Bible, which is too bulky for me to carry away'.[3]

After completing the *History,* Hume went to France again, for three years from 1763–66. This time he was in Paris, first as Secretary and then as Chargé d'affaires at the British Embassy. Hume was lionised and fêted by all, by almost all the *philosophes* such as Diderot and D'Alembert, and even more by the great aristocratic patronesses of the *salons*. Speculation has continued to the present day over how many, and precisely who, among these great ladies won his heart. To their mutual regret, Hume never met Voltaire, but he was able to procure introductions for Adam Smith, who had arrived in France in 1764 with the Duke of Buccleuch, his young charge. During his time in Paris Hume befriended Rousseau, who characteristically was feeling hounded, and arranged for him to be settled and royally pensioned in England. Rousseau stayed barely a year, however, and on returning to the Continent in 1767 declared their friendship to be at an end; Hume, and his friends in France, he believed, had long been conspiring to humiliate him and denigrate his writings. Letters from all parties to the affair were published, and much mirth attended the incident. The French had come to refer to Hume as *le bon David,* and they certainly appreciated the wit and irony of his writings more readily than his compatriots. His close friends, of course, knew him as affectionate, sociable and

amusing, but readers whose knowledge is restricted to the *Treatise* will have no conception of the man. For that, the *Letters* are indispensable.

On returning to London Hume became Under Secretary of State, handling diplomacy with foreign powers to the north of France, including the Russia of Catherine the Great. He was also in charge of home affairs for Scotland, and as official patron of the Scottish Church, he wrote the King's Address at the opening of the General Assembly in 1767 – and informed his friend the Rev. Hugh Blair, Regius Professor of Rhetoric and Belles-Lettres of the fact. He also tells Blair that 'reading and sauntering and lownging and dozing, which I call thinking, is my supreme Happiness, I mean my full Contentment'.[4]

In 1769, just thirty years after the appearance of the *Treatise*, Hume retired to Edinburgh, renewed old friendships and played host to all the important visitors to the city. Benjamin Franklin, for example, whom he had known for twenty years, stayed with him in 1771, and they undoubtedly discussed American independence, which Hume supported. In a typically affectionate letter to Adam Smith, he writes:

I am glad to have come within sight of you, and to have

THE SAVAGE MAN.

a View of Kirkcaldy from my Windows: But as I wish also to be within speaking terms of you, I wish we coud concert measures for that purpose. . . . I want to know what you have been doing, and propose to exact a rigorous Account of the method, in which you have employed yourself during your Retreat. I am positive you are in the wrong in many of your Speculations, especially where you have the Misfortune to differ from me. . . . On my Return, I expect to find a Letter from you, containing a bold Acceptance of this Defiance.[5]

In 1771 Hume moved from James's Court, off the High Street, into his new house at the south-west corner of St Andrew Square, one of the first phases of James Craig's plan for the New Town to reach completion. In retirement Hume continually revised new editions of his *History*, and worked on his *Dialogues Concerning Natural Religion*, which was published posthumously in 1779. This scintillating and profound work, modelled on Cicero, together with other posthumously published essays on suicide and immortality, enraged his fanatical enemies; they had mounted various attacks during his lifetime, including an attempt at excommunication during the General Assembly of 1756, and they were unduly provoked by the dignity with which he bore a long and fatal illness, probably intestinal cancer. Throughout his illness he was attended by his friend and doctor Joseph Black, and he kept in close touch with Smith, who was to act as his literary executor – Hume was himself Smith's executor, but that task fell to Black and James Hutton. Smith's famous letter describing Hume's death on 25 August 1776 is discussed in the next chapter. As moving in its own way is a letter Hume sent to the Comtesse de Boufflers; they had been close friends for fifteen years. She had been the mistress for many years to the Prince de Conti, but he never condescended to marry her, and now he had died. Hume's letter is dated 20 August.

Tho I am certainly within a few weeks, dear Madam, and perhaps within a few days, of my own death, I could not forbear being struck with the death of the Prince of Conti – so great a loss in every particular. My reflection carried me immediately to your situation in this melancholy incident. What a difference to you in your whole plan of life! Pray write me some particulars; but in such terms that you need not care, in case of decease, into whose hands your letter may fall.

My distemper is a diarrhoea, or disorder in my bowels, which has been gradually undermining me these two years; but, within these six months, has been visibly hastening me to my end. I see death approach gradually, without any anxiety or regret. I salute you, with great affection and regard, for the last time. DAVID HUME[6]

Benjamin Franklin, when a diplomat in Paris during the American War of Independence, by Carmontelle. Franklin visited Edinburgh in 1759 and again in 1771, when he stayed with Hume.

Philosophy

What distinguishes the great philosophers from each other and from their lesser peers is rarely the complete originality of their particular premises or conclusions; rather, it is the emphases they place, the routes they take, and the overall synthesis they offer, in the context as they see it, of sometimes quite familiar elements. Countless philosophers before Hume, for example, reflected on the how and why of change, and historians have established that very little of his account is strictly original. Nevertheless, in Scotland first, and subsequently throughout the English-speaking world, it was

Hume's account, however much it synthesised earlier views, that attracted attention and carried the day. What were its principal features?

CAUSATION. Hume was interested in the processes by which we acquire knowledge; the processes of perceiving and thinking, of feeling and reasoning. He recognised that much of what we claim to know derives from other people at second- or third-hand, or worse; he recognised, as others had before him, that our perceptions and judgments can be distorted by many factors, sometimes by what we are studying, sometimes even by the very act of study itself. The main reason, however, behind his emphasis on 'probabilities and those other measures of evidence on which life and action entirely depend'[7] is this:

> it is evident that all reasonings concerning *matter of fact* are founded on the relation of cause and effect, and that we can never infer the existence of one object from another unless they are connected together, either mediately or immediately. . . .
> Here is a billiard ball lying on the table, and another ball moving toward it with rapidity. They strike: and the ball which was formerly at rest now acquires a motion.[8]

In cases like this, when we observe the whole sequence, what exactly do we observe? And in the much commoner cases, when we wonder about the *unobserved* causes or effects of the events we observe, what do we do? In dealing with such questions Hume separates importantly different issues:

a) a question about the causal *relation*: what exactly is it for one event to be the *cause* of another? what is the evidence of *causal* relations between events?

b) a question about the causal *inference*: what entitles us to *infer* from the occurrence of one event, that another is its cause or its effect?

c) a question about the causal *principle*: why do we insist that *every* event has a cause, and what entitles us to do so?

d) three extra questions about *necessity*: (i) why do we insist that what distinguishes a genuine *causal* relation from a merely casual relation is the *necessity* of that particular pair of events occurring together? (ii) what entitles us to *infer* that if one event is the cause or effect of another, then it *must* have occurred with it, or immediately before or after it? (iii) why do we insist that *every* event *must* have a cause?

Hume recognises, in other words, that this notion of 'must' or 'necessity' is a peculiar feature of causal relations, inferences and principles, and challenges us to explain and justify the notion. He argues that there is no observable feature of events, nothing like a physical bond, which can be properly labelled the 'necessary connection' between a given cause and its effect; events simply *are,* they merely *occur,* and there is no 'must' or 'ought' about them. However, repeated experience of pairs of events sets up the habit of expectation in us, such that when one of the pair occurs we inescapably expect the other. This expectation makes us *infer* the *unobserved* cause or effect of the observed event, and we mistakenly project this mental inference on to the events themselves. There is no necessity observable in causal relations; all that can be observed is regular sequence: there is necessity in causal inferences, but because inferences are what observers do, we can say that this necessity is only in the mind. A further example may help to bring this point out.

Hume holds that there is no peculiar *property* common to all causes, and that merely examining events in isolation, as it were, can tell us nothing about their causes or effects. But when we realise that causation is a *relation* between pairs of events, we immediately realise also that very often we are not present for the whole sequence that we want to divide into 'cause' and 'effect'. So, Hume argues, our understanding of the causal relation is intimately linked with the role of the causal inference, because only causal inference entitles us to 'go beyond what is immediately present to the senses'.[9] What would Adam, innocent but alert, have been entitled to infer as he watched the first moving ball approach the first motionless ball? Nothing. He could have guessed, with equal propriety, that the balls became fish on contact, that two balls become one, that they disappear or, indeed, anything at all: 'the mind can always *conceive* any effect to follow from any cause, and indeed any event to follow upon another'.[10] Only when he has witnessed several collisions will he make the proper inference, because only then will sight of a moving ball trigger expectation of the other's movement: 'his understanding would anticipate his sight and form a conclusion suitable to his past experience'.[11] But now two very important assumptions emerge behind the causal inference: the assumption that 'like causes, in like circumstances, will always produce like effects', and the assumption that 'the course of nature will continue uniformly the same' – or, briefly, that the future will resemble the past.[12] Unfortunately, this last assumption lacks either empirical or *a priori* proof; that is, it can be conclusively established neither by experience nor by thought alone.

Hume frequently claims to base all his theses on experience, since only experience establishes matters of fact. Is it merely a matter of fact, however, that the future will resemble the past? As Bertrand Russell remarked, earlier this century, the problem is whether future futures will resemble future pasts, in the way that past futures really did resemble past pasts. Hume declares that 'if . . . the past may be no rule for the future, all experience becomes useless and can give rise to no inference or conclusion'.[13] And yet, he holds, the supposition cannot stem from innate ideas, since there are no innate ideas in his view, nor can it stem from any abstract formal reasoning. For one thing, the future can surprise us, and no formal reasoning seems able to embrace such contingencies; for another, even animals and unthinking people conduct their lives as if they assume the future resembles the past: dogs return for buried bones, children avoid a painful fire, and so on. It must be stressed that Hume is not deploring the fact that we have to conduct our lives on the basis of *probabilities*; he is not saying that inductive reasoning could or should be avoided or rejected. On the contrary, he tries to show that whereas formal reasoning of the kind associated with mathematics cannot establish or prove matters of fact, factual or inductive reasoning lacks the 'necessity' and 'certainty' associated with mathematics. His position, therefore, is clear: because 'every effect is a distinct event from its cause'[14] only investigation can settle whether any two particular events are causally related; causal inferences cannot be drawn with the force of logical necessity familiar to us from *a priori* reasoning, but although they lack such force they should not be discarded. In the context of causation, inductive inferences are inescapable and invaluable. What, then, makes 'past experience' 'the standard of our future judgment'?[15] *Custom*: it is a brute psychological fact, without which even animal life of a simple kind would be more or less impossible. 'We are determined by *custom* alone to suppose the future conformable to the past';[16] nevertheless, whenever we need to calculate likely events we must supplement and correct such custom by self-conscious reasoning.

Some implications. Hume issued a re-written version of parts of Book I of the *Treatise* in 1748, under the title *Philosophical Essays concerning Human Understanding;* ten years later he revised the title to *An Enquiry concerning Human Understanding.* In line with what he had said in the *Abstract,* Hume decided to concentrate on his analysis of causation, and on its implications. He first tries to reconcile the arguments of those who hold that all our actions

"Tea in the English manner" (1776) by M.-B. Olivier. Hume was familiar with this salon, of the Prince de Conti, through the Comtesse de Boufflers. The harpsichordist in the painting is Mozart.

are determined, and those who hold that we are genuinely free to do what we choose. He claims that the determinists are right to insist that every event has a cause, but mistaken in the view they take of necessity, failing to see that it belongs only to an inference in the mind; advocates of free will, on the other hand, are right to say that responsibility makes sense only if we are truly the agents of our actions, but mistaken in holding that 'free' in this sense means 'uncaused'. Hume's view is that our actions, like all other events, have causes, namely, the choices and decisions which immediately precede our actions, and for which we accept responsibility. However, although these mental happenings function as the motives of our actions, they themselves have causes, of which we are normally unaware and for which we are not held responsible. His point in discussing the free-will issue is to show that human actions can be understood, and are properly understandable, in terms of what he has said about causation in general – we notice patterns of behaviour, we infer motives precisely

in order to offer 'interpretations' of actions:

> were there no uniformity in human actions, and were every experiment which we could form of this kind irregular and anomalous, it were impossible to collect any general observations concerning mankind, and no experience, however accurately digested by reflection, would ever serve to any purpose.[17]

Such thoughts were important when he came to reflect on the nature of history, as we shall see. Here, however, two features of the discussion should be noticed. Firstly, we can see an example of Hume's attempt to introduce rigour into areas not notable for it; human behaviour is capable of causal explanation, and therefore also of prediction, he is saying, albeit not yet with the same degree of precision or certainty that we expect in the natural sciences. The second feature is related to this. So important is our belief that similar causes produce similar effects, that we hold to it even when we cannot find the required uniformities; and when we find something puzzling or inexplicable we neither suppose that the laws of nature

Mme de Boufflers and Mme la duchesse de Lauzun, by Carmontelle. Mme de Boufflers first wrote to Hume in 1761. They met in 1763, became close friends, and maintained a correspondence thereafter.

have changed, nor that we have encountered a causeless event. Absence of adequate evidence for a cause, is not taken as adequate evidence for the absence of a cause.

MIRACLES AND RELIGION. The cases which most clearly conflict with what Hume has said about causation are those of alleged miracles. Hume had prepared a discussion of miracles for the *Treatise*, but was advised to omit it as too overtly contentious. He included a later version of that discussion in the 1748 *Enquiry*, however, linked to another chapter on religious topics. It would be disingenuous to insist that, philosophically, the main arguments in these two chapters can be separated from, and assessed independently of, the religious examples. Hume knew that none of his contemporary readers would do so, and he was right. Dozens of pamphlets, sermons, chapters and books were published against him. It is important, nevertheless, to grasp that his discussion of miracles is not primarily about whether they occur – he rather brusquely defines them as impossible; rather, it is about the nature and reliability of evidence, questions which arise way beyond the narrow religious context. The recurrent term in his discussion is *testimony*, that is, reports of evidence.

Hume readily concedes that all of us have to rely on reports from other people; knowledge is a social phenomenon in the sense that agreement about what happened is important in defining what we count as knowledge. Moreover, none of us has enough first-hand experience of our own to make very extensive claims. Hume holds that, as a general rule, testimony is reliable, and he does so for two reasons: our memories are moderately reliable, and men have a natural inclination, strongly re-enforced by social sanctions, to tell the truth, and to feel shame if detected in falsehood. These general assurances, however, cannot help us in cases of doubt, so Hume suggests that in weighing the probability of evidence the content and the context of what a witness says must both be examined. We need to consider not only the type and quantity of evidence, but also the manner and motive in giving it. In the end we must rely on 'experience and observation'. But surely we must be told whose experience is to count, and why, and how the tests are to be performed. *Ex hypothesi*, we cannot appeal to our own experience in order to test reports by others of experiences unlike our own; and in weighing what people say we neither appeal indiscriminately to anyone, nor require the assent of everyone. Hume relies on a notion of experts, or qualified observers, to whom we can appeal for help. Typically we learn who count as

the experts whilst learning the procedures for making reports of the kind in question; the learning may be quite informal, even unconscious, and the experts range from the sublime to the ridiculous – at its lowest, anyone might count as an expert who seems to know more than oneself. Parents and teachers are the first experts children encounter, but their own friends also play this role on many occasions. Hume uses the notion of experts and agreement to secure both the social dimension of our judgments, and their objectivity.

On the topic of miracles, Hume asks whether it is more likely that primitive peoples truly reported extraordinary events, or falsely reported ordinary events or even events that did not occur at all. The pleasures of wonder and surprise, he thinks, can induce belief in strange tales, and ignorant people are naturally credulous. Moreover, unscrupulous power-seekers know how to exploit these human failings. Hume takes miracle stories to be reports of unique events, the cause of which is allegedly known by inference, not by experience, even though none of the conditions for establishing an inferred cause are satisfied. We are entitled to infer a cause, it will be recalled, with a greater or lesser degree of probability, when the event to be explained resembles others which we have directly experienced in conjunction with their causes. Many questions arise here. How much resemblance is needed to warrant such an inference? What properties or characteristics is one entitled to assign to such an inferred cause? Hume's extended reflections on such issues were published posthumously in his brilliant *Dialogues Concerning Natural Religion*.

Protestant theologians in Hume's day were eager to embrace what little they understood of Newtonian science and its methods, and they popularised an ancient argument known as the argument from design. This was supposed to establish the nature of God by means of inferences from the observable world around us – in Hume's words, it was 'an argument drawn from effects to causes'.[18] Schematically it ran like this: it is impossible to describe all the diverse phenomena in the known universe without implying some over-all plan behind it, which causally explains their nature and their inter-connections; such a plan, however, would need to be of such complexity itself, that it could be attributed only to some super-human being; moreover, there are sufficient clues in the universe, enough traces or footprints, to warrant the claim that the being is omniscient, omnivolent, omnipotent, and so on. In brief, the world could only be the way it is, because of the way God is; and we know something of the way God is, by the

"Moderates dispersing a Sunday school." The Moderates in the Kirk deplored the indoctrination employed by the evangelical "High Flyers", but here Kay suggests that Moderatism also had a fanatical side.

way the world is.

Sophisticated versions of this argument are still popular, but it received its most influential presentation in 1794, by Dr. William Paley, fifteen years after Hume's attack on Paley's predecessors appeared. These writers wanted to establish the nature of God in ways which would appeal to readers attracted by the rival secular, scientific explanations of the natural world. Hume maintains that their arguments lack a determinate base in experience, that they are untestable, unrevisable and claim a dogmatic finality and uniqueness inimical to genuine scientific inquiry. The unavoidable inductive arguments in such inquiry, after all, mean that in any given case we could turn out to be mistaken. He reminds us of his view that no event, considered by itself, points beyond itself to its causes or effects; these have to be discovered by experience and, what is more, *no* features of a cause need resemble any of the effect – they could be 'totally different'.[19] Factual inferences rest on the assumption of similarity of cases, and can be assigned various degrees of probability. In the absence of direct experience we are allowed only to postulate what is *sufficient* to bring about the alleged effects. Hume is quick to see that this fails to satisfy his own definition of what a causal relation is, and of how we can know one, since the crucial notion of necessity is lacking. He illustrates the point by asking what we can infer from watching the rising pan of a half-hidden pair of scales. We can infer that the weight on the hidden pan *exceeds* the known weight, but that is all, and the inference is almost vacuous. We can only guess *what* is on the hidden pan: it could be a bag of feathers, it could be an elephant. Hume holds that theologians first of all guess the cause, proceed to draw further inferences from this first inference, and then promise untold benefits for mankind in an unverifiable future. His conclusion is that allegedly 'unique' causes cannot legitimately be inferred from, or used to explain, allegedly 'unique' effects. When uniqueness is claimed for an event we can never know whether we have adequately identified or circumscribed it. Furthermore, if there is no direct evidence in favour of an hypothesis, we cannot justifiably assert that the world is, notwithstanding, *indirect* evidence of the nature of God. In addition, if we have no experience of a thing's attributes we cannot pick it out from among other things, and if we cannot do this even vaguely, we have no means to confirm that it exists. It is useless to postulate a cause whose attributes, by definition, are unknown. Of course, we can invent a name, any name – say 'Blictri' – and arbitrarily assign it

some attributes: but whilst this may reflect our needs in various ways, it brings nothing into existence, enables us to explain nothing, and provides our own actions with no special moral authority. Finally, there is too much pain, suffering and chaos in the world as we know it, to justify any inference to a fully competent cause of it all.

Although religions exercised perhaps less influence over man and society in the eighteenth century than in earlier times, their impact was still considerable, and on his death bed Hume declared that 'he had not yet finished the great work' of delivering his countrymen 'from the Christian Superstition'.[20] He had spent his early life in a deeply Calvinist environment, and he never looked upon those experiences with anything but loathing. He quickly came to the view that religions had their origins in primitive societies which were dominated by 'anxious fear of future events',[21] and which lacked all semblance of proper government. Religions ministered to these fears without seeking for their causes, so that the remedies they prescribed were, at best, placebos, at worst, devices for enhancing the power of the priests who dis-

Francis Hutcheson (1694-1746) by Allan Ramsay. An important influence upon the Scottish Enlightenment, Hutcheson laid great emphasis on the roles of sentiments and passions in men's lives.

pensed them. Priests, in Hume's view, were always enemies to liberty of thought, and typically generated superstition, faction, and a form of slavery. That is why 'the errors in religion are dangerous; those in philosophy only ridiculous'.[22] Through the 'absurdity and contradiction' of their doctrines, priests not only induce hypocrisy, by feigning beliefs impossible to entertain, but succumb to self-deception. Like many others, Hume was appalled at the carnage achieved in the name of one religion or another, but he held that the causes of such misery lay not only within the institutions inevitably linked with religions, but within the very doctrines themselves. In this connection he maintained that polytheism was probably older, and was certainly less threatening to individuals and society, than monotheism, because it supposed many causes at work, no one of which need be regarded as dominant. Monotheists, on the other hand, adopted a subtler thesis of a unitary, yet invisible, cause of all things, which could only be appeased,

if at all, by an élite group of people. Hume believed that although many people are attracted by the thought of a single, if incomprehensible, mind or plan behind the universe, the only proper stance on such large questions is that of suspended judgment. Whilst such an attitude might still leave space for some notion of faith, Hume held that hypotheses merely based on faith were generally untestable and useless as explanations; moreover, to resort to faith was to yield up one's distinctively human capacity to think and to reason. Similar considerations lay behind his dismissal of revelation or inspiration as a source of special knowledge.

MORAL PHILOSOPHY. It would be a gross distortion of his views to imply that Hume's analysis of causation, on the one hand, or of society, on the other, are solely directed at displacing certain religious doctrines and practices. We ought to look briefly at what he has to say about man in his social context, that is, his views on the moral life, broadly considered.

Hume regarded his own moral views as those of a common-sense man, albeit with a strictly secular outlook. Very briefly, he holds that man cannot be adequately defined or understood as an essentially rational animal, as so many earlier philosophers and theologians had proclaimed. Indeed, he holds that pure thought, or abstract reasoning of the kind associated with pure mathematics, is itself inert, and cannot motivate anyone to do anything; all that such thought can do is enable us to recognise relations between things. This recognition can somehow influence what does motivate us, namely, our sentiments, which are forms of the most basic desires to avoid pain and attain pleasure. In the *Treatise* Hume dramatically summarised his view that thought plays only a subordinate role in the moral life by declaring that 'reason is, and ought only to be, the slave of the passions':[23] it helps in the formulation of our goals, but not in our motivation towards them. When he came to rewrite this passage in 1751, however, he toned it down: 'no doubt *reason* and *sentiment* concur in almost all moral determinations and conclusions . . . (but) it is probable . . . that this final sentence depends on some internal sense or feeling, which nature has made universal in the whole species'.[24] Hume drew inspiration for such views from Shaftesbury and from Francis Hutcheson, Professor of Moral Philosophy in Glasgow until his death in 1746. One of the features which most distinguishes the philosophers of the Scottish Enlightenment from their successors in the French and German Enlightenment, is the emphasis on the essential part played by the passions in our lives; their influence is a brute psychological fact, to be neither condemned nor condoned, but a fact nevertheless that theories of man and morality ignored at their peril. Very often, as it happened, the French and German writers regretted the fact, thought it to be avoidable, and proclaimed the sovereignty of Reason. As we all know, Reason did not triumph: only Revolution.

In deciding what to do we all weigh the possible consequences, but the merit of an action, Hume holds, derives from the motive behind it. It is worth recording that Hume's language is sometimes confusing: he uses the term *sentiment* to mean both feeling and thought, and this makes his claim that passions or sentiments are the sole causes of action more plausible than it might otherwise appear. He draws a distinction between 'artificial' and 'natural' virtues. 'Artificial' virtues are those which we might nowadays describe as sociologically conditioned, in the sense that they are procedures we adopt, as individuals or groups, and often unselfconsciously, to help things run smoothly and to temper our self-seeking and divisive tendencies. For example, our sense of justice arises 'artificially, though necessarily, from education and human conventions'; indeed, at one place, Hume states that 'public utility is the *sole* origin of justice'.[25] 'Natural' virtues, by contrast, are said to be grounded in our universal tendency to share, quite literally, the feelings of others. Such 'sympathy' (and the notion is not equivalent to the modern idea of compassion) ultimately explains even the artificial virtues. Both artificial and natural virtues, then, are understood as qualities which human beings find useful or agreeable both in their own case, as owners of those qualities, and in other people whom they observe as spectators. Hume's notion of 'sympathy' proved fruitful, and was taken up and developed by Adam Smith, as was the idea of learning to judge ourselves impartially.

ART, TASTE AND AESTHETIC JUDGMENT. Hume's account of aesthetic judgments, brief though it is, is similar to what he says about moral goodness and moral judgment. 'Beauty', he claims, is a 'power' in objects which causes pleasurable sentiments in observers: it is not itself either a sentiment in the observer or a property of the object discernible by the *five* senses. Rather, it is a special property whose presence is *felt* only when certain kinds of people interact, under specific conditions, with specific things: we could say it is discernible by a sixth sense (a notion introduced by the French in the late seventeenth century). By talking about the thing which currently pleases or displeases some-

one, we can change that person's response to it; that is, we can change how they perceive it, think of it, or react to it, and in this way induce them to feel differently about it. Such emphasis on feeling, however, should not be taken to imply that our discussions are incurably personal or subjective. On the contrary, Hume tries to show that agreement is possible, and of a kind that is quite strong enough to satisfy our deepest yearning for so-called objectivity. Three conditions must be met: the conventions of language must be observed by all dis-

"The Connoisseurs", by David Allan. Hume held that qualified judges could resolve issues of taste, through "strong sense, united to delicate sentiment, improved by practice, perfected by comparison . . .".

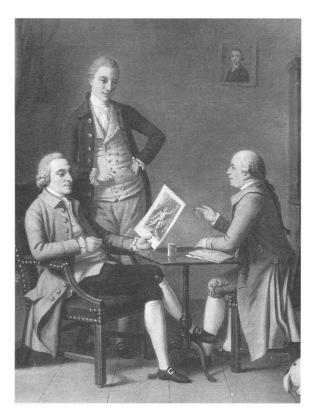

putants and, if necessary, clarified in the particular context; it must be possible to establish publicly shareable viewpoints and referents; finally, we must assume a shared psychological make-up among the disputants. Personal idiosyncrasies due to age or background should be recognised as such: idiosyncrasies. And the old saying that there can be no disputing in matters of taste should be seen as harmlessly, because only trivially, true. If the exercise of taste involves no judgment then, indeed, there can be no dispute or discussion; but if it does involve judgment, as most people think, then discussion is not only possible but desirable. Moreover, judgment, understood as public discourse, is always capable of reaching a pragmatic, if not a formal, resolution of difficulties.

Hume's remarks on art mostly occur when he is discussing features of our social life. That is why he considers art from the standpoint of human actions: the artist is trying to get something done, and spectators are trying to establish the why and the wherefore. Works of art, in this way, are pleasurable means of communication, and their acceptance depends on their making sense to spectators who can agree in their responses. Hume holds that as an historical phenomenon, art occurs only when man has time to turn aside from the brute necessi-

ties of living. Nevertheless, in the more leisurely context of his own epoch, the arts can be held to refine the temper and make men more sociable, because artists who are trying to please spectators have to consider their needs and interests. This point has an important consequence for criticism of the arts: because art is a human activity, one of the general criteria for understanding any human action applies to it – namely, knowledge of how the agent himself viewed the context and appropriateness of what he was doing. So we should consider works of art in terms of the audience for which they were intended, as well as in terms of their internal character, their genre, style and tradition. Hume holds that one can achieve the 'proper sentiment' towards most, and certainly towards the best, works of art. There are two elements in his claim. To be causally affected by a work's properties, we must adopt the right viewpoint – the right frame of mind, as well as the right physical standpoint. The second element is even more important. What distinguishes a *proper response* from a merely *passive reaction*, as when we bask in the hot sun, is the active contribution of the spectator. This involves an interpretation of the work's meaning and value, over and above identification of the aspects we find affecting; meaning, after all, cannot be detected by the five senses alone, any more than necessity. It involves the exercise of the mind.

Although they receive their most sustained treatment in a single essay, 'Of the Standard of Taste', which Hume published in 1757, his views on art and criticism still prove fruitful to thinkers today; moreover, they belong to a period when the modern notion of aesthetics was receiving its first tentative formulation. Public concerts were beginning to take place, the easel painting was becoming popular, and the first novels were appearing; except for those who travelled to Europe, however, most people saw very few paintings, had access to no museums, had little knowledge of Greek, as opposed to Roman, sculpture and architecture, and none at all of the art of other cultures. Hume's own tastes were almost inevitably those of his own time, governed by the literary models of antiquity. On his travels he carried copies of Virgil, Horace, Tasso and Tacitus. For style he admired Cicero, of course, and among moderns, Addison; in contemporary poetry and drama, he believed, the French held the palm. Shakespeare's genius ensured his pre-eminence, but his vulgarity and unevenness were regrettable; John Donne, on the other hand, was artificial, and Ben Jonson hopelessly servile to the ancients. For a time Hume allowed his better judgment to be warped into championing the cause

Frontispiece, by Bartolozzi, to Robert Adam's book on the palace of Diocletian at Split, that so influenced contemporary taste. Adam was a friend of Hume.

Portia and Shylock, by David Allan. Hume admired the heroic and inspired in Shakespeare, but judged him guilty of great lapses of taste.

of William Wilkie, author of *The Epigoniad*, as the Scots Homer, and he was delighted when his kinsman John Home's melodramatic play *Douglas* took London by storm, in 1756. In the same vein, however, he prepared a devastating paper under the title 'Of the Authenticity of Ossian's Poems', which he withheld from publication out of deference to his friend Hugh Blair; the challenge he makes to Macpherson to produce the evidence, and to establish the authenticity of his documents, echoing as they do the earlier discussion of miracle stories, lays down standards entirely acceptable to historians of our own day. Hume expressed no serious interest in painting or music, possibly because he did not encounter them, but he enjoyed dancing. Like all the major figures of the Scottish Enlightenment, except Adam Ferguson, Hume was a Lowlander born and bred. Does this explain why he held the noise of bagpipes to be a 'barbarous discord'?[26]

VIEWS ON HISTORY AND POLITICS. Hume's view of the nature of historical writing and understanding, which brings together his thoughts on evidence and human testimony, as well as on agency and motivation, rests on two fundamental tenets: firstly, agents act with certain intentions, but are necessarily ignorant, when they set out, of the outcome; secondly, observers know the outcome, but are doomed merely to conjecture the intentions necessary for understanding it. The unbridgeable gap between foresight and hindsight of the 'actor'

The execution of Charles I, ascribed to Weesop.

Hume's History of England *ends at 1688, but he wrote the Stuart volumes first, no doubt influenced by the events of the '45 and their aftermath. The execution of Charles I provided him with a classic case around which to formulate his own political philosophy. In the* History *(ch.LIX): "it is dangerous for princes, even from the appearance of necessity, to assume more authority than the laws have allowed them. But it must be confessed, that these events furnish us with another instruction, no less natural, and no less useful, concerning the madness of the people, the furies of fanaticism, and the danger of mercenary armies."*

and 'spectator', as Hume calls them, can baffle the most diligent enquirer. One important point here is the tension between the agent's passions, which alone can motivate him, and the spectator's reason, which functions in his understanding: 'Mens' views of things are the result of their understanding alone: Their conduct is regulated by their understanding, their temper, and their passsions'.[27] Spectators do have access, however, to data logically unavailable to the agent: in particular, to the longer term consequences of his acts, and to the varying significance ascribed to them from different perspectives, and in relation to different sets of issues. The judgments of hindsight are transient, nevertheless, because the possibility of re-interpretation is ever present in the light of succeeding events.

A central theme of Hume's historical reflections concerns the unavoidable struggle between liberty and authority. He is primarily concerned with liberty under the law, and with constraints upon it exercised by various kinds of authority; to a lesser degree he considers limits on personal liberty imposed by habit or education. For Hume, a discussion of liberty is not ultimately separable from a discussion of virtue, and thus of how to live as a social being: 'general virtue and good morals in a state must proceed entirely from the virtuous education of youth, the effect of wise laws and institutions'. The real threat to society stems from faction: 'Factions subvert government, render laws impotent, and beget the fiercest animosities among men of the same nation, who ought to give mutual assistance and protection to each other'.[28] On one point Hume is adamant: 'violent innovations no individual is entitled to make'.[29] In the middle of the eighteenth century, politicians and historians alike were sensitive to the reverberations of the Civil War, Restoration, and Hanoverian Succession; and nowhere were they more alert than in Scotland, especially after the '15 and the '45. Hume concedes that fifty years after the Civil War things were much better than before it: but the means to improvement, the revolution itself, was an evil which generated excess upon excess. And precisely because the consequences of excess cannot be foreseen, there is never a case for instigating a revolution or resisting the law. The stability and very structure of society depend on the upholding of law, and society faces its greatest peril when resistance to law is itself proclaimed as 'lawful or commendable'. Gradual change should be sought, in the recognition also, that the complexity of political questions means that 'there scarcely ever occurs, in any deliberation, a choice, which is either purely good, or purely ill. Consequences, mixed and varied, may be foreseen to flow from every measure: And many consequences, unforseen, do always, in fact, result from every one'.[30]

Throughout his writings Hume observes that personal inclinations, political interests, religious zeal, are constant threats to society. It is 'not enough for liberty to remain on the defensive', not least because, however carefully framed, no laws could 'possibly provide against every contingency'.[31] He explains man's natural impatience towards opposing views by citing the psychological and social needs for agreement, and the mutually re-enforcing effect of such agreement: these needs, however, can easily consolidate into habits which resist true freedom of thought. Moreover, organised factions typically depend on limiting thought by making habitual those passions which inhibit it and survive without it. Hume holds that toleration developed historically not as a result of positive policy, but from a slow recognition that attempts at repression merely stiffened resistance. He does not think, however, that toleration always wins through. In this context, Hume faces a dilemma which recurs throughout his philosophy: the dilemma of upholding moderation, and of stabilising the unavoidable tension between liberty and authority. Since there is no criterion of moderation in advance of a particular context with clear boundaries – for moderation is definable only by reference to limits – there can be no fully intelligible principle of moderation independently of cases: and how are such cases identified? Moreover, it is unclear how an attitude of moderation could, in practice, motivate anyone to displace deeply engrained habits, on the one hand, or fanaticism, on the other.

The aim of government, in Hume's view, is to establish and then to preserve just laws. But the laws must not suppose that man's nature can be very much changed. The law-makers, in other words, whether in the sphere of government or morality, must first seek to understand the nature of man. They must also grasp that threats to liberty stem from various sources. On the economic front Hume saw the national debt, with its attendant taxation levies, together with the prospect of nationalisation of property, as especially dangerous. He considers that low interest rates, controlled labour costs, and competitive pricing are all essential to ensure both successful foreign trade, and a buoyant home economy which motivates the labour force. Arbitrary and penal taxation, alike, undermine liberty; indirect taxation, particularly on luxuries, is preferable to other kinds which lead to speculation and switching of funds, both of which weaken an economy. Running up a national debt is a popular expedient among politicians, but should be condemned. By limiting the capacity of our successors to deal with their own immediate problems, it is likely to diminish their own respect for the traditions they inherit, and make them adopt a more cavalier policy towards their own,

unknown, posterity. The historical structure of society is thus undermined by bequeathing one's debts to later generations.

Hume disapproved of the concentration of capital in a few cities as much as he lamented the population drift towards them; and he attacked all isolationism in politics or economics. He recognised that diversification will be necessary when an economy rests on a few staple products, because such an economy is always vulnerable to decreasing demand, and to lower pricing by successful competitors. It might be added that he disapproved of State ownership on the grounds that a State can always secure itself against enquiry and accountability.

If law is to ensure liberty, there can be no case for a standing army. Apart from the fact that it is an irresistible tool for any tyrant, it is inimical to the delicate balance between liberty and authority. In the end, however, Hume believes that economic, social and political obstacles to liberty are traceable to mistaken philosophical views. This emerges, implicitly, from his discussions of religion and its institutions, and in his remarks on the influence of habit, ignorance and the passions. Religions trade on and consolidate man's passions, and in so doing effectively inhibit free inquiry.

But there are greater obstacles to knowledge of one's self and of others, because all the sources of knowledge are liable to distortion or misinterpretation. The majority of our claims to know something, as we have said, do not derive from firsthand experience, but are reports of what we have heard from other people who, themselves, probably learned it from yet others. Education, in the broadest sense, is a principal source of our beliefs, and in the *History* Hume deems education to be a fundamental obstacle to liberty. In the past, this was because education was dominated by religions, in unholy alliance with scholastic philosophy; but, more generally, education essentially involves habit forming, and this is intrinsically dangerous. Hume is not here talking about the life-preserving habits, such as sleeping or eating, nor even the habit of expecting the future to resemble the past: these he regards as entirely natural, and beyond either the beneficial or harmful influence of education. He is concerned, rather, with social conditioning, because man's whole existence as a social being, from the family upwards, makes him an easy victim of unscrupulous indoctrination. The herd instinct, along with the desire for agreement, approval and acceptance, may be essential, at some level, for survival; but they are also malleable characteristics. Paradoxically, we might say that the conditions for

Inveraray Castle, by John Clerk of Eldin. When Hume attended service in the old Kirk, while a guest at the castle, the minister preached on "Unreasonable scepticism".

social existence can also lead to slavery. When Hume declares that the bulk of mankind are 'governed by authority, not reason' he means that they are literally governed by magistrates whose task is to uphold the law, and metaphorically governed by habits and passions independent of reason. To tamper, therefore, with the principles and instruments of government, 'merely upon the credit of supposed argument and philosophy, can never be the part of a wise magistrate'.[32] Nor of a wise philosopher.

SCEPTICISM. Hume was by no means ashamed of his sceptical stance and his sceptical arguments, although his opponents, using the same label, regarded it extremely unfavourably. As a general term of abuse *sceptic* covered all those who challenged orthodox views, asked difficult questions (even when no one else claimed to know the answer), omitted mention of God or canvassed views that left little or no room for a God, denied the existence of things for which words nevertheless existed, or merely confessed ignorance. On all these grounds Hume qualifies for the label. At different times he explicitly denies that we have innate ideas; that the causal relation is observably anything other than constant conjunction; that there are observable necessary connections anywhere; that there is either an empirical or demonstrative proof for the assumptions that the future will resemble the past, and that every event has a cause; that there is an irresolvable dispute between advocates of free will and determinism; that formal reasoning is crucially involved in everyday life; that there is a case for believing reports of miracles; that there is explanatory force to the design argument; that extreme scepticism is coherent; that he can find the experiential source of our ideas of self, substance or God.

In spite of this list, which can easily be supplemented, Hume thought of his own position as one of only mitigated or moderate scepticism. This needs to be explained. In antiquity, the sceptical philosophers formulated sets of arguments which challenged claims to knowledge: the fundamental question concerned the 'criterion', or test, for distinguishing truth from falsity. Some argued that in the face of insufficient evidence, all judgment must be suspended, and no resort made to probabilities. Others, however, urged that in practical life probability is enough; things have to get done, and we do not need the last ounce of evidence. Cicero, and Hume following him, adopted this latter view. Hume was frequently misunderstood, however, as denying the truth of certain claims, when he was simply asking how we know them to be true. Thus,

Hume holds that there is an external world, independent of our senses, and that this is a common sense belief, whilst questioning how the belief can be satisfactorily justified. Again, as he crossly told a correspondent, 'I never asserted so absurd a proposition as *that any thing might arise without a cause*';[33] his interest was in the origin, nature and justification of the belief which we unquestionably do have, that every event has a cause. On many matters he held that we submit blindly 'to the current of nature', and he regarded this as a sceptical conclusion to his enquiries, because our own reasoning seemed to play so little part in the adoption or justification of such beliefs. Dogmatism of any kind, however, is one of the greater evils, so a 'true sceptic' will be as diffident of his doubts as of his assertions.

Influence and Disputed Questions

However much we may think that his contemporaries misunderstood Hume's views, there is no doubt that they reacted strongly to them. Adam Smith derived many of his notions in moral and political philosophy from Hume, extending them where need be – as in the case of 'sympathy' and 'the impartial spectator'. Adam Ferguson, likewise, developed his conception of civil society against the background of Hume's reflections. In America, James Madison and Alexander Hamilton studied Hume's political writings and *History* with

"The Triumph of Truth", *by Sir Joshua Reynolds, shows James Beattie, Professor of Moral Philosophy at Aberdeen, presiding over the defeat of the sceptics, Hume and Voltaire.*

great care whilst formulating their views on the future structure and direction of their nation. In France, too, Hume's political, economic and historical writings were widely admired and discussed by the leading intellectuals before the Revolution. In Scotland, Thomas Reid, Professor of Philosophy first in Aberdeen and then in Glasgow, devoted a great deal of time to rebutting Hume's views on the nature of both knowledge and morality. Professor James Beattie, also of Aberdeen, secured passing fame, particularly in Germany, for a diatribe against Hume, and all over Britain theologians published numerous attacks on the great infidel. One of the most troublesome notions for many of Hume's contemporaries, however, was that of causation: fierce debates took place between practising scientists, and James Hutton devoted hundreds of pages to the issue in his own vast philosophical treatise, which eventually appeared in 1794. In Germany, Immanuel Kant (1724–1804),

having credited Hume with waking him from a dogmatic slumber, also devoted a considerable portion of his philosophy to formulating a cogent alternative to Hume's position. It is no exaggeration to say that almost all of Western philosophy since the end of the eighteenth century can be associated with the rival views of Hume and Kant.

In terms of sales the most popular of Hume's works was the *History*. It went through 150 editions within a century of publication, whereas the *Treatise* had to wait nearly as long for a second printing. In the nineteenth century a few philosophers claimed Hume as their mentor, such as August Comte in France, and J. S. Mill and T. H. Huxley in England; William James, in America, drew much inspiration from him. There has been an astonishing resurgence of interest in Hume's work since the 1960s, although in the earlier part of this century his name had been kept alive in Scotland. In the first place dispute has centred on the appropriate contexts for understanding Hume's work and the due weight to be given to his various claims, made over a 40-year span in works of different kinds. Hume was trying to displace many of his readers' views on the nature of man and society, and his own knowledge of their beliefs profoundly influenced the style, content and emphasis of his approach. In this context there is dispute over Hume's conception of philosophy and its roles, and over the nature and scope of his scepticism.

On more particular topics there is considerable disagreement about the need for, or the possibility of, modifying his account of causation to cope with developments in modern science, especially at the level of very small or very large phenomena. Do appeals to statistical frequencies avoid the sceptical elements in Hume's position? Are his own views on inductive argument and the weighing of probabilities fundamentally sound? If our sensory experience is a seamless continuum, as some people maintain, does it make sense to divide it up into events with beginnings and ends? If we cannot explain how we identify, separate and classify events, can we talk of separate causes and effects at all? Hume emphasised the importance of resemblance or similarity in his theory of causation: similar causes are assumed to produce similar effects. Things are similar, however, only in certain respects. How do we decide on the relevance and existence of similarities?

His views on the nature of the self provoke lengthy argument in legal and medical spheres, as well as among philosophers; and his views on freedom and determinism, the roles of reason and sentiment, and the nature of justice, are much debated. His economic views are now closely compared with those of Adam Smith. Studies of seventeenth- and eighteenth-century Scottish legal thought, and the precise theological issues of the day, together with attempts to establish the nature of Hume's rather slight scientific knowledge, are likely to lead to revised interpretations of his work. One sign of a great thinker is that later readers deem it a cultural duty to define their position in relation to his and to treat him, however anachronistically, as a contemporary. With the attention now being given to the whole range of his works, including the *Essays* and the *History*, it is unlikely that Hume's views will suffer neglect in the near future.

The context in which Hume was writing would strike most modern readers as almost entirely alien. He was the first major Scottish philosopher to publish all his works in English – Reid, although older than Hume, published his works late in life. He was writing before most of the philosophers

and political theorists, musicians and poets, artists and, above all, scientists, whom we study today. In 1763, it still took 16 days to reach London by coach from Edinburgh, and there was only one coach a month. Books were relatively expensive and Hume was addressing a small élite, to whom religion was still a social and political force. He was not, and could not have been, discussing twentieth-century issues. Certain philosophical problems, however, seem to transcend the occasions on which they happen to be discussed; if they are not strictly perennial problems, they nevertheless seem to recur in different forms in different contexts. Modern readers study Hume's works because so many of the issues he raised have their parallels in our own times; and formulation of the questions is a necessary step towards preparing the answers.

Hume often declares that, in the end, philosophy is an unnatural endeavour, in the sense that most people do not need it and that life goes on without it. Academic philosophy might even be harmful, as well as useless; and although it suits certain sorts of unusual people, even they are expected to function effectively and responsibly in the public world. Hume saw his own role as philosopher as that of an 'Ambassador from the Dominions of Learning to those of Conversation';[34] among his tasks were the study and preservation of those traditions which alone make sense of the social and historical context we live in, and which constitute common opinion and act as a check on the wilder flights of speculation. One of the strongest bonds of society, he holds, is communication; in the fullest sense this notion involves an understanding of oneself and one's relations with others, together with a conception of how to live and conduct oneself. It is not surprising, therefore, that Hume made bold to claim that 'the science of man is the only solid foundation for the other sciences'; nor that he also declared: 'Be a philosopher: but amidst all your philosophy, be still a man'.[35]

Notes

For ease of reference to Hume's books, section or chapter numbers are quoted, rather than page numbers, because they are common to all editions. The numerous editions also make it impossible to do more than refer to the essays by their title.

1. All these passages are quoted from David Hume, *Essays, Moral, Political and Literary*, edited by T. H. Green and T. H. Grose (London, 1875), vol.ii, pp.445-9.
2. *The Letters of David Hume*, edited by J. Y. T. Greig (Oxford, 1932), vol.i, pp.115-29.
3. *Letters*, i, p.210.
4. *Letters*, ii, p.134.
5. *Letters*, ii, p.206-7.
6. *Letters*, ii, p.335.
7. *An Abstract of A Treatise of Human Nature.*
8. *Abstract.*
9. *Treatise of Human Nature*, i, iii, 2.
10. *Abstract.*
11. *Abstract.*
12. *Abstract.*
13. *An Enquiry concerning Human Understanding*, iv.
14. idem.
15. idem.
16. *Abstract.*
17. *An Enquiry concerning Human Understanding*, viii.
18. *An Enquiry concerning Human Understanding*, xi.
19. *An Enquiry concerning Human Understanding*, iv.
20. Draft letter from William Cullen to William Hunter, on the death of Hume, Glasgow University Library, Thomson-Cullen Papers, 161.
21. *The Natural History of Religion*, xiii.
22. *Treatise*, i, iv, 7.
23. *Treatise*, ii, iii, 3.
24. *An Enquiry concerning the Principles of Morals*, i.
25. *An Enquiry concerning the Principles of Morals*, iii.
26. In the unpublished essay, 'Of the Authenticity of Ossian's Poems', contained in *Essays*, vol.ii, p.419.
27. *History of England*, liii.
28. In the essay, 'Of Parties in General' (1742).
29. In the essay, 'Of the Original Contract' (1748).
30. In the essay, 'Of the Protestant Succession' (written in 1748, published in 1752).
31. *History of England*, xlviii and xlvii.
32. In the essay, 'Idea of a perfect Commonwealth' (1752).
33. *Letters*, i, p.187.
34. In the essay, 'Of Essay Writing' (1742).
35. *An Enquiry concerning Human Understanding*, i.

Bibliography

There is no standard or uniform edition of Hume's works, but most of them are available in paperback. Convenient editions of Hume's *Essays*, and also of his *History*, are published in the *Liberty Classics* series (Indianapolis, 1985). There are many editions of the two *Enquiries*, and they are printed together, edited by P. H. Nidditch, along with the *Abstract* (Oxford, 1975). Nidditch has also edited the *Treatise* (Oxford, 1978). The best edition of the *Dialogues Concerning Natural Religion* is by N. Kemp Smith, who also provided a long introduction (Indianapolis, n.d.).

The only modern and comprehensive biography is by Ernest Mossner, *The Life of David Hume* (Oxford, 2nd edition, 1970): it is an immensely enjoyable work.

Readers new to Hume may like to begin by reading some of the *Essays*, or the *Dialogues Concerning Natural Religion*; the chapters on the Cromwellian period, in the *History*, also make very good reading. Philosophy students often begin with the two *Enquiries*, before making their way to the much more difficult *Treatise*.

Many commentaries on Hume are rather difficult to read, or focus on issues of specialist concern. An excellent guide to the wealth of discussion this century is given by Roland Hall, *50 Years of Hume Scholarship* (Edinburgh, 1978). A good general introduction to many of Hume's views is provided by Terence Penelhum, *Hume* (London, 1975). His moral philosophy is sympathetically discussed by J. L. Mackie, *Hume's Moral Theory* (London, 1980). A good discussion, wider than its title implies, is provided by David Miller, *Philosophy and Ideology in Hume's Political Thought* (Oxford, 1981).

An advanced discussion of causation in a modern context is provided by T. L. Beauchamp and A. Rosenberg, *Hume and the Problem of Causation* (Oxford, 1981).

A wide-ranging work, which includes discussion of Hume's historical and political writings, is D. W. Livingston, *Hume's Philosophy of Common Life*, (Chicago, 1984). My own *Hume's Sentiments: Their Ciceronian and French Context* (Edinburgh, 1982) includes a study of Hume's views on religion and on art.

Adam Smith

D.D.RAPHAEL

DAVID HUME is famous both as a philosopher and as a historian. His close friend Adam Smith is now known to the world for his achievement as an economist, but in his own day he was greatly respected as a moral philosopher too. It is neither surprising nor unjust that Smith's great work of political economy, *An Inquiry into the Nature and Causes of the Wealth of Nations*, should have placed in the shade his earlier contribution to ethics, *The Theory of Moral Sentiments*, but both deserve to be remembered and both are eminently worth reading for their enduring contribution to their subjects and also as literature. There are, in addition, some shorter works which repay attention, notably an essay on the History of Astronomy, and scholars are now able to study reports of early lectures on jurisprudence and on rhetoric, which help one to see how a notable philosopher turned into a brilliant economist.

The *Wealth of Nations* is indeed a toweringly successful work. The nineteenth-century historian, H.T.Buckle, said that 'looking at its ultimate results, [it] is probably the most important book that has ever been written, and is certainly the most valuable contribution ever made by a single man towards establishing the principles on which government should be based'.[1] It is foolhardy to describe any book (other than the Bible, if that can count as one book), even with the qualification 'probably', as the most important ever written, but Buckle had good cause to note the profound results of Smith's work and in particular of his placing economics at the centre of politics. Economics has of course moved far beyond the treatment given to it by Adam Smith but, historically speaking, the *Wealth of Nations* remains the seminally influential work of political economy to a degree which can

hardly be matched by a single early book in any other field of thought and policy.

Life

Adam Smith was born at Kirkcaldy, Fife, in 1723. It is commonly said that the date of his birth was 5 June, and this indeed appears to be confirmed by the inscription on his tombstone; but since 5 June is the date on which he was baptised, we must conclude that his birth was in fact earlier, though perhaps by only a few days. He was named Adam after his father, who had died in January at a relatively early age and after a marriage of less than three years. It was a second marriage for Adam Smith senior, since he had been left a widower in 1717. His second wife, Margaret Douglas, was a young woman in her twenties, and the premature death of her husband meant that she had to cope as best she could with a stepson, Hugh, and with her own son, Adam, both of them rather delicate. Hugh died in his early forties, like his father before him. Adam grew up to be more robust and lived to the age of sixty-nine. The mother, despite the anxieties of her youth, reached her ninetieth year and died in 1784 only six years before her son. He had remained unmarried and his mother shared his home in Edinburgh from 1778, as he had shared hers in Kirkcaldy before that. They were understandably very close to each other emotionally, a widowed mother and a posthumous only child. This may explain why Adam Smith did not marry, but his affection for his mother did not prevent him from falling in love at least twice, and one of a recently discovered batch of letters indicates that even at the age of fifty-three he still thought he might marry and have children.[2]

Margaret Douglas Smith was not left indigent by

the death of her husband, nor did she lack the comforting support of her own kin. Her brother and her sisters all lived in Fife and she visited them frequently. On one such visit to her brother at Strathenry, her son Adam, then aged three, was carried off by a group of vagabond tinkers. His mother would obviously have been distressed, as would his uncle, who managed to recover the child after a few hours. Whether the incident had any effect on the little boy himself is more dubious, but W. R. Scott was ready to surmise that 'the shock and, more especially, the constraint would remain deeply impressed on his sub-conscious mind, and this would engender an attitude which would be antipathetic to any enforced compliance and receptive to everything which was in the direction of freedom'.[3] Scott was, however, rather prone to fanciful conjecture, and I myself think that Smith's passion for freedom is more likely to have had its source in the influence of Francis Hutcheson at Glasgow University.

Smith attended the local burgh school at Kirkcaldy, where he was given a solid grounding in Latin, Greek, and mathematics, together with a taste for the performance of drama. He proceeded to the University of Glasgow in 1737 at the age of

fourteen. That seems young by modern standards but Smith was in fact older than the average entrant in those days. Most students began at the age of eleven or twelve, and one might well wonder how far they understood the quite sophisticated lectures of the Moral Philosophy course which they attended in their third year. Adam Smith at sixteen will have been more capable of appreciating the subject and it was in this field that he found his *métier*. The Professor of Moral Philosophy at the time was Francis Hutcheson, who has been called the father of Scottish philosophy and who strongly influenced Hume as well as Smith. The influence on Smith lay less in the specific character of Hutcheson's ethical theory than in arousing curiosity about law, government, and economics, going along with an enthusiasm for social and economic freedom. Smith always referred to Hutcheson in terms of admiration and affection. He was equally fulsome in his praise of another of his Glasgow teachers, Robert Simson, Professor of Mathematics, whom Smith described as one of the two greatest mathematicians of his time.[4] Simson does have a significant place in the history of mathematics for his restoration of Greek geometry, though Smith's estimate of him is excessive. According to a fellow-

Glasgow. The University, late 17th century.
Oxford. Balliol College, early 18th century.

ADAM SMITH · 71

student, Smith's own interests as an under-graduate at Glasgow lay chiefly in mathematics and natural philosophy. The stimulus of Simson's teaching no doubt contributed much to that.

Having completed the three-year curriculum at Glasgow in 1740, Smith was awarded a Snell Exhibition to Balliol College, Oxford. This award is still made annually to enable especially talented students of Glasgow University to proceed to more advanced study at Balliol. Both institutions have benefited greatly from it, but in the eighteenth century the gain to the Scottish students was limited. The standard of teaching at Oxford was miserably low, as we learn from the unanimous opinion of Adam Smith, Joseph Butler, Edward Gibbon, and Jeremy Bentham. Balliol, however, did have a good library and Smith made excellent use of it. He read a wide range of Greek and Latin literature, retaining much of it in his memory for use in his writings many years later. He also read a fair amount of French literature and took pleasure in translating memorable passages into English. His reading of classical literature naturally included ancient philosophy. He supplemented this with some modern philosophy, not a great deal, to judge from his works, but it did include Hume's *Treatise*

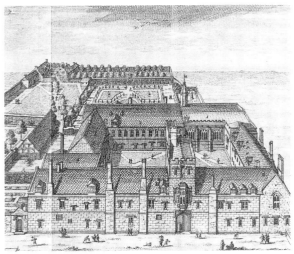

of Human Nature, published very recently in 1739–40. Smith himself in later years frequently recalled that he had been reprimanded at Oxford for reading the book and that his copy had been confiscated. One report has it that this was the reason why he left after six years, when his Snell Exhibition still had four years to run. At any rate he did decide in 1746 that he had had enough of Oxford

Kirkcaldy. Plan and elevation of the Smith family home (after an old plan).

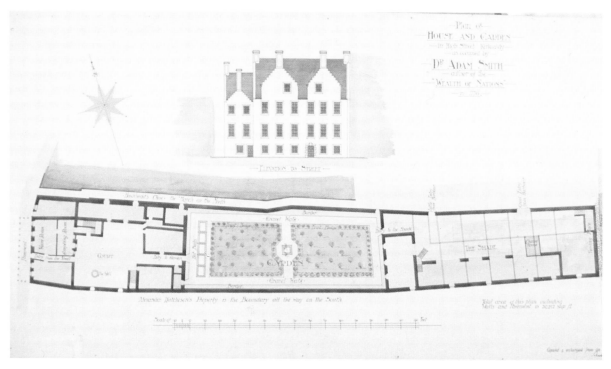

and he returned to Kirkcaldy in August of that year.

In 1748, through the good offices of three advocates, Henry Home (afterwards Lord Kames), Robert Craigie, and James Oswald of Dunnikier (a friend from schoolboy days and at that time MP for Fife), Smith was invited to give a course of lectures in Edinburgh on rhetoric and *belles-lettres*. The lectures had no connection with the university, but the intention of the organisers was to broaden the education of budding lawyers, and Smith's audience consisted largely of students of law and theology. Smith repeated the course in the two subsequent years, and in the latter at least, he gave an additional course of lectures on civil law for the law students. Both series of lectures were warmly appreciated and the audience came to include a number of prominent citizens as well as the students.

A direct result of Smith's success in Edinburgh was to be offered appointment to the Chair of Logic at the University of Glasgow, which became vacant at the end of 1750. He was due to begin his Logic teaching at Glasgow in the autumn of 1751. Shortly before doing so he was asked if he would also teach part of the Moral Philosophy course since the Professor of Moral Philosophy, Thomas Craigie, was seriously ill. Craigie in fact died at the end of November 1751 and Smith was transferred, at his own request, to the Moral Philosophy Chair for the following session. The scope of the Moral Philosophy course, which included the philosophy of law and the principles of politics, appealed to him much more than that of Logic. Although Smith wrote some early essays on the theory of knowledge and the history of logic and metaphysics, he never found that side of philosophy as congenial as ethics and its closely related social studies. He held the Chair of Moral Philosophy at Glasgow with great distinction and enjoyment for twelve years, from 1752 to 1764.

Despite a lack of natural gifts as a speaker, either in quality of voice or in ease of eloquence, Adam Smith was an extremely successful teacher and in other respects an exemplary professor. The originality and discernment of his philosophical views far surpassed those of his predecessors, including his own admired teacher Hutcheson. His pastoral care of his students was as concerned as anyone could desire, and his contribution to the administration of the university was quite exceptional.

Following the traditional practice of the time, Smith's main course of lectures for the Moral Philosophy class dealt with natural theology, ethics, and 'jurisprudence', the last section covering the history and general principles of law and government, including the principles of political economy. From the ethics section Smith distilled his first book, *The Theory of Moral Sentiments*, published in 1759. He planned to follow this up with a book based on the

Henry Scott, 3rd Duke of Buccleuch, by Gainsborough. The Duke regarded Smith "as a friend whom I loved and respected, not only for his great talents, but for every private virtue".

PHILOSOPHERS

latter part of his lectures and concentrating on the principles of natural justice which underlie positive systems of law, the practices of government, and the workings of economic life. In the course of time, however, his thought about economics pre-occupied his attention and grew to form the *Wealth of Nations*. Smith still hoped to supplement this with a further book on the history and theory of law and government, and he evidently had written a considerable part of it towards the end of his life; but he never completed it to his own satisfaction and ordered his executors, Joseph Black and James Hutton, to destroy the manuscript, along with others, just before his death. We have some idea of the scope of the projected book from two reports of his lectures on jurisprudence which have survived, but a comparison of the economics section of these reports with the *Wealth of Nations* suggests that the planned book on law and government would like-wise have been vastly superior, in structure and persuasiveness, to the lectures which outlined its substance.

Smith's book on ethics was warmly received, not so much for the philosophical merits of its abstract theory as for the attractive presentation of its ideas in simple language and imaginative illustrations. Edmund Burke in a review described the style as 'rather painting than writing'.[5] The book was read and applauded in France and Germany, making its way at first in the original English version and before long in translation. It must have been known in other countries of Europe too, for the reputation of Adam Smith brought students from Geneva and

Moscow to Glasgow University in 1761, specifically in order to study under him. A more profound effect on Smith's personal fortunes arose from the admiration accorded to the book in London. A leading politician, Charles Townshend, was step-father to the third Duke of Buccleuch, then a school-boy at Eton. Townshend sounded out Smith about the possibility of acting as tutor to the Duke when he should leave school and travel abroad for his further education. The invitation was crystallised in 1763 and as a result Smith gave up his Glasgow Chair in 1764 in order to accompany the Duke of Buccleuch on a 'grand tour'.

It was not unusual for a Scottish university pro-fessor to take a post as tutor for a time to a young nobleman, but it was unusual to resign his pro-fessorship in consequence. More commonly the professor asked for leave of absence. There were different views about the propriety of taking ex-tended leave of absence in such circumstances. Smith thought it was wrong and he therefore re-signed his professorship. That seems a drastic step and indeed David Hume, when giving Smith the first news of Townshend's intention, assumed that Smith would not be willing to give up his university post.[6] Townshend, however, had not spoken idly in saying that he would make it worth Smith's while. He offered not only a salary of £500 a year but also a pension for life of £300 a year after the tutorship period was ended. Even the latter figure was higher than the combined income which Smith received from his professorial stipend and the students' fees. So Smith would have a degree of security well beyond that afforded by a university post and, perhaps more important, the freedom to devote himself entirely to the books he wanted to write.

Smith left Glasgow in January 1764, just about half way through the university session. The tale of his last meeting with his class is worth repeating because, like his resignation of the Chair, it reflects his scrupulous sense of moral conduct. He arranged for a substitute to deliver the remainder of his lectures at a salary to be determined by the univers-ity and paid wholly by Smith, with no cost to the students. Indeed he insisted on paying back to the students the fees which he had received from them, so that the teaching which he himself had given them would also be free. The students tried to resist this last provision. At the end of his final lecture to them Smith explained the position and called up the first of them to take back his fee. 'The young man peremptorily refused to accept it, de-claring that the instruction and pleasure he had already received was much more than he either

Voltaire (François Marie Arouet, 1694-1778) by J. A. Houdon. Playwright, novelist, poet, essayist, atheist and philosopher, Voltaire touched human activity in almost every sphere and has been described as "the most celebrated man in Europe".

had repaid or ever could compensate, and a general cry was heard from every one in the room to the same effect. But Mr. Smith was not to be bent from his purpose. After warmly expressing his feelings of gratitude and the strong sense he had of the regard shown to him by his young friends, he told them this was a matter betwixt him and his own mind, and that he could not rest satisfied unless he had performed what he deemed right and proper. "You must not refuse me this satisfaction; nay, by heavens, gentlemen, you shall not;" And seizing by the coat the young man who stood next to him, he thrust the money into his pocket and then pushed him from him. The rest saw it was in vain to contest the matter, and were obliged to let him have his own way.'[7]

After meeting in London, Smith and the Duke of Buccleuch left for France in February 1764. They were joined by the Duke's younger brother, Hew Scott, in the autumn. They spent eighteen months in Toulouse, two further months travelling about in the South of France, then two months in Geneva, and finally ten months in Paris. The whole period of two and a half years abroad contributed as much to the education of Adam Smith as to that of his pupils. He had already begun work in Glasgow on his projected treatise on political economy and had

gleaned much relevant information from discussion with Glasgow merchants and from his own observation of the industrial and commercial life of Scotland. He now had the opportunity to compare with it what he could see and hear of the economy of France. In Toulouse he was a keen observer also of social and political institutions. At Geneva he was delighted to meet, on several occasions, and to converse with Voltaire, whom he admired excessively, not only as a spokesman for freedom of thought but also as a playwright, poet, and historian. Above all, Smith benefited from his experience of Paris. Like Hume before him, he was a great favourite with the ladies at fashionable salons. He enjoyed the theatre, which he attended regularly. More valuable still were his frequent meetings with the group of thinkers who called themselves *les économistes* and who then came to be known as the physiocrats.

Their leader was François Quesnay, an eminent physician by profession but also the originator of a distinctive theory of economics. Another member of the group was Turgot, who was just completing his book, *Réflexions sur la formation et la distribution des richesses*, and who was later to become Minister of Finance under Louis XVI. The physiocrats maintained that national wealth depended entirely on agriculture; it was the only form of production which created a genuine surplus over costs; the task of other forms of production was to turn the products of agriculture into consumable goods. This theory led them to oppose the conventional wisdom of 'mercantilism', which advocated governmental support and protection for manufacture and trade. Smith regarded the primary doctrine of the physiocrats about agriculture as exaggerated, but their opposition to mercantilism and their consequent defence of free trade corresponded to the views which he himself had reached. He undoubtedly learned much from them, especially Quesnay's explanation, in his *Tableau économique*, of the role of the circulation of money in the economic process. Smith had a high regard for Quesnay and intended to dedicate the *Wealth of Nations* to him. In the event, however, Quesnay died before Smith's book was completed.

Smith's esteem for Quesnay's ability as an economist went along with personal gratitude to him as a doctor. In August 1766 the Duke of Buccleuch suffered from a fever and Quesnay, despite being unwell himself at the time, agreed to Smith's pressing request to attend his pupil. Two months later Smith again called in Quesnay when Hew Scott fell ill. This time the illness was more serious and in fact proved fatal. On each occasion Smith wrote, in

Skirmish at Lexington, 1775, the opening clash of arms of the American War of Independence. Like Hume, Smith believed that the British had treated the colonists "with savage injustice", and advocated that restrictions on trading should be lifted.

letters to the boys' stepfather and sister, detailed accounts of the maladies and of the measures taken to counter them. His own deep concern, as one standing *in loco parentis*, is movingly apparent. When Hew Scott died, arrangements were at once made for Smith and the Duke to return to London with Hew's body. That was the end of the continental education.

Smith remained in London for about six months. Apart from shepherding a new edition of the *Moral Sentiments* through the press, he continued to work on his economics book, taking the opportunity to acquire information for the historical sections. No doubt he also continued his association with the Duke of Buccleuch. The Duke's mode of life was soon to be changed by marriage, and once that event had taken place, in May 1767, Smith returned to his mother's house in Kirkcaldy and devoted himself entirely to the writing of the *Wealth of Nations*.

The book grew under his hands and took longer than he expected. There is evidence in a letter of 1770 from Hume that Smith was then planning to take his manuscript to London for publication, but in fact he remained in Kirkcaldy for three more years and then worked at the final revision in London for three further years. During the latter period he regularly read parts of his manuscript to knowledgeable people such as Benjamin Franklin and Richard Price in order to take account of their comments and criticisms before settling on a final version. His friendship with Franklin will no doubt

have given him up-to-date information about America. Smith was deeply interested in the worsening dispute between Britain and the American colonies, a topic on which he developed a distinct and original view.

The *Wealth of Nations* was published on 9 March 1776. Surprisingly for a long academic work with much technical detail, it was immediately popular and the first edition was sold out after six months. Edward Gibbon, in a letter to Adam Ferguson, aptly summarised its virtues and the reasons for its success: 'What an excellent work is that with which our common friend Mr. Adam Smith has enriched the public! An extensive science in a single book, and the most profound ideas expressed in the most perspicuous language.'[8] David Hume, who was better qualified to judge the value of the work as a treatise on economics, was equally loud in its praise, although he did not expect it to be popular so quickly. It soon began to exert an influence on public policy. Some of Smith's recommendations for taxation were given effect in the Budgets of 1777 and 1778 introduced by Lord North, the Prime Minister and Chancellor of the Exchequer. Other members of the Government consulted Smith in 1778 about the policy they should adopt for ending the war with the American colonies, and in 1779 about a proposal to grant free trade to Ireland. Smith's arguments for free trade generally and for taxation policy were taken up with especial enthusiasm by William Pitt the Younger and were given practical application in various measures of

Panmure House, Edinburgh, where Smith settled in 1777.

Margaret Smith (d.1784), artist unknown. Smith's mother was "the object of his affection for more than 60 years".

Pitt's administration.

The year 1776 was doubly memorable for Smith, since the publication of his great work was soon followed by the death of his dearest friend, David Hume. Although the two men did not meet often, they had come to have the warmest affection for each other. Hume's esteem for Smith's intellectual achievement in the *Wealth of Nations* was matched by his respect for Smith's personal integrity. Smith for his part admired Hume more than anyone else in the world. He considered his friend to be the greatest philosopher of the age and a man of incomparable moral character. Hume's calm courage in the face of death has become a legend, largely through Adam Smith's account of it. To Smith's great surprise, his account stirred up as much acrimony as approbation. He had ended it by describing Hume 'as approaching as nearly to the idea of a perfectly wise and virtuous man, as perhaps the nature of human frailty will permit'.[9] This judgment was a deliberate imitation of the final sentence of Plato's dialogue *Phaedo*, which describes the last day of the life of Socrates. The allusion was understood by some readers, such as Edmund Burke, who commented to James Boswell that Hume 'had been preparing all along to die without showing fear', plainly a Socratic aim.[10] Boswell, once an admiring pupil but now a disillusioned critic of Adam Smith, urged Samuel Johnson to denounce the 'vain and ostentatious infidelity' exhibited by Hume and praised by Smith.[11] Johnson did not oblige and assured Boswell that Hume's apparent lack of fear on his deathbed was a pretence.[12] However, Smith's piece was publicly denounced by George Horne, President of Magdalen College, Oxford, in the name of 'the People called Christians'. Horne would have been even more incensed if he had known of a private letter in which Smith had gone over the same ground with the initial remark that 'Poor David Hume is dying very fast, but with great cheerfulness and good humour and with more real resignation to the necessary course of things, than any whining Christian ever died with pretended resignation to the will of God'.[13]

In 1777 Smith was appointed, at his own request, to a vacant post of Commissioner of Customs in Scotland. Edward Gibbon (and no doubt others) thought it odd that this should be the chosen occupation of 'a philosopher who . . . had enlightened the world by the most profound and systematic treatise on the great objects of trade and revenue which had ever been published in any age or in any

William Pitt, the younger (1759-1806) by Gillray.
Pitt was Prime Minister from 1783 to 1801, and from 1803 to 1806.

Smith's monument, Canongate Church, Edinburgh.

country';[14] but Smith himself was well content. It enabled him to live in the Scottish capital with his elderly mother and to see his most congenial friends as often as he desired, particularly Joseph Black and James Hutton. He was paid a stipend of £600 a year, and in consequence he thought he should give up the pension which he still received from the Duke of Buccleuch. The Duke rejected the suggestion, however, saying that the pension had been granted unconditionally. The combined income of £900 a year was a very substantial one for that time. Smith acquired a spacious home, Panmure House, in the Canongate and brought over from Kirkcaldy his mother and his cousin, Janet Douglas, to share it with him. Soon afterwards he arranged for a nephew of Janet Douglas to join them so that he could be educated in Edinburgh. Even so, Smith's style of life was not lavish and he quietly gave away large sums of money to charitable causes. He took very seriously his duties as Commissioner of Customs and was exceptionally diligent in his attendance at meetings of the Board. He had always been absent-minded and probably became more so in his later years, to judge from the tales told about him in this Edinburgh period. The failing did not impair his capacity for administration in his Glasgow days and there is no reason to suppose that it interfered with his efficiency at the Board of Customs.

Smith visited London again briefly in 1782 and for a longer spell in 1787. In the course of the second visit Smith met the Prime Minister, William Pitt the Younger, frequently. There is a pleasing, and reasonably reliable, story of their meeting at the Wimbledon villa of Henry Dundas, a member of the Government. Smith was one of the last to arrive and when he appeared the company stood up to greet him. He asked them to be seated but Pitt replied: 'No, we will stand till you are first seated, for we are all your scholars.'[15]

Later in 1787 Smith was elected Rector of Glasgow University, an office which gave him great pleasure and which he held for two years. In his letter to the Principal accepting the honour, Smith recalled the days of his professorship at Glasgow in these terms: 'The period of thirteen years which I spent as a member of that society I remember as by far the most useful, and, therefore, as by far the happiest and most honourable period of my life.'[16] Perhaps this thought gave him an added incentive to return, a few months later, to his long projected revision of *The Theory of Moral Sentiments*. The result of that revision, completed in December 1789 and published in the spring of 1790, was the greatly expanded sixth edition. The additions do not alter the

William Pitt, the younger (1759-1806) by Gillray.
Pitt was Prime Minister from 1783 to 1801, and from 1803 to 1806.

essential structure of Smith's ethical theory but they do reflect an outlook of more maturity in the estimation of character and also in allusions to religious doctrine.

Smith died on 17 July 1790. His grave in the Canongate churchyard is marked by a plain monument describing him simply as the author of *The Theory of Moral Sentiments* and the *Wealth of Nations*.

Smith's monument, Canongate Church, Edinburgh.

View of Greenock, 1786.
Trade from the Clyde ports grew rapidly at mid-century, and Smith's views on free trade influenced leading merchants and bankers of his acquaintance.

Works

Wealth of Nations. Pride of place must be given to the *Wealth of Nations.* It was not the first scientific treatment of economics, nor does it show profound originality in any one feature. The achievement of the book is to bring together for the first time so much of the economic life of society into a coherently related system, illustrated at all points by a wealth of empirical evidence. At the same time it is written in everyday language, easily understood by the non-specialist. Students of economics at Oxford used to be advised – perhaps they still are – to read through the whole of the *Wealth of Nations* as their first assignment, in order to obtain an intelligible conspectus of the entire field of their subject. The same advice can be given to anyone who is not a student of economics but would like to be reasonably informed about it.

The primary theme of the book is indicated by its full title, *An Inquiry into the Nature and Causes of the Wealth of Nations.* The term 'wealth' emphatically does not mean money. Smith insisted that the real wealth of a nation consisted in commodities, things that could be used and enjoyed. Like Hume and the physiocrats, he opposed the mercantilist view that a country's wealth was the amount of money it had acquired in the form of gold and silver. The purpose of Smith's inquiry is to show what national wealth really is, to explain how it has grown in modern commercial society, and consequently to make policy recommendations for the continuance of that growth. In order to explain economic growth he has to analyse the workings of the economic system, and this analysis or model is the most dominant and the most impressive feature of the first half of the work. Smith then relates the analysis to the history of economic growth and emphasises the key role of 'natural liberty'. This leads on to his advocacy of free trade and his criticism of the protectionist policies of mercantilism. He does not, however, think that there is no room at all for governmental control in economic affairs, and the final part of the work, taking up almost a third of the total space, deals with the necessary duties of a government in raising revenue and in carrying out functions which cannot be successfully left to private enterprise.

In his lectures on rhetoric Smith speaks of two alternative methods of conducting a didactic discourse. One is to begin with the data to be explained, taking up each set of things in whatever order seems convenient or familiar, and to find a

The final stages in pin manufacture, during which spirals are cut for the heads, wound round the shafts, annealed, and flattened. The pin is then coated with tin, washed, dried, polished and packed.

principle of explanation for each set as it comes up. The other method is to begin the exposition with a single basic principle, or a very few such principles, and to show how all the phenomena under inquiry can be explained by following out the connected consequences of the basic principle or principles. He names Aristotle as exemplifying the first method and Newton the second. Needless to say, he regards the Newtonian method as superior and he recommends it both for philosophy and for natural science. Smith undoubtedly thought that he had followed his own advice in composing his two books, the one on moral philosophy, the other on political economy. Each of them begins with what he takes to be the basic principle or concept of explanation and identifies it in the title of the first chapter.

In the case of the *Wealth of Nations* the basic explanatory concept is the division of labour, that is to say, specialisation by each worker on a particular job or function instead of doing everything for himself. Smith believes that the division of labour is the primary causal factor in economic growth. The view is plausible only if the idea of the division of labour is understood to include technological progress, whereby new tools or machines foster new, more specialised, skills. Smith thinks it is reasonable to put the two things together because he argues that the initial invention of new tools is a consequence of the division of labour. If you concentrate on one job or one function, instead of being distracted by a variety, you have the freedom of mind to invent methods of making the work easier. It is true that, at an advanced stage of manu-

facture, new machines are invented by engineers, not by the men on the job; but in the early stage of production, Smith says, it was the manual workers themselves who invented new tools or improved old ones. For that matter, the engineers who produce the later inventions are themselves the product of an increasing division of labour, like other 'philosophers' (Smith includes in this term scientists and technologists) whose function it is to observe and speculate.

Smith illustrates the effect of the division of labour by means of a simple example, the manufacture of pins. In the making of a pin there are about eighteen operations. A small factory employing ten men, who share these operations between them, produces about 50,000 pins in a day. If one man had to do all the operations, and if he lacked the specialised machines which the division of labour has brought about, he would take almost a day to produce one pin.

That shows the difference made to the producer. Smith then turns to the consumer, again with a simple telling example, the coat of a common labourer. It is the joint product of a host of skilled workers, a shepherd, a wool-sorter, a wool-comber, a dyer, a spinner, a weaver, a fuller, and many more. Some of these could not carry out their trade without material supplied by merchants and carriers. They in turn rely on shipbuilders, sailors, and manufacturers of sails and ropes. A similar long list would be needed to account for the rest of the labourer's clothes and for his household effects. The labourer depends for his comforts on the work of thousands of other people. And while those

Ramsay, The Gentle Shepherd, *illustrated by David Allan.*
Smith chose the coat of a common labourer as his most extended
example of the division of labour.

comforts appear simple and modest when compared with the luxuries of the rich, yet the difference between the two is no greater than the degree to which the labourer's comforts exceed those of 'many an African king, the absolute master of the lives and liberties of ten thousand naked savages'.[17] The European labourer has political mastery over nobody, but he has a material standard of life which requires the services of thousands and is far superior to that of the African chief who can command thousands. This colourful contrast indicates the scale of economic growth in modern commercial society and the remote consequences of the division of labour.

The benefits of a division of labour arise from exchange. The butcher, the baker, and the candle-stick-maker gain from their specialism because they can exchange their surplus meat, bread, and candlesticks for all the other things that they need. When a primitive system of barter is replaced by buying and selling through the medium of money, the concept of the market takes a central place in the economic system. Smith's analysis of the economy is an account of the natural laws exhibited by the working of the market.

His emphasis on the division of labour as the fundamental cause of economic growth is one original feature of his exposition. Another is his perception that the division of labour is limited by the extent of the market. Since the reason for a division of labour is the possibility of exchanging products, an advance in the division and sub-division of labour will take place only if there are more customers for the specialised products. That, Smith points out, is why you will find a greater specialisation of occupations in a town than in a village. The implications of the perception extend beyond the town to the national community and to international trade, where a vastly larger number of potential customers can be reached, provided that cheap transport is available and provided also that there are no obstacles to freedom of trade.

In explaining the workings of the market, Smith begins with an account of prices. The price of goods in the market depends both on demand, what customers are prepared to pay, and on the cost of production. Smith distinguishes three factors in the cost of production, the wages of the workers, the profit of those who have invested capital in the machines and materials needed to produce the goods, and the rent charged by landowners for the use of their land in the course of production. He then proceeds to an important distinction between market price and what he calls natural price. The

Glasgow, the Trongate. The statue of King William was a favourite meeting-place for merchants.

Children at work in coal mines. Smith warned against the brutalising effect of the division of labour: 'it corrupts the courage of the worker's mind and the activity of his body'.

wages, where Smith relates the natural rate of wages to the relative power of employers and workers, to the difference between a developing, a static, or a declining economy, and to the differences between more and less unattractive occupations. He assumes that all work is in principle unattractive, 'toil and trouble', needing to be balanced by the attraction of monetary reward. The toil and trouble can lie not only in the arduous, dirty, or dangerous character of the actual work but also in the effort or length of training or the subsequent insecurity of success, so that the high fees of a lawyer, for instance, are said to be justified on the same grounds as the wages of a miner. Smith goes so far as to suggest that in an economy which followed the laws of the market with perfect freedom (and with free access for all to education and training), the inequalities of pay would balance the inequalities of toil and trouble, so that all occupations would yield an equal amount of net satisfaction. This rather implausible view is Smith's economic interpretation of the traditional notion of political theory that the ideal state of nature was one of perfect liberty and equality.

The analysis so far can apply to a static economy: the price obtained in selling a commodity repays the cost of its production when the money is distributed to the three groups of people involved in the production. Smith's chief purpose, however, is to analyse a dynamic economy in which there can be a continual growth of wealth. He therefore goes on to give a detailed account of the financial aspects of the economy, the functions of capital and income, of money and banks, and the particular importance of saving.

market price is the price actually received in the market, and of course it varies considerably from time to time. The so-called natural price is a theoretical concept; it is the idea of a price which tends to recur over a long term. Smith compares it to a centre of gravity around which the market price fluctuates. It represents a sort of equilibrium of market forces. When the market price goes down, there is a smaller return to producers in the form of wages, profit, and rent. Consequently some of them are induced to transfer the use of their labour, capital, or land to other forms of production. That causes a drop in the supply of the low-priced commodity; it fails to meet the demand and so can now realise a higher price, which in turn can attract back workers, capitalists, and landowners. Conversely if the market price rises above the natural price, more producers come in, supply exceeds demand, and the price falls back again to its 'natural' level.

Since the natural price is closely related to a natural level of the costs of production, consisting of wages, profits, and rent, Smith proceeds to an analysis of the way in which these costs are determined. Economists call this his theory of distribution, an explanation of the way in which the money paid for goods is distributed among the three factors which make up the cost of production. The account is particularly elaborate and interesting on

Sedan chairmen, by Kay, after Allan. An 18th-C. example of a service industry.

Smelting ore at Leadhills, by David Allan. An 18th-C. example of heavy industry.

Sedan chairmen, by Kay, after Allan. An 18th-C. example of a service industry.

Smelting ore at Leadhills, by David Allan. An 18th-C. example of heavy industry.

When goods are sold, part of the money is used for immediate consumption and part for the purchase of materials, tools, and other things needed to carry on future production. The second part is capital and is itself sub-divided into two sections, fixed capital and circulating capital. Fixed capital is used for the means of production that stay put: machines and tools, buildings, the improvement of land. Circulating capital is that part which circulates among producers, buyers, and sellers: money, materials, finished goods. The total stock of circulating capital is continually being depleted; money, obtained as wages, profit, or rent, is exchanged for goods and these are in due course drawn off from the category of circulating capital as they are transferred to the category of commodities for immediate consumption or to that of fixed capital. The withdrawals from the stock of circulating capital have to be replaced by new production. So both consumption and fixed capital depend on circulating capital.

Only part of the labour force is engaged in production, and those workers have to supply what is needed for consumption by the whole society. People whose work consists in the rendering of services cannot contribute to the stock of circulating capital; the value of their work is used up at once, while production provides, as it were, stored-up work which can be used in the future. An increase in national wealth requires an increase in production, and that can be achieved either by increasing the number of productive workers or by increasing efficiency with improved machines or additional sub-division of labour. Whichever method is used, additional capital is needed, to pay additional wages or to buy new machines. The additional capital can be obtained by saving, that is to say, spending less on immediate consumption and using what is saved to increase production. The process is cumulative, since the savings of one year do more than provide additional employment for one year. As we have seen, productive workers produce more than is required for their own needs, so the additional labour financed by saving generates scope for yet further saving and thus for further economic growth.

There is no guarantee that the workings of the market will lead to increased wealth. While the history of civilisation as a whole exhibits a general tendency to economic progress, the economy of a particular society can decline as well as grow. Just as saving can add to the number of productive workers and increase output, excessive spending on immediate consumption can cut the amount of circulating capital so that it is insufficient to maintain the existing labour force, and if this goes on the

Wigs: to illustrate how the foibles of the rich inadvertently provide employment for the poor.

Lace woman, by David Allan. The poor earned a living by selling luxuries to the rich, in this case braids and trimmings, displayed from the pole.

result is a general decline in national wealth. Smith believes that the more natural tendency is towards economic growth for reasons of human psychology. The desire to spend for the sake of present enjoyment can be wild and unrestrained but is intermittent. The inclination to save, however, comes from 'the desire of bettering our condition, a desire which, though generally calm and dispassionate, comes with us from the womb, and never leaves us till we go into the grave'.[18]

Human psychology is indeed at the root of the whole of Smith's elaborate analysis of the economic system. It all depends on the effect of cool self-interest. This leads people to exchange, to go in for the specialisation of the division of labour in order to reduce their toil and trouble, and to accumulate capital by saving in order to better their condition. The whole system comes about naturally. Although it produces an extraordinary degree of mutual dependence and mutual benefit, it owes nothing to deliberate planning. Each person simply follows the natural tendency to think of his own interest, yet the result of the interplay of self-interested motivation is an unexpected and unintended benefit to the community as a whole. Smith was not the first to glimpse this economic truth, but he was the first to perceive its magnitude and its central importance, which he impressed upon his readers with a striking metaphor: the individual 'intends only his own gain, and he is . . . led by an invisible hand to promote an end which was no part of his intention'.[19] In this passage of the *Wealth of Nations* the metaphor refers to the increase of national wealth, 'the annual revenue of the society', and more generally to promoting 'the public interest'. Smith had used the same metaphor earlier in his ethics book to refer to the distributive effects of economic growth; it benefits the poor as well as the rich by increased employment. Since the rich do not actually consume much more than the poor, their great houses and fine possessions give work and sustenance to many more people; 'they are led by an invisible hand to make nearly the same distribution of the necessaries of life, which would have been made, had the earth been divided into equal portions among all its inhabitants'.[20]

When Smith says that self-interested individuals are led by an invisible hand to benefit society or to help the poor, he is not making economics depend on theology. He uses the metaphor simply for colourful effect. His point is that the wider consequences come about automatically and are not the result of any deliberate plan by individuals or groups. They exhibit the virtues of 'the obvious and simple system of natural liberty'.[21] This belief

underlies Smith's arguments for *laissez-faire*, although the arguments themselves are directed against particular restrictions on freedom and are supported by solid empirical evidence.

His plea for freedom is not confined to international trade. He also attacks restrictive practices in industry which hinder competition and mobility in the supply of labour. Corporations retained rules about apprenticeship which had outlived their usefulness; the training of apprentices was unduly long, the number accepted was unduly small, and when the apprentice was qualified he was confined to one skilled trade. It should be noted that the removal of these restrictive practices would require governmental intervention, so that Smith's ideology of natural liberty does not always mean that government should stand aside. On the other hand Smith also attacked the English Poor Law, which restricted mobility by inducing the poor to remain in the parish of their birth. Change on this score would involve a lightening of public control.

When Smith turns to the major policy topic of free trade, he begins with an argument of general principle but he then makes his case in detail by examining the disadvantages of protectionist measures in the form of bounties, duties, and the prohibition of imports. Here again his recommendations do not all point in the one direction of removing governmental control. He thinks that protectionist measures are justified in the interests of national defence and also in order to meet on fair terms the protectionism of other countries. We have to adapt ideal solutions to the limitations of the real world. 'To expect, indeed, that the freedom of trade should ever be entirely restored in Great Britain, is as absurd as to expect that an Oceana or Utopia should ever be established in it.'[22]

This spirit of realism is more characteristic of Adam Smith than the underlying ideology of natural liberty and equality. His earlier book, *The Theory of Moral Sentiments*, is similar. There too we find an occasional idealistic exaggeration, as in the statement, quoted earlier, that the distribution of necessities by the invisible hand comes near to natural equality. On the whole, however, Smith keeps his feet firmly on the ground in the ethical work, as in the economic, and builds his theory upon the evidence of empirical fact. In both cases the basic relevant facts are psychological and sociological.

Theory of Moral Sentiments. The principal aim of *The Theory of Moral Sentiments* is to give a psychological explanation of moral judgment. Earlier in the eighteenth century British moral philosophy had been dominated by debate about the place of

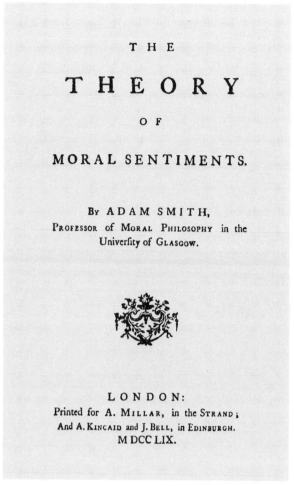

THE

THEORY

OF

MORAL SENTIMENTS.

By ADAM SMITH,
PROFESSOR of MORAL PHILOSOPHY in the
Univerſity of GLASGOW.

LONDON:
Printed for A. MILLAR, in the STRAND;
And A. KINCAID and J. BELL, in EDINBURGH.
M DCC LIX.

reason and feeling in moral judgment. On the one side were thinkers who followed a rationalist theory of knowledge. They believed that genuine knowledge was of necessary truth and was most obviously exemplified in mathematical reasoning. They argued that moral judgment depended on a rational understanding of necessary moral principles. On the other side were those who applied the empiricist theory of knowledge to ethics. They believed that genuine knowledge of the real world was afforded by experience in the form of perception by the senses. Judgments of value, in their view, are based upon a different form of experience, feeling or 'inner sense'. Adam Smith took it for granted that the rationalist case in ethics had been demolished by Hutcheson and Hume. He therefore followed the empiricist approach of those two thinkers but considered that he could improve upon the particular explanation which each of them gave.

Hutcheson had argued that moral judgment is the

Thetis comforts Achilles weeping for the death of Patroclus, from a French translation of the Iliad *(1776). Illustrations to Homer, across the centuries, are very informative on issues of taste, including sympathy.*

expression of feelings of approval or disapproval, and that the natural human tendency to have these feelings is an innate capacity which can be called a 'moral sense', analogous to the 'sense' of beauty. Hutcheson held that the object of moral approval is always a form of benevolence. (The object of disapproval, in his view, is not positive malevolence, which is hardly ever found in real human beings, but a failure to show normal benevolence.) He regarded approval and benevolence as different species of love, a loving esteem directed upon a loving kindness. This aspect of Hutcheson's theory is plainly influenced by Christian doctrine, but the exposition appeals simply to observable facts of psychology.

Hume took the psychological explanation further. Hutcheson had noted that the aim, and the normal effect, of benevolence is to produce happiness or remove unhappiness. Hume used this fact to explain the observer's feeling of approval. The observer sympathises with the feelings of people affected by a kind action; he shares in imagination the pleasure which they receive from it. His sympathetic feeling shows itself as approval. There is no need to postulate an innate moral sense.

Adam Smith followed Hume in explaining moral approval by sympathy. He treats sympathy as the basis of his ethical theory just as he treats the division of labour as the basis of his economic theory. He aims, however, to make an advance upon Hume's explanation by elaborating the account of sympathy so as to cover two different forms of moral judgment. The first is the judgment that an action is right or proper, and the second is the judgment that an action is meritorious.

According to Smith, approval of an action as right or proper arises from sympathy with the agent's motive. The spectator of an action can imagine himself in the agent's shoes. If he finds that he would share the feelings which motivate the actual agent, this perception of agreement in feelings is a form of sympathy, and the spectator expresses it in approval of the agent's motive as proper or appropriate to the situation. If the spectator finds that he would not share the agent's feelings, this perception of disagreement is a form of antipathy, which is expressed as disapproval of the agent's motive as improper.

The second type of moral judgment, concerning the merit or demerit of an action, depends upon sympathy with the person affected by the action. If the person affected is benefited by the action, he normally feels gratitude. The spectator, imagining himself in the shoes of the person affected, finds that he too would feel gratitude. That perception

constitutes sympathy with the beneficiary and is expressed by approving the action as meritorious, deserving of reward. If the person affected by an action is harmed by it, he is likely to feel resentment. The spectator who sympathises with that resentment expresses his sympathy this time as a disapproving judgment of the action as having demerit, deserving of punishment. A judgment of merit or demerit, however, is dependent upon a prior judgment of propriety or impropriety. In order to sympathise with a sufferer's resentment, a spectator must first be out of sympathy with the agent's motive in doing the hurtful action; if he should sympathise with, and so approve, the agent's action (perhaps as a necessary chastisement or as a necessary means to prevent greater hurt), he would not share the resentment of the person affected. Similarly, Smith would say, the spectator can sympathise with a beneficiary's gratitude only if he judges the beneficent action to be a proper one; if the spectator considers the action to be improper (e.g. because the agent is giving away stolen goods), he cannot share or approve of the beneficiary's gratitude.

The explanation of merit and demerit in terms of sympathy with gratitude and resentment forms the first step in Smith's account of justice, in which he does make an advance upon the theory of his predecessors. His explanation of propriety in terms of sympathetic agreement with the agent's motive is less successful. It leads him to an analogy with truth and to the suggestion that judgments concerning the truth of opinions depend simply on agreement with those opinions.

However, the most impressive part of Smith's ethical theory is his account of conscience as an imagined impartial spectator. Hutcheson, Hume, and Smith all base moral judgment on the attitude of spectators towards the actions of others. What about the judgment of an agent concerning his own actions? That question had been neglected by Hutcheson and Hume, and the neglect had left their theories vulnerable to the criticisms of their rationalist opponents, who tended to regard conscience or the sense of duty as the central factor in moral judgment. Smith suggested that conscience, an agent's moral judgment of his own action, is formed by imagining oneself a spectator of one's own action. This gives the judgment the necessary impartiality and at the same time highlights the socialising function of sympathy. The reactions of society, in the form of approval and disapproval, provide a 'mirror' in which a person can see 'the beauty or deformity' of his own conduct and character.[23] We all like to be approved and therefore we take up the judgments of society into our judgments about ourselves. Smith does not, however, leave it at that. He does not regard conscience as simply a crude reflection of popular attitudes. There are, after all, occasions when a man's conscience goes against majority opinion. This, according to Smith, is because he is better informed about the relevant facts and his own motives than mere spectators can be. Conscience is not a simple reflection of the feelings of actual external spectators, but the judgment of an imagined spectator who joins the impartiality of a spectator's point of view with the fuller knowledge which the agent possesses.

The concept of imagination plays as important a part in Smith's theory as the concept of sympathy. Moral judgment, whether concerning others or oneself, requires an act of imagination, thinking oneself in another person's shoes, in order to see whether one shares his feelings. This emphasis upon imagination is something that Smith had learned from Hume, although he employs the concept in his own way. It has a central role also in Smith's interesting excursion into the philosophy of science, to be found in a long essay on the History of Astronomy which he wrote in the earlier part of his life but kept aside for a projected book on the history of the arts and sciences. It is one of the few manuscripts which he allowed his executors to leave undestroyed before his death, and it was published posthumously in *Essays on Philosophical Subjects*. As a contribution to the history of science it is exceptionally well informed for its time, but its continuing interest today lies in its philosophical theory of scientific systems as imagined structures to fill up the gaps in observed data. Since Smith, like most people in his day, drew no firm distinction between science and philosophy, it is a reasonable inference that he would apply the theory to his own (and any other) system of economics and of ethics. It is a relativistic theory without being wholly sceptical. It follows the spirit of Hume's 'mitigated scepticism', and it depends very much on learning from history.

Disputed Questions

The interpretation of the ideas of any great thinker is liable to vary in different ages. Interpretation must involve selection, and many interpreters in making their selection are partially influenced by the dominant concerns of their own time. This has certainly been true of interpretations of the *Wealth of Nations*. In the nineteenth century it was taken to be concerned above all with the advocacy of free trade, and Adam Smith was regarded as a forerunner of 'Manchester liberalism'. That view has been heavily qualified in the twentieth century, when scholars have noted the limited character of Smith's libertarian ideas and have emphasised instead the value of his work as a study of economic growth. No doubt there is room for further variation in the future.

Scholarly opinion has changed also on the extent to which the *Wealth of Nations* is indebted to the French physiocrats. Smith undoubtedly improved his understanding of the economic system by drawing on Quesnay's model of a circular flow of money, and he went along with the physiocrats in assigning to agriculture the cardinal role in production, although he thought that they exaggerated it. He did not, however, derive from them his conception of natural liberty and the doctrine of free trade which depended on it. The claim that he had worked out his main principles, including that of natural liberty, as early as 1750 was made by Smith himself in a paper of 1755.[24] Any scepticism about

Adam Smith, by John Kay.
"In his external form and appearance there was nothing
uncommon . . . but even in company . . . he appeared to be in a
fervour of composition" (Dugald Stewart).

this claim was dispelled by the discovery, in 1895 and in 1958, of reports of Smith's lectures on jurisprudence. Recent scholarly work on those reports and on other manuscript material has established detailed information about the development of Smith's systematic thought. A particularly impressive paper was published in 1973 by R. L. Meek and A. S. Skinner.[25] The lectures on jurisprudence have been used by other scholars, notably Donald Winch and Knud Haakonssen, to elicit a picture of Smith's position in political thought.[26] There is room for further inquiry on this topic and for speculation about the kind of theory he had in mind for his uncompleted book on the history of law and government.

A group of historians has lately been relating the political thought of the Scottish Enlightenment to a tradition of 'civic humanism' emanating from the Italian Renaissance. While it is possible to find some points of comparison between this tradition and the moral and political ideas of Adam Smith, other historians have argued, more convicingly in my opinion, that Smith's political thought should rather be assigned to an alternative tradition of 'natural jurisprudence'. Debate on this issue is likely to continue.

There has been some dispute about Adam Smith's perceptiveness as an economic historian. He was undoubtedly perceptive in his discussions of economic history before his own time. The dispute is whether he realised the extent and the significance of the changes taking place in the middle of the eighteenth century, whether, in short, he appreciated the beginnings of the Industrial Revolution. Some scholars have argued that Smith was a bookish man, who obtained his factual data from treatises, works of history, and legal documents, and that even so he relied too much on outdated material. Others have pointed to evidence in the *Wealth of Nations* of a man who looked at the real world around him as well as at books and who was indeed aware of the growing pace of technological innovation. It seems to me that the second group has had the best of the argument, but perhaps the controversy has not yet been decisively resolved.

Differences of opinion about the *Moral Sentiments* have been due to ignorance on the part of economics scholars who have looked at the work solely as an adjunct to the *Wealth of Nations*. It can indeed be instructive on that score but it is essentially an exercise in moral philosophy. There was in the nineteenth century a long-standing dispute about the so-called 'Adam Smith problem', an alleged inconsistency between the psychological assumptions of Smith's two books. It was said that the

The Author of the Wealth of Nations

Moral Sentiments insisted on the sympathetic or benevolent tendencies in human nature, while the *Wealth of Nations* emphasised self-interest as the effective motive of action. The supposed inconsistency was largely due to a failure to read the *Moral Sentiments* carefully. That book highlights sympathy as the basis of moral judgment, not as the motive of moral action. More recently Jacob Viner, a scholar of great distinction in the interpretation of the *Wealth of Nations*, contrasted the *Moral Sentiments* as a youthful idealistic work, typical of traditional theological philosophy. When he read it more carefully in later years he came to doubt his earlier view but still retained some misconceptions. For reliable interpretation of the *Moral Sentiments* one has to go to scholars trained in philosophy and acquainted with the history of moral philosophy. A thoroughly sound and enlightening account was given by T. D. Campbell some years ago.[27] There is, however, scope for further work about the historical development of Smith's ethical

THE WEALTH OF NATIONS. 5

BOOK I.

Of the Caufes of Improvement in the productive Powers of Labour, and of the Order according to which its Produce is naturally diftributed among the different Ranks of the People.

CHAP. I.

Of the Divifion of Labour.

THE greateft improvements in the productive powers of Labour, and the greater part of the fkill, dexterity, and judgment with which it is any where directed, or applied, feem to have been the effects of the division of labour.

THE effects of the divifion of labour, in the general bufinefs of fociety, will be more eafily underftood, by confidering in what manner it operates in fome particular manufactures. It is commonly fuppofed to be carried furtheft in fome very trifling ones; not perhaps that it really is carried further in them than in others of more importance : but in thofe trifling manufactures which are deftined to fupply the fmall wants of but a fmall number of people, the whole number of workmen muft neceffarily be fmall ; and thofe employed in every different branch of the work can often be collected into the fame workhoufe, and placed at once under the view of the fpectator. In thofe great manufactures, on the contrary, which are deftined to fupply the great wants of the great body of the people, every different branch of the work employs fo great a number of workmen,

theory and about its relation to his jurisprudence and to the sociological ideas of the *Wealth of Nations.*

Another unsettled and intriguing question is Adam Smith's position on religion. The first edition of the *Moral Sentiments* (1759) contains unmistakable signs of a retention of Christian doctrine. Later editions of that book, passages in the *Wealth of Nations,* and some remarks in private letters furnish equally unmistakable signs of scepticism about revealed religion, and I think there is evidence enough that Smith's friendship with Hume was chiefly responsible for the change. But it seems that Smith was never won over completely to Hume's scepticism about natural religion also. Perhaps he was not sure himself just where he stood. I doubt if the problem worried him deeply. Although Smith was in conventional terms more sympathetic to religion than Hume was, the truth or falsity of religious belief did not touch his heart in the same way. Smith's aim in life was to contribute to scientific understanding and to the improvement of the human condition. The metaphysical implications of these two things were of interest to him but were not crucial.

Notes

References to the works of Adam Smith follow the conventions of the Glasgow Edition (Clarendon Press, Oxford, 1976–83), allowing location in any other edition also.

1. H. T. Buckle, *History of Civilization in England* (London, 1857-61), vol.i, p.194; cf. vol.ii, p.443.
2. Letter of Adam Smith to Earl Stanhope dated 8 May 1777; Kent County Archives, file U1590 C15.
3. W. R. Scott, *Adam Smith as Student and Professor* (Glasgow, 1937), p.25.
4. *The Theory of Moral Sentiments* (hereafter *TMS*), III.2.20. The passage was added in the sixth edition of 1790.
5. *The Annual Register, 1759,* p.485.
6. *The Correspondence of Adam Smith,* eds E. C. Mossner and I. S. Ross (Oxford, 1977) (hereafter *Corr.*), p.36.
7. John Rae, *Life of Adam Smith* (London, 1895), p.170, quoting A. F. Tytler.
8. Ibid., p.287.
9. *Corr.,* p.221.
10. *Boswell in Extremes, 1776-1778,* eds Charles McC. Weis and Frederick A. Pottle (New York, 1970; London, 1971), p.270.
11. James Boswell, *The Life of Samuel Johnson,* ch.35.
12. Ibid., ch.36; cf. *Boswell in Extremes,* p.155.
13. *Corr.,* p.203.
14. Ibid., p.228.
15. Rae, *Life of Smith,* p.405.
16. *Corr.,* p.309.
17. *Wealth of Nations* (hereafter *WN*), I.i.11.
18. *WN,* II.iii.28.
19. *WN,* IV.ii.9.
20. *TMS,* IV.1.10.
21. *WN,* IV.ix.51.
22. *WN,* IV.ii.43.
23. *TMS,* III.1.3.
24. Dugald Stewart, 'Account of the Life and Writings of Adam Smith', IV.25; reprinted in Adam Smith, *Essays on Philosophical Subjects.*
25. R. L. Meek and A. S. Skinner, 'The Development of Adam Smith's Ideas on the Division of Labour', *Economic Journal,* vol.83 (1973).
26. Donald Winch, *Adam Smith's Politics* (Cambridge, 1978); Knud Haakonssen, *The Science of a Legislator* (Cambridge, 1981).
27. T. D. Campbell, *Adam Smith's Science of Morals* (London, 1971).

Bibliography

A substantial section of this essay covers, in revised form, the same ground as parts of my book *Adam Smith*, published in the Past Masters series by Oxford University Press (1985) and available in paperback. Readers who would like to know more about Adam Smith may find it helpful to begin with that book.

Those seeking a comprehensive biography should turn to John Rae, *Life of Adam Smith* (London, 1895; reprinted with additional material by Jacob Viner, New York, 1965). A fair amount of new information is contained in *Adam Smith* by R.H.Campbell and A.S.Skinner (London, 1982), a book which also gives clear, concise surveys of Smith's writings and lectures. Another short book of similar character, *Adam Smith: The Man and His Works* by E.G.West (New York, 1969), is more lively but rather sketchy and not always accurate.

Smith's own two books can be read with pleasure by the interested layman. *The Theory of Moral Sentiments* should be read first. An annotated edition by D.D.Raphael and A.L.Macfie is available in the Glasgow Edition of the *Works and Correspondence of Adam Smith* (Oxford, 1976). The best modern version of *An Inquiry into the Nature and Causes of the Wealth of Nations* is likewise in the Glasgow Edition (Oxford, 1976), introduced and annotated by R.H. Campbell and A.S.Skinner, and textually edited by W.B.Todd. An earlier scholarly edition of the work by Edwin Cannan (London, 1904) is still useful and has been reprinted in paperback. A cheaper paperback edition, limited to the first three of its five books, has been edited by Andrew Skinner for Penguin Books (Harmondsworth, 1970) and contains a long, lucid introduction.

For commentary on the *Moral Sentiments* readers should consult T.D.Campbell, *Adam Smith's Science of Morals* (London, 1971). The *Wealth of Nations* has been the subject of an enormous amount of commentary, most of it specialised. For non-specialists I recommend Andrew S.Skinner, *A System of Social Science: Papers relating to Adam Smith* (Oxford, 1979), and Chapter 2 of Mark Blaug, *Economic Theory in Retrospect* (3rd edition, Cambridge, 1978). Readers who feel able to tackle a more elaborate discussion can proceed to Samuel Hollander, *The Economics of Adam Smith* (Toronto, 1973).

Joseph Black

R.G.W.ANDERSON

BY THE END of the eighteenth century Edinburgh had gained world-wide recognition as one of the principal centres of scientific and medical studies. This position had not been achieved by any natural process of institutional development but by a positive policy of the Town Council early in the century to establish a medical school as a centre of excellence. Chairs had been established in all branches of medicine, some of which had been filled by men of great distinction. Students were attracted in large numbers from near and far – sometimes very far indeed: from North America, the Caribbean and Russia. Well-established Colleges of Surgeons and Physicians regulated their respective professions, periodicals, pharmacopoeias and textbooks were published, a large purpose-built infirmary had been constructed (to a design by William Adam) and the student medical society had received a Royal charter.

By the 1790s, the *éminence grise* of Edinburgh science and medicine was Joseph Black. 'No lad could be irreverent towards a man so pale, so gentle, so illustrious' wrote Henry Cockburn,[1] while an anonymous poetaster commented 'Disputes he shunn'd, nor car'd for noisy fame; And peace forever was his darling aim'.[2] The basis of Black's reputation was established by the chemical and physical investigations which he had conducted some forty years earlier. As a student he carried out research for a medical thesis which was immediately recognised as being of fundamental importance. This dealt with the properties of alkalis and their relationship to fixed air (carbon dioxide). Later, as a young professor in Glasgow, he considered the nature of heat in relation to different states of matter. But then his studies in philosophical chemistry came to an abrupt end and his

interests changed. This discontinuity in Black's career coincided with his appointment to the Chair of Medicine and Chemistry back in Edinburgh, and it remains an unexplained feature of his enigmatic and, in some ways, paradoxical character.

Black was both sociable and diffident. He had close relationships with many of the brilliant intellectual circle in Edinburgh, being especially intimate with the physician William Cullen and the geologist James Hutton. He was a clubbable man, regularly attending the convivial meetings of the Poker Club and the Oyster Club, a smal! group of industrialists and intellectuals whose founder members were Black himself, Hutton and Adam Smith. He often dined with the eccentric Lord Monboddo and his circle of friends.[3] After dinner, when the mood took him, he would sing a song. He appreciated music, played the flute, and could draw skilfully. He never married but he enjoyed the company of intelligent women. For exercise, he rode.

Yet Black followed a way of life in which 'the love of peace and quietness' (as James Watt commented[4]) was paramount. He could not be persuaded to publish an authentic account of his discoveries in heat, though frequently urged to do so by many of his friends right up to his old age. (A pirated edition, taken from lecture notes, had earlier appeared.) Unlike Hume, Smith and Hutton, Black never wrote a book to consolidate his reputation. Yet his fame spread throughout Europe. He was elected to the Imperial Academy of St Petersburg, the Société Royale de Médicine and the Académie Royale des Sciences of France. Catherine the Great tried to persuade Black to come to Russia to establish a medical and chemical seminar in St Petersburg.[5] In fact there was ex-

when work on the new building started. He appealed strongly for a house for the chemistry professor to be included in Adam's plan, arguing that he needed to spend many hours in the laboratory to prepare for his next day's lecture demonstrations. He was successful in persuading the Trustees for Building the New College on this point but as only small sections of the college were built in Black's lifetime, he remained in his residence in Nicolson Street until his death. Here 'his house was not unoccupied; for the uniformity of his single life was often agreeably chequered by the welcome visits of his numerous friends, the descendents of the respectable pair at Bordeaux'.[8]

Student and Teacher

Joseph Black was born on 16 April 1728 in Chartron, a suburb of Bordeaux, the fourth of twelve children. His father, though of Scots origin, came from Belfast while his mother, Margaret Gordon, was the daughter of an Aberdeenshire merchant who had also settled in Bordeaux. Joseph was initially taught at home but at the age of twelve he was sent to Belfast to attend a school. In 1744 he left Ulster to continue his education at Glasgow University. As was usual at the time, he entered the arts class where he probably (though it is conjectured) studied Latin, Greek, logic, ethics and natural philosophy.[9] He matriculated in 1746, which would have enabled him to graduate master of arts on completing the five-year course. But Black did not choose to graduate at this time.

Though there was the potential for science teaching at Glasgow when Black arrived from Belfast – there were chairs in natural philosophy, anatomy

tremely little chance that he might have accepted the invitation and he always seems to have been unhappy to travel. After re-establishing himself in Edinburgh he only left Scotland once, in 1788, when he visited Birmingham, Oxford and London. Shortly after he had returned, he wrote in predictable style: 'I have had much better sleep since I came home than when in England'.[6] During the summer vacation, for a change of air, he rented houses at Leith Links and the Meadows, both then on the outskirts of Edinburgh.

Although it is difficult to ascertain Black's religious views from his personal papers, some minor evidence of his attitude can be adduced from the University archives. In Glasgow in 1765 he argued against the provision of a college chapel. Again, in 1789, when the architect Robert Adam was drawing up plans for a major new university building at Edinburgh (to replace the jumble of adapted buildings which had been used for two centuries), Black wrote that he disapproved of the inclusion of a chapel, which he considered to be 'in imitation of the english and foreign Colleges'.[7] There is no mention of Black churchgoing himself.

Black was serious-minded and assiduous. He played an active role in the administration of first Glasgow and then Edinburgh University as a member of the Senatus Academicus. At Senate meetings, Black fought hard for resources to improve his classroom and laboratory facilities: his own success at teaching had made them inadequate. A new laboratory was built for him at Edinburgh in 1781, though this had to be demolished

George Drummond (1687-1766) by John Alexander. Drummond served on the Town Council for thirty years, and was Lord Provost six times. He was the driving force behind the building of the Royal Infirmary, the expansion of the University, and the creation of the New Town.

and botany (combined), and the practice of medicine – in fact little instruction was provided for students. This was to change early in 1747 when, in rapid succession, John Carrick was succeeded by William Cullen in the new appointment of lecturer in chemistry. Cullen had been brought up in an agricultural environment (his father was factor to the estates of the Duke of Hamilton) and he had had a varied career as ship's surgeon, private physician and mature student, graduating doctor of medicine at Glasgow in 1740. Shortly after his return as a teacher, Cullen rapidly obtained funds from the University to establish a laboratory and to teach. Cullen was to be a major influence on Black, and they developed a friendship which was to last until Cullen's death 43 years later. Of this period, Black wrote 'D. Cullen about this time began also to give Lectures on Chemistry which had never before been taught in the University of Glasgow and finding that I might be useful to him in that Undertaking he employed me as his assistant in the laboratory and treated me with the same Confidence and friendship and direction in my Studies, as if I had been one of his children. In this situation I lived three years.'[10]

Up to this time, most chemistry, when it was taught at all, was intended to provide medical students with a background for the materia medica part of their course. Cullen's syllabus (a published version, dated 1748, exists) was different and innovative, dealing in part with industrial processes including soap making, brewing, distilling and vinegar manufacture. Philosophical chemistry was also well covered, with concepts such as elective attractions and affinities being treated. It is perhaps surprising that we find in Cullen's own notes for his students the comment 'Some persons may expect very particular Inquiries on the subject of certain Arts': the expectation of Glasgow students must have been changing with some rapidity. The area which the lectures dealt with most summarily was in fact chemistry as applied to medicine: Cullen wrote in his lecture notes 'Pharmaceutical Courses of Chemistry have not deserved the place they have hitherto held in our Schools . . . they are not fitted to lead us to a general knowledge of Chemistry'.[11] Here he was referring to his uninspired course of study at Edinburgh from 1734 to 1736 given by the professor of medicine and chemistry, Andrew Plummer. The content of the lectures was closely based on Plummer's drug manufacturing business for local pharmacies.

Black studied medicine in Glasgow for three years, but he left in 1752 without graduating to attend the medical course in Edinburgh. Here he lived with his cousins James Russell and Adam Ferguson, who both later occupied the chair of natural philosophy. Edinburgh's medical faculty, in contrast to Glasgow's, enjoyed a European reputation. It had been established in 1726 (though there had been a few earlier medical appointments on an irregular basis) with a specific publicly-stated aim: to establish a centre of excellence so that Edinburgh students would not be forced to travel elsewhere for their education. Indeed, it was hoped to attract English and foreign students to Edinburgh.[12] The master-mind behind the scheme was George Drummond, Lord Provost six times between 1725 and 1764. Leyden University, where Herman Boerhaave had developed and was teaching a new medical curriculum, was Drummond's model. The four professors of medicine appointed at Edinburgh had all studied at Leyden, as had the professor of anatomy, Alexander Monro primus. Drummond was also instrumental in the building

Pioneers of Edinburgh Medicine. a) Sir Robert Sibbald (1641-1722); b) Monro primus (1697-1767); c) William Cullen (1710-1790); d) John Rutherford (1695-1779).

Two varieties of calculi found in the human bladder, and a lithotome caché *developed in the 1750s to remove them by surgical means.*

JOSEPH BLACK · 97

of the Infirmary which opened in 1748. An earlier hospital had been established in a small house in 1729 but it was inadequate for Drummond's ambitions, which were influenced by the clinical teaching which Boerhaave had instigated at the St Cecilia Hospital in Leyden. In February 1748 John Rutherford, professor of the practice of physic at Edinburgh started to use the operation room of the new Infirmary for clinical lectures, and two years later a special 10-bed ward was opened for his teaching. It may well have been interest in Rutherford's teaching which drew Black to Edinburgh. Writing to his father two years later, Black remarked that he had 'been taught everything upon the Practice which can be learned in a College. I have also seen some real Practice and have even practised a little myself'.[13] In this same letter, Black remarked that he had considered travelling to London for further clinical experience (not an uncommon course of action for medical students) but that he had decided against the idea for the time being because of lack of contacts there and because the flourishing state of Edinburgh medicine reduced the need for this experience. There is no evidence that he ever did go to London for this purpose.

One of Black's major concerns at Edinburgh was the production of a thesis, a requirement for graduation in medicine. This task was not always taken very seriously by students, but Black deeply involved himself in chemical experiments on alkalis for this purpose. There is some indication that Black's interest in the relationship between fixed air and causticity had been aroused earlier, at Glasgow. Causticity, the property produced when alkaline earths such as chalk are roasted in a lime kiln, had been the matter of some considerable attention by the medical profession. Indeed two Edinburgh professors, Robert Whytt (theory and practice of medicine) and Charles Alston (materia medica), both published works on the subject in 1752 and were in vigorous dispute. This arose from a disagreement as to whether shells or chalk produced, after roasting and dissolution, the more effective lime-water for dissolving urinary stones.[14] (The mechanical removal or crushing of calculi was a painful, frequently performed, surgical operation in the eighteenth century.) Arising from the argument, Whytt believed that chalk became caustic during calcination by absorbing fiery particles, while Alston thought that the causticity was a property of the lime itself. It was well known that the efficacy of lime was reduced on exposure to the atmosphere, and that a crust formed on limewater. Whytt explained this phenomenon by the

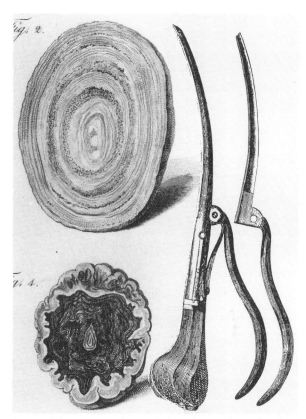

loss of fiery particles, while Alston thought that perhaps the air itself produced the crust.

Against this background, Black conducted his investigations into the properties of an alkaline earth with properties similar to limestone, magnesia alba (basic magnesium carbonate). His declared reason for this choice of topic was that he hoped to discover a more powerful remedy for dissolving calculi than lime-water, though he also felt it was judicious for a student to avoid the disputes of his Professors. Black initially believed that magnesia alba was simply another progenitor of quicklime and lime-water, and his research started with limited aspirations. As it happened, the experiments ultimately led him to a new theory of causticity and later to the chemical differentation of fixed air (carbon dioxide) from atmospheric air. Details of the experiments and Black's reasoning are dealt with below (see pp.109ff).

Black started on his experiments in 1753, having delayed the final phase of his undergraduate career because, as he explained in a letter to his father, he was occupied at the Infirmary and with private patients.[15] (Black was rather frequently making excuses in his correspondence.) In fact he was finding the more practical aspects of his medical work left insufficient time for his chemical interests, and

Professors at leisure in Glasgow University garden (1762).

he apologised for this in another letter to his former teacher at Glasgow, Cullen. The thesis was ready by the summer of 1754. Apart from the chemical part, a shorter and less substantial opening section dealt with the effect of magnesia alba on acidity of the stomach. Black was embarrassed by the relatively trivial nature of this part, but felt it necessary to include it because of its medical connotations.[16] In June 1754, 170 copies of *De Humore Acido a Cibis Orto et Magnesia Alba* were printed, a dozen of which were despatched to Cullen, who was asked by the author whether he considered it worth publishing in a journal. A few months later copies were sent to his father in Bordeaux, with a suggestion that one should be presented to a family friend, Montesquieu.[17] This was done, and doubtless Joseph shared his father's pleasure at the favourable comments made by the elderly philosopher.

Black stayed on in Edinburgh after graduation, continuing his work on alkalis and their property of causticity. When he presented his paper to the Philosophical Society in June 1755 (he had become a member in the previous year) the scope of his reported experiments had extended to considering the relationship between quicklime, fixed air and chalk.[18] Here Black showed that fixed air could be transferred from potash to slaked lime in solution (lime-water). He then refined the paper for publication and it appeared in the second volume of the Society's *Essays and Observations, Physical and Literary* in English (rather than in Latin, the required language for his thesis). His work as a physician continued over this period.

By this time, the much-derided Plummer was getting elderly and his chemistry course, never stimulating, was becoming increasingly outdated, having been given annually for some 30 years. Plummer had tried to dispose of his teaching duties some years earlier, but now he was stubbornly clinging to his chair. Henry Home, Lord Kames, approached Cullen and suggested that he should teach privately in Edinburgh so he might develop a suitable base from which he could succeed to Plummer's post. Before Cullen could be persuaded, Plummer suffered a stroke in the summer of 1755. Three replacements were suggested: Cullen, Francis Home (a physician with interests in agriculture and bleaching) and Black. Black, being available immediately, stepped into the breach and started his first course of chemistry teaching.[19] But this was a temporary measure and a month later Cullen was appointed joint professor with the incapacitated Plummer, resigning from Glasgow and starting his teaching in Edinburgh in January 1756. This left Cullen's medical chair in Glasgow vacant,

which was filled by Robert Hamilton. Black took advantage of these changes and was initially appointed to the professorship of anatomy and botany in Glasgow (Hamilton's vacated chair), but a year later he transferred to the chair of medicine. He did not relish his medical teaching and was self-critical of his abilities in this work. He also held the tenureless lectureship in chemistry for which there was voted annually a stipend of £20;[20] in this teaching he took greater satisfaction.

Established in Glasgow, Black pursued his teaching, his medical practice and his research. His experimental work was to take a different direction from his Edinburgh studies, and was directed towards developing theories of heat.[21] Here again his interest may have been stimulated initially by Cullen. Cullen was particularly interested in Boerhaave's treatment of heat in the *Elementa Chemicae* of 1732. In particular he was fascinated by the fact that when some salts dissolve in water the temperature rises, while for others the temperature drops. Cullen also considered the lowering of temperature caused by the evaporation of fluids. Black was aware of the experiments which Cullen was conducting early in 1755 while he was still in Edinburgh, and this led him to consider the phenomenon of heat transfer to or from a body on liquefaction or solidifaction, evaporation or condensation, without a change of temperature being registered on the thermometer. Experiments were conducted over a long period – probably from 1756 to 1764; it was Black who introduced the term 'latent heat' to describe the effect. Further experiments were conducted to demonstrate that different substances have different, and characteristic, capacities for heat. Between 1764 and 1766 Black was assisted by his assiduous student William Irvine. These experiments will also be considered in greater detail below (p.113). Unlike his earlier studies on causticity, Black never overcame his reluctance to publish the theories of heat. Perhaps there was no need to: by the middle of the 1760s he had established his position as a leading philosophical chemist.

Glasgow was a stimulating place to return to. Shortly after arriving there Black said he met 'a young man possessing most uncommon talents for mechanical knowledge and practice, with an originality, readiness and copiousness of invention, which often surprised and delighted me in our frequent conversations together . . . I therefore contracted with him an intimate relationship.'[22] This young man was the future engineer James Watt, who was introduced to Black by Robert Dick, professor of natural philosophy. Dick had arranged for Watt to be employed as 'Mathematical Instrument Maker to the University' and Black was to use his talents to equip his laboratory and in other, more domestic, ways (such as constructing him an organ and supplying him with an alarm clock). In November 1758, Black formally went into partnership with Watt and Alexander Wilson, a typefounder who later became the professor of astronomy at Glasgow. Watt supplied his skills to Black, for which the partnership was charged (70 days work early in 1759). Watt also acted as a general retailer of a wide variety of merchandise,[23] Black's purchases being recorded in a business-like way. Later, when Watt was to recall these days he was anxious to state that his relationship with Black was not one of pupil-master. He had not attended Black's chemistry class, declaring that he would have possessed a more solid knowledge of chemistry had he done so.[24] However, Black was to help finance Watt's early endeavours at Glasgow, debts which were not paid back for several years after they had parted company in 1766.

Not a great deal is known of Black's chemistry teaching at Glasgow as no student's lecture notes survive. Thomas Reid, professor of moral philosophy, attended the course in 1765 at the age of fifty-five 'with a juvenile curiosity and enthusiasm'.[25] Black probably started incorporating the results of his investigations into heat into the course in 1757. Undoubtedly the theory of causticity was

included. His reputation started to spread and foreign students began to arrive at Glasgow. Clearly Black was a most popular teacher and was provided, in 1763, with an expensive new laboratory costing £350, though only after the Rector overruled the Principal and the professor of logic, who declared the existing laboratory adequate.[26] Black was always interested in his practical facilities: while at Glasgow he designed new and more sensitive furnaces, had them made by Watt and installed them in his laboratory. The contents of Black's laboratory in 1766 are in fact known, because of the need to make a formal handover of equipment before he left for Edinburgh. It would seem that the laboratory was used by students during their course (Cullen had previously complained 'the laboratory has been open to you but I am sorry to find that so few of you have frequented it'). The contents extended little beyond basic apparatus such as furnaces, stills and glassware. A separate inventory listed Black's personal effects which could be purchased by the University if they

wished: it includes 'The Street Crystal Lamp' and his tea kettle.[27]

The Edinburgh Chair

Almost inevitably Black was destined to return to Edinburgh. The chain of events was initiated by the ageing Rutherford retiring in 1766. It had long been speculated that Cullen would replace him as professor of the practice of medicine. But Rutherford, as was usual when professors retired, had influence as to whom his successor would be and favoured the priggish, traditional (and Boerhaavian) John Gregory, professor of physic at King's College, Aberdeen. After much politicking, Rutherford's party prevailed, and Gregory was appointed. By chance, Robert Whytt died a month later and Cullen, though he felt aggrieved at his treatment, was eventually prevailed upon to put his name forward as a candidate and was appointed professor of the institutes of medicine. There were, prior to this process, efforts to get Black to transfer to Edinburgh to teach chemistry. Pamphleteering had started as early as 1764, one making the appeal:

> Dr Black was given a public and very approved specimen of his genius in chemistry . . . I presume there is

not a man in Edinburgh, who even pretends to be acquainted with natural knowledge, and can refuse his assent to what we have said of Dr Black's worth, or can have the least hesitation, in allowing that this gentleman would be a very valuable acquisition to the University of Edinburgh. . . . Though the students of medicine are extremely well satisfied with the course of chemistry given here by Dr Cullen; yet so high is their opinion of Dr Black, that last summer a proposal was made, for associating such a number as, on going to Glasgow, might engage Dr Black to give a summer course.[28]

Black was duly elected to the chair of medicine and chemistry at Edinburgh and, in the manner of the pied-piper, drew most of the Glasgow medical students with him. It was to be the last change of appointment which Black would make.

In a recent study of chemistry in the Scottish Enlightenment, the historian Arthur Donovan comments that 'Black's move to Edinburgh . . . marked, for reasons which remain unknown, the end of his career as a creative philosophical chemist'.[29] This assessment of the sudden decline of Black's research interest in fundamental scientific questions is generally accepted. An earlier biographer, William Ramsay, tried to explain this:

Model of a Newcomen Steam Engine.
While repairing this model in 1757, Watt concluded that it
would be more efficient to cool the steam in a separate condenser
instead of in the cylinder itself. This innovation was the basis of
his fame and fortune.

'Black furnishes an example of what is not infrequent; of a man doing his best work at an early age. In his case, the cessation of his originative activity was due in greater measure to his poor health'.[30] Such an explanation can be challenged. Black's health was less than robust and he worried about it a great deal. The topic dominates many letters in the long correspondence with James Watt ('my health upon the whole no worse – but have been driven to one of the last shifts of a valetudinarian, a flannel shirt').[31] But Black's activity did not decline – rather it diversified, and philosophical chemistry was a victim of his growing financial and institutional interests.

Back in Edinburgh, Black pursued his teaching with vigour. His courses became immensely popular, and he developed a widespread reputation for his skill in lecture demonstrations which was frequently commented on by those who had attended them. His income from teaching depended entirely on the numbers of students registering for the classes (the chair he occupied was unsalaried) and it was in his financial interest to develop the renown of being a lecture demonstrator extraordinary. This did not pass without

critical comment and some disapproved of his showmanship. Black was responsible for purchasing and maintaining his apparatus (no grant was provided). Some of his apparatus still survives, being presented by the University to the Industrial Museum of Scotland in 1858.[32] It has a home-spun quality about it and if it is representative of what Black used it indicates that he was unwilling to purchase high quality instruments which were readily available from specialist makers in London and Paris in the eighteenth century. It would seem that Black was more interested in displaying his skills of manipulation than in demonstrating spectacular experiments. Henry Brougham, attending Black's last course of lectures in 1796, wrote 'In one department of his lecture he exceeded any I have known, the neatness and unvarying success with which all the manipulations of his experiments were performed . . . I have seen him pour boiling water or boiling acid from a vessel that had no spout into a tube, holding it at such a distance as made the stream's diameter small, and so vertical that not a drop was spilt.'[33]

Black's course extended from mid-November to mid-May each year. He lectured five times a week, the course comprising about 120 lectures. Many copies of student lecture notes survive (not all were taken down by students – many were written out by professional scribes). The basic structure of the course varied little from the evidence of the earliest notes (of 1766) to those of the latest (1796). After the introduction, which consisted of definitions and an outline history of chemistry, there were four main sections: the general effects of heat (expansion, fluidity and inflammation), the general effects of mixture, chemical apparatus, and the 'chemical history' of bodies. This last, and largest, section was divided into salts, earths, inflammable substances, metals and waters. Though the content of the lectures was to some extent kept up to date by Black's wide circle of correspondents and his own reading, the course must have seemed very dated by the time he retired. The unchanging structure of the course could simply not accommodate the rapidly changing nature of chemistry in the second half of the eighteenth century. The lectures were published after Black's death, being edited (and to some extent reconstructed) by John Robison, professor of natural philosophy at Edinburgh from 1773 and a long-standing colleague. Robison initially considered his task almost as an act of piety. As he proceeded, he came to relish the work less and less, finding the language of Black's own notes for his lectures 'artless and very often disagreeable in words and in phrases' and one of

HEADINGS OF DR BLACK'S LECTURES
TAKEN DOWN BY JOHN MCCARTNEY IN 1787

Lecture   *Introduction*
1   Advice to Students
    General nature of the Science of Chemistry
    Books proper to be perused and consulted
2   The history of the rise and progress of Chemistry
4   Definition and use, with the definitions of authors
    particularly Boerhaave
5   Division of the course into five parts
    The More General and
    The more particular doctrines to which is added
    The Art of Pharmacy

General Doctrines
1st of Heat
2   of Mixture
3   of the Instruments of Chemistry

Heat
6-10   Nature and Cause of heat
11   Expansion
12   Thermometers
13   Fluidity
14 & 15   Latent heat
16 & 17   Volatility
18   Spontaneous evaporation
19   Ignition
20 & 21   Inflammation

General effects of mixture
22   Experiments with various mixtures
23   Specific gravity
24   Chemical attraction
25   Elective attractions explained

Instruments
26   Vessels
27   Forms for various operations
    Sublimation
    Glass vessels
28 & 29   Means of producing heat – breathing, friction,
    electricity, mixture, fermentation, sun's rays,
    fewels
30-33   Furnaces (including assay furnace, blowpipe,
    glass house furnace, retort furnace, athanor)

Particular Doctrines
33   Objects divided into 5 classes
33-36   Salts
37   Alkalis
39-41   Acids
42-50   Compound salts
52-59   Earths
    Absorbent or Alkaline Earths, Quick Lime,
    Magnesia Alba
60-64   Fixed or Mephitic air
    Properties of alkalis
    Clays, stones

Inflammables
69-70   Phosphorous
71   Sulphur
    Charcoal
72-75   Vinous or ardent spirits
76-78   Oils, aromatic, unctuous
79   Bitumen
    Coal

Metals in General
80   Their great usefulness
    Alchemy not to be regarded
    General qualities
    Effects of heat
81-84   Calces – their properties
85   Arsenic
86-89   Mercury
90-92   Antimony
    Bismuth
93   Zinc
    Lead
94 & 95   Tin
96-99   Iron (including cause and prevention of rust,
    black ink, pyrites, ores)
100   Copper
102-4   Gold and silver
    Platina
    Regulus of Cobalt
105   Nickel
106-108   Explanations of the table of elective attractions

Waters
109-110   Give rise to meteors, vegetables and animals
    Spring waters
    Trials for discovering fixed air, acids, alkalis,
    sulphur etc
    Sea water

Vegetables
111 & 112   Their immense variety beauty and use
    Physiology not understood
    Sap, wood, gum, aromatic oils, unctuous and
    expressed oils, saline matters, sugar, farina
113   Putrefaction

Animal Substances
114   Principles the same as those of vegetables
    Solids
    Fluids
115-117   Secreted fluids
    Excrementitious
    Useful (including semen, mucus, saliva, milk)

Pharmacy
118   The art of collecting, preserving and preparing
    the substances employed by physicians
    Collecting them
    Preserving them
    Preparing them – putrifaction of juices
    Saline, earthy, inflammable, metallic vegetable
    and animal substances
    The ultimate operations for adapting the sub-
    stances to the use of the patient

the major topics 'tedious beyond bearing'.[34]

One of the main areas where Black's concepts became dated was in the theory of combustion. The traditional approach explained the pheno- menon in terms of the phlogiston theory. This underlying philosophy did not simply involve a particular lecture or group of lectures: it pervaded large areas of the course. Phlogiston was said to be an invisible, weightless substance which was given off when inflammable bodies were burnt or metals calcined. The theory had been propounded by Johann Joachim Becher in the late seventeenth cen- tury and was refined by George Stahl. Its accept- ance by chemists was almost universal though there were certain problems in interpreting some effects such as weight increase on calcination. When Black's contemporary, the English chemist Henry Cavendish, discovered hydrogen in 1766, it was first thought that this gas was in fact pure phlogiston. As the era of pneumatic chemistry burgeoned, more and more gases were chemically characterised. A particularly prolific investigator was the English dissenter Joseph Priestley, who made careful investigations of combustion and photosynthesis. When he heated the calx of mer- cury strongly, a gas was evolved which supported burning and living systems. This Priestley believed was atmospheric air without its phlogiston com- ponent: he called it dephlogisticated air. At about the same time the French chemist Antoine-Laurent Lavoisier produced and studied the gas, and came to appreciate that it was a new species, oxygen, which participated positively in the combustion process. His theory had been formulated by 1777. The phlogiston concept became redundant, and so far-reaching were the consequences that the sup- planting of it by Lavoisier's theory became known as the Chemical Revolution.

Black was very slow to accept this fundamental change. A student's lecture notes of the 1783–84 session read: 'Some chemists in France suppose that no bodies contain the phlogiston. Dr B sup- poses that bodies contain the Phlogiston'. Black corresponded with Lavoisier in 1790 and was clearly not entirely won over to the new theory. He said that he had 'been habituated 30 years to beleive and teach the doctrine of Phlogiston. . . . I felt much aversion to the new system. . . . This aversion however proceeded from the power of habit alone has gradually subsided. . . . Your plan . . . is infinitely better supported than the former Doc- trine.' In a letter of 1792 there are still doubts: 'I find the French theory so easy and applicable that I mostly make use of it'. Black's caution, when most chemists had accepted the oxygen theory, lost him

credibility with his students, who by 1785 were certainly discussing Lavoisier's doctrines with enthusiasm in their own Chemical Society.[35]

In spite of Black's hesitation to adopt what proved to be the most significant chemical theory of the century, his popularity as a lecturer did not decline. In the 1790s, the average number of students attending his lectures was 225. By no means would all of these ultimately graduate in medicine at Edin- burgh. A significant number were students from the continent of Europe who travelled to various medical schools for their education and would graduate elsewhere. Some of the foreigners were already established chemists: for example Lorenz Friedrich von Crell, when he attended in 1769, was professor of philosophy and medicine at Helm- stadt, Germany, and Johan Gottlieb Gahn, was working as a professor of mining, assigned to improve copper smelting techniques at the Stora- Kopparberg, Sweden, when he came in 1772. Some 132 students from America attended the Edinburgh medical school from 1769 to 1794, a very substantial number, considering that this period spans the War of Independence.[36] It is likely that all would have attended Black's class. At a different social level it is clear that artisans also came. The best documented example is Archibald Geddes, man- ager of a Leith glassworks 'who soon engaged his

Professor's attention by the readiness and propriety with which he applied to the improvement of his manufacture the instructions which he received in the lecture'.[37] Black also gave separate courses of lectures for lawyers. James Boswell attended one of these in 1775, but with little enthusiasm. One of Black's students peevishly recorded that the early start of these special courses made him too tired to lecture to his students later on in the day.[38] In spite of the outdated form his teaching took by 1796 (when he retired) it is noteworthy that there are four nineteenth-century editions of the lecture course: Robison's of 1803, an American edition of 1806/7 and two German ones of 1804 and 1818.

As well as his commitments as professor of medicine and chemistry, Black was deeply involved in two other occupations, that of physician and industrial consultant. About the former little is known. More can be discovered about the industrial matters because a substantial number of letters to Black on the subject are known. As he tended to draft replies on his incoming letters, both sides of the correspondence is often available.

Black practised as a private physician at Glasgow and Edinburgh. He mentioned that private patients were occupying him as early as February 1753; he attended Adam Ferguson in May 1797. There is no reason to believe that he did not practise throughout his career (though Robison says that he 'restricted his attendance to a few families of intimate and respected friends'). Only the most famous of his patients are known.[39] Sir Walter Scott wrote that as a boy he might have died from consumption had it not been for Black's advice that his tuberculous nurse should be dismissed. David Hume consulted Black in his last illness, Black appreciating the incurable nature of the disease and informing him of the hopeless prognosis. About Black's involvement with the Royal Infirmary and the Royal College of Physicians, slightly more is known. He served as a manager to the Infirmary on at least four occasions between January 1771 and January 1794. The main duty was to make regular inspections and report the findings to the Board of Managers.[40] He served on only one, very brief, occasion as one of the two ordinary physicians of the Infirmary. On 2 October 1775 he replaced John Steedman, who was in poor health. But only one month later, at an extraordinary meeting of the Managers, Black resigned because of his own bad health. It is not altogether clear why this happened; no letters to Watt survive for this period (Black was very candid about his health in writing to Watt). However several manuscript student lecture notes

are dated 1775/76, so presumably Black's health did not prevent him from teaching.

Black had become a member of the Faculty of Physicians and Surgeons of Glasgow in 1757, and was admitted a fellow of the Royal College of Physicians of Edinburgh in 1767. He played a significant role in the life of the college, serving as its president from 1788 to 1790 (at the same time as his pupil, Daniel Rutherford, discoverer of nitrogen, was secretary). Black was a member of the revision committee for the sixth, seventh and eighth editions of the College's *Pharmacopoeia Edinburgensis* of 1774, 1783 and 1792. He took a particular interest in mercurial and antimonial preparations, dealing with those in detail in his lectures and distributing printed tables to students which compared the entries in the Edinburgh with the London pharmacopoeia. Black also arranged for the Edinburgh and Leith Glass-house Company to manufacture accurate phials for measuring out drugs. The same firm made Nooth's apparatuses, complicated glass

---

The PREPARATIONS of ANTIMONY are,

I. Thofe in which the ANTIMONY is only reduced to a fine POWDER.

> Antimonium præparatum. Ed. et Lond.
> Tablettes de Kunkel. Meuder.

II. In which the COHESION of the BRIMSTONE, and METAL is diminifhed, and the laft is therefore left more difpofed to be affected by ACIDS.

> Kermes Mineralis
> Sulphur antim. præcip. vulgo fulphur aurat. Ed.
> Sulphur antimonii præcipitatum. Lond.
> Pilulæ Æthiopicæ. Ed.
> Æthiops antimonialis. N. D.
> Regulus antim. medicinalis. N. D.
> Crocus antim. medicinalis. N. D.

III. In which the BRIMSTONE is feparated, but the METAL is preferved intire.

> Regulus antimonii
> Regulus antim. martialis.

IV. In which the BRIMSTONE is totally or moftly feparated, and the METAL itfelf is more or lefs calcined.

1. By HEAT and AIR.

> Vitrum antim nii. Ed. et Lond.
> Vitrum antimonii ceratum. Ed.
> Nix antimonii.

Leadhills, c.1780, by David Allan. Boys are breaking down lumps of lead before it is fed to the furnaces. Black carried out assays at Leadhills for the owner (the Earl of Hopetoun, in the background).

vessels used for preparing artificial carbonated mineral waters (for domestic purposes, as an alternative to visiting healing wells or attending spas), and was probably advised by Black to do so. His influence was to diversify the products of the glasshouse (which had previously only made bottles for beer) and make medical and chemical ware available from a local source.[41] In the 1790s, Black became interested in the work of Thomas Beddoes who was treating patients with gases at his Pneumatic Institution in Bristol. An apparatus was sent to Black by Watt, Black writing to say that he intended treating a friend who was in 'a deplorable state of Hypochondriacism' with dephlogisticated nitrous air (laughing gas).[42] Such are the scraps of evidence of Black's involvement with medical practice in Edinburgh. It is certain that Black was considered a prominent figure in the Edinburgh medical establishment and was appointed to the ultimate sinecure: Principal Physician to King George III in Scotland.

Much more is known about Black as an industrial consultant. Scotland was rapidly industrialising, from a very low base, in the latter part of the eighteenth century.[43] Some credit for this must go to the Board of Trustees for Manufactures in Scotland. Following the Act of Union of 1707, an annual sum of money had been set aside for seven years to encourage the coarse woollen industry. A further

sum of £14,000 was added and, in addition, the surplus from the Malt Tax when its yield exceeded £20,000 per year. To begin with, no mechanism was established for the distribution of funds, but in 1727, the Board of Trustees was set up. In its first year of operation £6,000 was made available for the herring, the linen and the woollen industries. Black and his colleagues were closely involved in proposals put to the Board, and in adjudicating proposals of others made to it. Of particular concern in mid-century was development of schemes for improving the bleaching of linen.

Linen was a major and expanding commodity throughout the eighteenth century in Scotland.[44] A crisis had arisen because the bleaching agent, potash, made from wood ashes, had risen in price by 50 per cent between 1750 and 1760. An alternative to potash, used in the country, was sour milk, though this process took weeks for each batch of linen. Black's colleague, Francis Home (by now professor of materia medica), suggested that dilute solutions of sulphuric acid should be used as a substitute for sour milk. Home was awarded a premium of £100 by the Board in 1756. Black also examined the problem and suggested that by adding lime to potash, caustic potash was obtained which had a much more powerful bleaching action than potash alone. But it was said that the solution tended to have a destructive effect on the cloth and

Black's furnace, diagram by Reuss, showing internal construction. Such portable furnaces, originally designed by Black, were in widespread use for over a century.

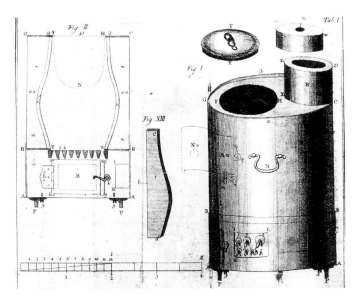

its use was banned in Scotland and Ireland. However, the Irish Linen Board changed its views in 1770 and Black's paper (first compiled in 1763) 'An Explanation of the Effect of Lime upon Alkaline Salts; and a Method Pointed Out whereby it may be Used with Safety and Advantage in Bleaching' was published in the second (Dublin) edition of Home's *Essays on Bleaching* of 1771. It is the only substantial publication of Black's which concerns an industrial process.

Another approach to the bleaching problem was to look for a cheaper way of making potash. Cullen himself had investigated the possibility of burning conifers in the remoter parts of the Highlands to provide the alkali and considered whether ferns or seaweed would be economically favourable. For this he was rewarded by the Board. Black also became interested in this approach and analysed burnt kelp (a form of seaweed) from different sources for its alkali content. He showed that high prices were sometimes paid for kelp with poor yields, demonstrating, for example, that kelp from Mull, only slightly cheaper than that from Colonsay, produced only about one-seventh the quantity of potash.[45] For this work Black too was rewarded, in 1783, with a premium by the Board though most commercial bleachers had to continue to import ashes to Scotland. In that same year Black and Hutton were asked by the Board to judge the effectiveness of an air furnace whose construction it was sponsoring. Although rather pessimistic about the likelihood of success of the furnace, they recommended the payment of a further small sum of money to enable the inventor to continue his trials.[46] Black took a particular interest in furnace construction and though he published nothing on the subject himself, a long description of a design of his for laboratories was published by a German attending the lecture course, August Christian Reuss.[47] 'Black's furnace' was available from laboratory suppliers well into the twentieth century.

In 1784, Sir John Dalrymple, sometime Solicitor to the Board of Excise, and entrepreneur, described Black as 'the best judge, perhaps in Europe, of such inventions'. (In this case, Black had been judging the financial viability of the tar trade.) Black was consulted by a considerable number of industrialists on an extraordinarily wide range of topics. In the surviving correspondence these include sugar refining, alkali production, bleaching, ceramic glazing, dyeing, brewing, metal corrosion, salt extraction, glass making, mineral composition, water analysis and vinegar manufacture. In addition his opinion was sought on agricultural matters.

As well as advising on industrial matters and performing analyses for those engaged in these pursuits, Black himself invested in local industries. In 1794 he made a substantial investment in the Edinburgh and Leith Glass-house Company and the inventory accompanying his will indicates that he had invested in the Culcreach Cotton Company.[48] On his death, Black left a considerable sum even though he had lost most of his early capital when the Ayr Bank of Douglas, Heron and Company failed in 1772. Undoubtedly a good part of Black's fortune (Ferguson said that it was twice that which had been expected) was amassed by careful investment.

In one area of Black's problem-solving for industry considerable evidence survives. This is the documentation which concerns the tar works of Archibald Cochrane, Earl of Dundonald.[49] Lord Dundonald had discovered that a solution for dealing with the destructive effects of worms eating their way through ships' hulls was to coat the hull with tar. He had set up a tar works at Culross, on the Firth of Forth, producing tar by distillation of coal in closed vessels. Dundonald's business skills were wanting, and though the process seemed potentially profitable he had immediate financial problems and Black was called in as consultant to check the technological and financial viability of the scheme. Black's careful estimates show that he took many factors into account, including whether the country was in a state of war or not – in time of war, the demand for tar would be much greater and its value higher. He also considered the increased profitability which would arise by selling waste products of the process: varnish from the

Portable laboratory of the late 18th C., developed for analysis of minerals in the field.

Letter from the Leith Commissioner of Police asking Black for advice about the water supply.

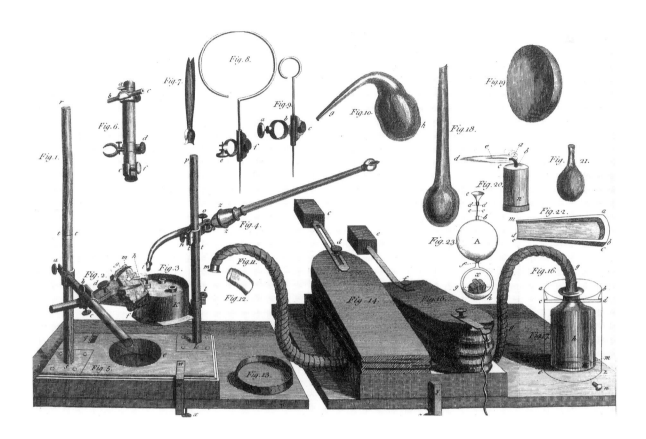

Title-page of Black's MD thesis, "On the acid humours arising from food and magnesia alba".

JOSEPH BLACK · 109

rosin, coke which might be used for iron production in the nearby Carron iron works, and so on. Dundonald was guided by Black to proceed and applied to Parliament for an extension to his patent, which was granted for twenty-one years from 1785. Black's advice proved correct: by 1788 Dundonald's British Tar Company was yielding a clear annual profit of £5,000.

Another major industrial figure who benefited from Black was Henry Cort who had developed improved methods of iron production: coke-smelted pig-iron and puddled, rolled bar-iron. The processes had been patented in 1784 and Cort was anxious that iron produced by them would be adopted by the Navy for anchors, bolts and blocks. Cort visited Black in that year, bringing a sample of iron for him to examine. Black was convinced of its quality, but Cort had difficulties in getting the products of his innovatory processes accepted. Three years later he solicited a testimonial from Black, which was published in a pamphlet.[50] From then onwards the processes were speedily taken up. Seeking the imprimatur of Joseph Black was a sensible course of action: Dalrymple's judgment was a widely accepted opinion.

In spite of Black's abandonment of fundamental research after a few years and in spite of his varied and successful interests in chemistry thereafter, the early part of his career was frequently recalled during his lifetime. Henry Brougham attended the last course of lectures which Black gave some thirty years after his productive 'philosophical' period had ended. He remembered 'We knew there sat in our presence the man now in his old age reposing under the laurels won in his early youth. I have heard the greatest understandings of the age giving forth their efforts in its most eloquent tongues . . . but I should without hesitation prefer for mere intellectual gratification, to be once more allowed the privilege which I in those days enjoyed, of being present while the first philosopher of his age was the historian of his own discoveries.'[51] These discoveries must now be looked at in great detail; they have always been regarded as Black's major achievements.

Fundamental Research

It is often claimed that the work on causticity, both for the thesis of 1754 and the Philosophical Society paper published in 1756 was the first in which a balance was used to determine a chemical process. This is not strictly true – assayers had been using balances for centuries before – but it is probably the first time one was used in a planned, cyclic scheme of quantitative experiments. Friedrich Hoffman

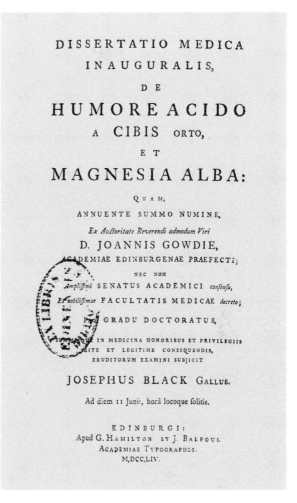

DISSERTATIO MEDICA
INAUGURALIS,
DE
HUMORE ACIDO
A CIBIS ORTO,
ET
MAGNESIA ALBA:
QUAM,
ANNUENTE SUMMO NUMINE,
Ex Auctoritate Reverendi admodum Viri
D. JOANNIS GOWDIE,
ACADEMIAE EDINBURGENAE PRAEFECTI;
NEC NON
Amplissimi SENATUS ACADEMICI consensu,
Et nobilissimae FACULTATIS MEDICAE decreto;
PRO GRADU DOCTORATUS,
IN MEDICINA HONORIBUS ET PRIVILEGIIS
RITE ET LEGITIME CONSEQUENDIS,
ERUDITORUM EXAMINI SUBJICIT
JOSEPHUS BLACK GALLUS.
Ad diem 11 Junii, horâ locoque solitis.

EDINBURGI:
Apud G. HAMILTON ET J. BALFOUR,
ACADEMIAE TYPOGRAPHOS.
M,DCC,LIV.

had, in 1722, distinguished between magnesia alba and chalk. Black chose to investigate magnesia alba, preparing it by the reaction of potash on Epsom salts. He found that the product reacted with acids, giving off a gas in much the same way as chalk. Black then heated the magnesia alba, expecting it to produce a substance analogous to quicklime. Like quicklime, the resulting magnesia usta (magnesium oxide) did not effervesce with acids; but unlike quicklime it was not caustic or soluble in water: there was no limewater equivalent. Black now applied the balance, noting the loss in weight following heating magnesia alba. He considered that this might have been due to the air which had been driven off. He postulated that this air might have been introduced to the Epsom salts from the added potash. He now reacted the magnesia usta with potash, recovering magnesia alba which weighed very nearly the same as what he had started with. In other experiments he found that magnesia usta reacted with acids to form the

HMS Victory, *in the Bay of Naples.*
Black was asked to explain why iron nails corroded so quickly in copper-bottomed ships, including the Victory.

Double bellows used by Black to produce air for a blowpipe, "an indispensable instrument for every mineralogist".

same salts as magnesia alba, but without the air being produced in effervescence. The difference between the magnesia alba and usta was therefore the fixed air, which could be introduced to the latter by potash. These conclusions Black published in his thesis.[52]

In his subsequent paper Black took his experiments and conclusions to a further stage.[53] He confirmed Alston's view on chalk and lime: when chalk is heated strongly, an air is given off. The caustic qualities of the lime do not derive from the absorption of fiery particles from the heating process but from the lime itself. The quicklime is soluble and the resulting caustic solution is a property of the quicklime. In experiments analogous to those previously performed, Black showed that both chalk and quicklime combine with the same quantity of acid to form salts, and that a given weight of chalk can be recovered by forming quicklime and then reacting this with potash. The explanation is the same: the quicklime combines with air contained in the alkali. Black then considered a paradox: quicklime in solution should combine with air dissolved in the water to form a small amount of chalk as an insoluble precipitate. An explanation why this did not happen might have been that on solution of the quicklime, the air might have been driven off.

Black tested this by placing two vessels under a bell jar and reduced the pressure with an air pump. The same quantity of air bubbles from the liquids of both vessels: clearly his original explanation was not the answer. The air in the quicklime solution was not the sort which formed a chalk precipitate and thus fixed air and atmospheric air could be differentiated chemically. Black was the first to do this for any gas. He showed that fixed air would not support life (the well-known 1787 engraving by John Kay of Black lecturing shows a cage containing a bird awaiting its fate) and that it was produced in fermentation, on burning charcoal and on respiration. There is a story of Black's verification of the last property: he hoisted up into the roof of a church a quantity of caustic alkali which filtered through rags. When analysed after a ten-hour church service had finished, the congregation of 1,500 persons were found to have rendered the alkali 'mild and crystalline'![54]

It is less easy to trace the development of Black's heat concepts because of the lack of a publication by Black himself. Robison provided suggestions about the evolution of Black's ideas, but it has recently been pointed out that Robison's recollections and interpretations need to be treated with considerable caution.[55] Adam Ferguson's comments may be more reliable, though they were written some 40 years after the events they were describing.

Black was aware of certain seeming anomalies, such as Fahrenheit's observation that heat is emitted from supercooled water which then freezes to form ice, and the fact that water, when it is heated, does not all suddenly boil away when the boiling point is reached. He was able to distinguish between the quantity of heat in a body and its intensity (or temperature), realising that the thermometer could be used to determine quantity of heat if temperature was measured over a period of time while the body was being heated or was cooling. Black turned his attention to the measurement of latent heat. Taking two long-necked flasks, he poured similar quantities of water in both and placed them in a freezing mixture. In one he added a little alcohol to prevent it freezing. They were then taken out of the mixture (at the same temperature) and were allowed to warm up naturally. While the non-frozen mixture warmed up several degrees, the ice remained at freezing point. If it were assumed that the two flasks absorbed heat at the same rate, Black showed that the heat absorbed

by the ice in ten hours would have raised the temperature of an equal volume of water to 139 or 140 degrees. This was a measure of the latent heat of fusion. Another experiment to determine this constant was then tried. A known weight of ice was plunged into a similar quantity of hot water at a measured temperature. The resulting temperature after the ice had melted was considerably less than the mean temperature. In this experiment the latent heat of fusion was measured as 142 or 143 degrees Fahrenheit. The result of these experiments were presented to a meeting of the Literary Society in Glasgow in 1762.

Black then extended his work to the vaporisation of water. He poured known quantities of water into a pan set on one of his furnaces and measured the time taken to heat the water to boiling point, and then the time taken for the water to boil away altogether. He then calculated the rate at which the water was heated to boiling point, in degrees of heat, and, assuming that the heat continued to be

A series of absorption bottles.

transferred at the same rate, the degrees of heat needed to vaporise all the water. Thence the latent heat of vaporisation of water could be calculated. Later, more refined experiments to measure this quantity were conducted with William Irvine. These involved bubbling steam through a weighed quantity of water, noting the increase in temperature, and weighing the vessel at the conclusion of the experiment to determine the weight of steam condensed. These experiments were completed in the autumn of 1764.

Black's other major discovery at this time was that different bodies have different capacities for heat. This, too, was prompted by an experiment of Fahrenheit. When equal volumes of mercury and water, at different temperatures, were mixed, the temperature of the mixture at equilibrium was closer to the former temperature of the water than the former temperature of the mercury. This was unexpected because of the far greater density of mercury. Black concluded that the capacity of bodies for heat varied in a way which was not easily explained by their bulk properties. The phenomenon was appreciated by Watt who realised that to improve the efficiency of Newcomen steam engines (fairly widely used for drainage of mines) it was necessary to reduce the quantity of heat wasted in heating the cylinder, and this could be achieved by the use of a material which had a low 'specific heat'. Up to the time of Black's return to Edinburgh, Black and Irvine measured the specific heats of a variety of substances. Irvine continued the work after Black had departed and he himself succeeded to the chemistry lectureship in Glasgow in 1769.[56]

Retrospective Assessment

Dr Black was perhaps fastidiously nice in his notions of a philosophical performance, and too severe in his observations on the hurried publications of some chemists, which he called slovenly, and to consider as literary manufacture for profit. . . . But such was Dr Black's aversion to all hypothesis and conjecture in any experimental science, that he could not enjure the title of a *system* to be given to any body of chemical doctrines yet published. . . . In the last years of his life, he was convinced of the propriety of this scrupulousness, by the precipitancy with which he saw young men, who had scarcely left the forms of the school, publishing in all quarters of Europe.[57]

Thus Black's editor, John Robison, commented in the introduction to the *Lectures*. It is perhaps Black's fastidious niceness, his very perfection, which can account for the failure of Edinburgh chemistry school to develop beyond its basic pedagogical role. At a time when chemistry was rapidly evolving, Black chose as his amanuensis Thomas Charles Hope (who became his eventual successor), whose attitudes were similar to his own in his later life. Hope was pre-occupied with teaching to the exclusion of involving himself in other scholarly pursuits such as encouraging laboratory work by students, publishing and personal research. Unlike Black he was dull, pompous and uninspiring. Early in the nineteenth century Edinburgh had superb facilities for teaching chemistry but it was the German universities to which the initiative passed in founding the research schools.

Joseph Black's final act of delicacy was his own death. On 6 December 1799 his servant found him seated on a sofa, between his thighs a bowl of milk carefully balanced. He had expired in this position without spilling a drop.[58]

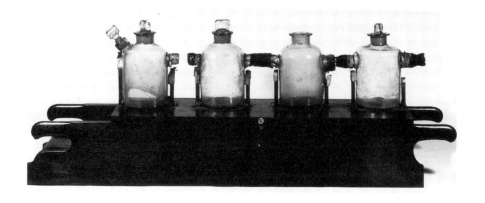

Black's balance, the most renowned item of his surviving apparatus. With another, more sensitive, balance he weighed to .01 gm.

JOSEPH BLACK · 113

Bibliography

Both publications on alkalis, the thesis of 1754 and the paper to the Philosophical Society, have been reprinted a number of times. Recent editions are a translation of the Latin thesis into English by Thomas Hanson, *On Acid Humour arising from foods and on White Magnesia* (Minneapolis, 1973), and the Alembic Club Reprint, *Experiments on Magnesia Alba, Quicklime, and other Alcaline Substances* (Edinburgh, 1963). Black did not publish his investigations on heat and the most comprehensive account (though one which must be treated with caution) is John Robison's two-volume edition of Black's *Lectures on the Elements of Chemistry delivered at the University of Edinburgh* (Edinburgh, 1803). It is reported that this has been reprinted recently in the United States.

Concerning Black's correspondence, Sir William Ramsay's *Life and Letters of Joseph Black M.D.* (London, 1918) contains transcripts of a number of letters and other personal papers (many of the manuscripts are now in Edinburgh University Library). The correspondence with James Watt, which is still in private hands, can be found in print in Eric Robinson and Douglas McKie, *Partners in Science* (London, 1970).

For recent scholarship on Black, by far the most penetrating study is A. L. Donovan's *Philosophical Chemistry in the Scottish Enlightenment* (Edinburgh, 1975) which also deals with William Cullen's and James Watt's chemistry, as well as with that of lesser figures. Donovan's account stops on Black's return to Edinburgh in 1766. Henry Guerlac provides an excellent, short biography of Black in the *Dictionary of Scientific Biography,* vol.ii (New York, 1970). A set of papers read at a symposium held in the Royal Scottish Museum, Edinburgh, in 1978 to celebrate the 250th anniversary of Black's birth has been published by the Museum, edited by A. D. C. Simpson: *Joseph Black 1728-1799* (Edinburgh, 1982). Black's practical chemistry and his teaching are dealt with by R. G. W. Anderson in *The Playfair Collection and the Teaching of Chemistry in the University of Edinburgh 1713-1858* (Edinburgh, 1978).

A bibliography of Black's printed works, papers on Black and an iconography has been prepared by R. G. W. Anderson and G. Fyffe, and will be published shortly by the Science Museum, London.

Notes

1. Henry Cockburn, *Memorials of his Time* (Edinburgh, 1856), p.42.
2. Quoted by Christopher Lawrence, 'Joseph Black: The Natural Philosophical Background' in A. D. C. Simpson (ed.), *Joseph Black 1728-1799* (Edinburgh, 1982), p.4.
3. Robert Kerr, *Memoirs of the Life of William Smellie*, vol.i (Edinburgh, 1811), p.411.
4. Eric Robinson and Douglas McKie, *Partners in Science* (London, 1979), p.81.
5. John H. Appleby, 'John Grieve's Correspondence with Joseph Black and some contemporaneous Russo-Scottish Medical Intercommunication', *Medical History*, vol.29 (1985), 402.
6. William Ramsay, *The Life and Letters of Joseph Black, M.D.* (London, 1918), p.91.
7. R. G. W. Anderson, *The Playfair Collection and the Teaching of Chemistry at the University of Edinburgh 1713-1858* (Edinburgh, 1978), p.23.
8. Joseph Black, *Lectures on the Elements of Chemistry*, vol.i (Edinburgh, 1803), p.lxxi.
9. Peter Swinbank, 'Experimental Science in the University of Glasgow at the Time of Joseph Black', in Simpson (ed.), *Joseph Black*, p.26.
10. Ramsay, p.4.
11. Anderson, p.11.
12. J. B. Morrell, 'The Edinburgh Town Council and its University, 1717-1766' in R. G. W. Anderson and A. D. C. Simpson (eds), *The Early Years of the Edinburgh Medical School* (Edinburgh, 1976), p.51.
13. Ramsay, p.18.
14. A. L. Donovan, *Philosophical Chemistry in the Scottish Enlightenment* (Edinburgh, 1975), p.89.
15. *idem*, p.173.
16. *idem*, p.191.
17. *idem*, p.178.
18. *idem*, p.201.
19. Anderson, p.12.
20. Swinbank, p.32.
21. Henry Guerlac, 'Joseph Black's Work on Heat', in Simpson (ed.), *Joseph Black*, pp.13-22.
22. Robinson and McKie, p.253.
23. Peter Swinbank, 'James Watt and his Shop', *Glasgow University Gazette*, vol.59 (1969), 5.
24. Robinson and McKie, p.416.
25. Thomas Reid, *Works*, vol.i (Edinburgh, 1813), p.21.
26. Anderson, p.20.
27. Swinbank, 'Experimental Science', pp.33, 34.
28. *Address to the Citizens of Edinburgh* (Edinburgh, 1764) (copy in National Library of Scotland).
29. Donovan, p.182.
30. Ramsay, p.144.
31. Robinson and McKie, p.28.
32. Catalogued in Anderson.
33. Henry Brougham, *Lives of the Philosophers in the Time of George III* (London and Glasgow, 1855), p.20.
34. J. R. R. Christie, 'Joseph Black and John Robison', in Simpson (ed.), *Joseph Black*, pp.47-52.
35. W. P. Doyle, 'Black, Hope and Lavoisier', in Simpson (ed.), *Joseph Black*, pp.43-46.
36. J. Rendell, 'The Influence of the Edinburgh Medical School on America in the Eighteenth Century', in Anderson and Simpson (eds), *The Early Years of the Edinburgh Medical School*, pp.95-124.
37. Black, *Lectures*, vol.i, p.lxx.
38. Basil Cozens-Hardy (ed.), *The Diary of Sylas Neville* (London, 1950), p.216.
39. Andrew Doig, 'Dr Black, a Remarkable Physician', in Simpson (ed.), *Joseph Black*, pp.37-41.
40. Anderson, pp.23, 30 (note 70).
41. *idem*, p.143.
42. Robinson and McKie, p.306.
43. Archibald Clow and Nan L. Clow, *The Chemical Revolution* (London, 1952).
44. Alastair J. Durie, *The Scottish Linen Industry in the Eighteenth Century* (Edinburgh, 1979).
45. Andrew Fyfe, 'On the Comparative Value of Kelp and Barilla', *Transactions of the Highland Society*, vol.5 (1820), 29.
46. Edinburgh University Library MS Gen.873, vol.i, ff.137-45.
47. August Christian Reuss, *Beschreibung eines Neuen Chemischen Ofens* (Leipzig, 1782).
48. Anderson, p.24.
49. Clow and Clow, pp.389-423.
50. Henry Cort, *A Brief State of Facts Relative to the New Method of Making Bar Iron* (1787).
51. Brougham, p.21.
52. Joseph Black, *Dissertatio Medica Inauguralis, De Humore Acido a Cibis Orto et Magnesia Alba* (Edinburgh, 1754).
53. Joseph Black, 'Experiments on Magnesia Alba, Quicklime, and some other Alcaline Substances', *Essays and Observations, Physical and Literary*, vol.2 (1756), 157-225.
54. Black, *Lectures*, vol.ii, p.87.
55. Christie, in Simpson (ed.), *Joseph Black*, pp.43-6.
56. Andrew Kent, 'William Irvine, M.D.', in Andrew Kent (ed.), *An Eighteenth Century Lectureship in Chemistry* (Glasgow, 1950), pp.140-50.
57. Black, *Lectures*, vol.i, p.lxiv.
58. Robinson and McKie, p.317.

James Hutton and John Clerk of Eldin on the Salisbury Crags
(detail).

James Hutton

JEAN JONES

HUTTON'S impact on geology rivals Hume's influence on philosophy, Smith's on economics and Black's on chemistry, although his fame never equalled theirs in his lifetime and he remains less well known today. Friend and exact contemporary of Smith and Black, Hutton was the last of the three to publish by some thirty years, since he did not put forward his comprehensive theory of the earth until 1785. Basing his reasoning on diligent observation, he stated that the surface of the earth is simultaneously being destroyed by erosion and recreated from sediments which are first laid down in the sea and then consolidated and elevated by heat. He further concluded that this cycle had been repeated, and would be repeated, an indefinite number of times over an infinitely long period and that therefore no vestige of an original earth remained and nothing could be known of it. With these bold suppositions he freed geological thinking from any restrictions of time scale and laid the foundations of the modern science.

Life

The son of a well-to-do merchant, who was at one time City Treasurer and Master of the Merchant Company, Hutton was born in Edinburgh on 3 June 1726. His father and elder brother died when he was young, leaving him with his mother and three sisters. He was sent to the High School (now the Royal High School) and afterwards to his native university. His friend and biographer John Playfair, Professor of Mathematics and later of Natural Philosophy at Edinburgh University, states that it was at the university that Hutton first became fascinated by chemistry, a fascination which lasted the rest of his life and from which 'he took his departure in his circumnavigation both of the

material and intellectual world'.[1]

In 1743, at the desire of his family, Hutton was apprenticed to a solicitor, the law being one of the most respected and lucrative professions in the capital. His spell in the solicitor's office was unfruitful and was soon terminated for he was 'often found amusing himself and his fellow apprentices with chemical experiments'.[2] The following year he went back to the University as a medical student, perhaps because this was the only way he could prosecute his study of chemistry, then taught as an adjunct to medicine. In 1747, for reasons unknown to us, he decided to complete his education abroad (not, in itself, uncommon at that period) and after nearly two years in Paris 'where he pursued with great ardour the studies of chemistry and anatomy'[3] he moved to Leyden, a university which had close links with Edinburgh and which had been the inspiration and model for Edinburgh's own medical school. Hutton graduated there a few months later, presenting a 34-page thesis entitled *Dissertatio Physico-medica inauguralis de sanguine et circulatione microcosmi* (Inaugural Physico-medical dissertation on the blood and the circulation of the microcosm). Modern scholars led by François Ellenberger have commented on the emphasis he lays on cyclical processes in the natural world even at this early date.

Hutton's career now took several unexpected and unexplained changes of direction. He lingered some months in London and then returned to Edinburgh where he soon abandoned any idea of being a doctor. In later years he is reputed to have said 'the more medical knowledge we require, the more we know how little efficacious the art is'.[4] He remained in the city for two years and, in conjunction with a former fellow student named John Davie,

*Tronmen (chimney sweeps) by Kay, after David Allan.
The firm of Hutton and Davie had a contract with the Tronmen
to buy soot, the raw material from which they manufactured
salammoniac.*

established a chemical works to manufacture salammoniac (ammonium chloride), which was used commercially as a flux in metallurgy as well as in its better known capacity as smelling salts. Previously all the salammoniac used in Britain was imported from Egypt. Hutton and Davie synthesised it by a process they had invented some years before, using soot as their raw material. The project prospered and, with Davie in charge of the day-to-day management, eventually brought both partners considerable wealth.

His business established, and a career in medicine rejected, Hutton next turned his attention to agriculture. His reasons for doing so are unclear though he had inherited two farms from his father, Slighhouses, a 140-acre arable farm near Duns in Berwickshire, and a hill farm on the southeastern edge of the Lammermuirs called Nether Monynut. At the time agricultural improvement was at its height. The efforts of early 'improvers' – such as Lord Cockburn of Ormiston and Sir Archibald Grant of

Monymusk – were famous and respected, and the impetus had spread to small landowners and was filtering down to tenant farmers. Hutton himself claimed, forty years later, that 'at an early period of my life I acquired a taste for agriculture'.[5] He applied himself to his new vocation with typical thoroughness, spending two years in East Anglia studying the improved methods of husbandry that had been developed there and making agricultural pilgrimages through Picardy, the Low Countries and much of England. 'In the course of them to amuse himself upon the road, he first began to study mineralogy, or geology . . . he [became] very fond of studying the surface of the earth, and was looking with anxious curiosity into every pit, or ditch, or bed of a river that fell in his way.'[6] From this time onwards Hutton's agricultural and geological studies went hand in hand, to their mutual benefit.

In 1754, at the age of 28, he settled at Slighhouses, where he engaged in an exhausting struggle to bring the land into good order. Neither enclosed nor drained, it was formed into long ridges, or run-rigs, by which farmers for centuries had striven to create a well-drained position for their crops. Instead, the rigs lost all their topsoil to the ditches at either side and were, besides, wasteful of ground and laborious to work. As Hutton wrote to a friend, sometime in the first year: 'ridges of this kind have cost me more than twenty ploughings' and he added, with a characteristic mixture of bawdiness and brevity, 'I a'n't like, in haste, to wax too fat, nor fart, nor fling neither'.[7]

Hutton remained at Slighhouses for about 13 years, years filled with study, observation and experiment which laid the basis for many of his future achievements, particularly in geology. He put into practice the improved farming techniques he had studied in East Anglia, and also busied himself with experimental work. Most importantly, studying the structure of the land wherever he went and seeking explanations for all that he saw, as he had already done for years on his journeys in England and on the Continent, he began to shape his geological observations into a coherent theory of the earth.

Such knowledge as we possess of his agricultural activities is derived mainly from his long, unpublished manual, 'The Elements of Agriculture', which he began writing in the 1750s, and altered and expanded at intervals over the next 40 years. In two volumes covering nearly 1100 pages, it deals with a comprehensive range of topics, such as types of soil, crops (particularly newly introduced crops such as turnips, clover and cultivated

grasses), fertilisers, the design of farm implements, and animal husbandry. Hutton is concerned, first and foremost, to advocate techniques which will preserve the fertility of the soil. He therefore bases his method on the careful rotation of crops; cattle to manure the fields that are laid down to grass; and the judicious use of inorganic fertiliser. He is also concerned with the comparative cost of old and new methods, including those which involved the division of labour, 'the source of wealth which Mr. Smith has so beautifully illustrated', and with the fundamental place of agriculture in the national economy and the government's duty to encourage it.

> The husbandman maintains the nation in all its ease, its affluence and its splendour. There is therefore a reciprocal duty which the state owes to the husbandry of the country.[8]

This duty entails controlling rents and the length of leases, and disseminating useful information, such as meteorological data or the results of recent agricultural research.

Since the 'Elements of Agriculture' is a text book rather than an autobiography it gives us a very incomplete account of Hutton's own work at Slighhouses. There is enough material, however, to

show that he was a methodical and scientific farmer who experimented continuously and, where he could, measured results quantitatively. He grew plants in the dark and then tested the effect of various intervals of light; he studied the relationship between soil fertility and the ability of a plant to propagate; he tried out coal ash, salt and seaweed ash as fertilisers, finding only the last successful; he devised a way of testing the calcium content of marl (based on Black's classic work) to enable farmers to use it effectively as a fertiliser; he experimented with different ways of treating wheat before it was planted, in an attempt to eradicate smut – one of the most prevalent and lethal cereal diseases; and he studied turnip diseases, and the bark beetle *Ips* which ravages Scots Pine.

However, according to later commentators, his most lasting achievement as a farmer was a technical one, the improvement in ploughing methods that he effected in the district. When he returned from East Anglia, he brought with him some Suffolk ploughs which could be pulled by two horses guided by a single ploughman. This was a startling innovation, for the Scots plough, the only plough in common use in Scotland at that date, was so large and heavy that it required a whole team of horses and bullocks to pull it, and two or three men to control them. The neighbours came to mock but stayed to applaud, and many of them took advantage of the innovation. Within a decade James Small, who lived at Blackadder Mount just ten miles from Slighhouses, designed his famous swing plough, but it must have become available just as Hutton was leaving Slighhouses, and there is no record that he ever used it.

In 1764 Hutton set out on a tour of central and northeast Scotland with George Clerk Maxwell. A man of enterprise and public spirit who was one of the Commissioners for the Forfeited Annexed Estates (the estates which the government confiscated after the '45), Clerk Maxwell worked hard to assess the potential of the estates under his care, inspecting them himself and commissioning extensive mineralogical and agricultural surveys. It seems likely that on the 1764 journey he, at least, was on Estates business. Hutton's object, according to Playfair, was 'mineralogy, or rather geology, which he was now studying with great attention'.[9] They travelled through 'a great deal of the inland Highlands', thence to Inverness and Caithness, and home by the coast.

About 1767 Hutton abandoned farming and went back to live in Edinburgh. According to his own account he had become disheartened when a ploughman he had brought from East Anglia

proved a disappointing deputy. Hutton's comfortable income may also have affected his decision to leave Slighhouses, for thereafter – if not before – he was under no compulsion to earn his living in any regular fashion. As well as the salammoniac business, he had other commercial interests, for he appointed a factor to receive 'the rents, mails and duties . . . of the houses shops and others in the Town of Edinburgh pertaining and belonging to me'.[10]

After Hutton settled in Edinburgh he devoted the rest of his life to business, scholarship and to the company of his friends. At first he lived in rather cramped lodgings – a visitor remarked 'his study is so full of fossils and chemical apparatus that there is scarcely room to sit down' – but in 1770 he bought a plot of land on St John's Hill, looking directly on to the Salisbury Crags, and there built the house in which he lived with his three sisters until his death in 1797.

He kept up his agricultural pursuits. He experimented with different types of fertiliser in his vegetable garden (writing earnest notes about cauliflowers to his friends) and he was growing trial plots of madder, and testing plants of various ages for the quality of their dye, when his friend Joseph Black and George Mackintosh, the Glasgow

manufacturer who invented 'Turkey red', were in correspondence. At least one lengthy meteorological experiment on heat and plant growth was also carried out during his days in Edinburgh. In spite of all this, his skill as a farmer seems to have been largely unnoticed, or discounted, by his scientific contemporaries in Britain, perhaps because he avoided any public, or semi-public, projects. In particular, he never joined the Highland and Agricultural Society, the most powerful and, as it has proved, the most long lasting of the innumerable agricultural societies which had sprung up all over the country. In France, however, Hutton's agricultural achievements were recognised by his election as 'associé étranger' of the influential Société Royale d'Agriculture de Paris.

As soon as he returned to Edinburgh – or perhaps even earlier – Hutton became deeply involved in the greatest commercial enterprise of the period, the construction of the Forth and Clyde Canal. The idea of a canal was first seriously considered in the early eighteenth century, but did not become a reality until the great era of British canal building some forty years later. The route, and the composition of the company to build it, were settled only after a long and acrimonious debate, in which Hutton joined, but eventually the Company of the

Proprietors of the Forth and Clyde Navigation was established by Act of Parliament in 1768 and empowered to raise £150,000. Hutton and Clerk Maxwell, who both held five £100 shares, were for seven years members of the executive committee which supervised its day-to-day management.

It was an ambitious operation: the canal is nearly 39 miles long, 63 feet wide and was originally 7 feet deep. Since construction began at the eastern end Edinburgh was chosen as the headquarters of the Committee. Between 1767 and 1774 Hutton attended 84 committee meetings, 15 of them on the site. Clerk Maxwell always excepted, the other committee members tended to appear mostly at the meetings in town which were held in various coffee houses and taverns. Here they discussed arrangements for purchasing the necessary land and equipment; wages; supplies of wood, lime and Pozzolana earth (which hardens under water when mixed with lime); the design of aquaducts and locks and many other matters.

The meetings on the site lasted two or three days, and were often uncomfortable and arduous. The committee members rode the proposed route with the surveyor, Robert Mackell, working out the gradient, the cost and the water supplies; they examined borings; they calculated the amount and quality of stone that could be procured from local quarries to build the locks; and they inspected the work already completed. Here, indeed, was Hutton's knowledge of geology put to good effect.

By 1775, with 28 miles of the canal completed, the committee was reconstructed and moved to Glasgow, and Hutton appears on it no more. The canal was eventually opened in 1790, and thereafter for 100 years it made a substantial contribution to the economic prosperity of the nation. From the end of the nineteenth century it lost its traffic to the railways and it was finally closed in 1962.

The first work that Hutton ever published may have been an offshoot of his interest in the canal. Called *Considerations on the Nature, Quality and Distinctions of Coal and Culm*, it was published in 1777 with the aim of persuading the government to abolish the tax on Scottish culm (small, stony, low-grade coal) carried by sea which was then taxed at the same rate as coal. The tax had long been a source of grievance and its fault from Hutton's point of view was that it discouraged transport along the canal to the sea. The difficulty lay in distinguishing the point at which coal became culm. Hutton proposed a simple test which could easily be applied by excise officers: small coal, if heated on a shovel, cakes, whereas culm does not. Although we do not know how much attention the

government paid to Hutton's well argued pamphlet, the tax was eventually lifted.

Hutton's early years in Edinburgh coincided with the heyday of the Scottish Enlightenment and he counted the most brilliant men in the city among his friends, notably William Robertson; Adam Ferguson; Lord Monboddo, at whose 'learned suppers' he was a frequent guest; Adam Smith; and Joseph Black. Only Hume is missing from the list and no-one has yet discovered how well Hume and Hutton knew each other. Outside Edinburgh, Hutton's closest friend was James Watt whom he met, through Black, in the 1760s.

Hutton's friendship with Black 'was a distinguishing circumstance in the life and character of both'.[11] Black's voluminous correspondence shows that they were continually together and indicates that they shared much of their research: for example, they tested the effects of heat and pressure on sea shells by heating them up in a Papin's digester; they analysed earths sent by aspiring farmers; and at the request of the Board of Manufactures (the eighteenth-century equivalent of the Scottish Development Agency) they tested a new design of furnace for smelting iron ore. Together they knew most of the eminent scientists and industrialists in Britain – men like Erasmus Darwin (grandfather of Charles and a distinguished physician), Josiah Wedgwood, Sir Joseph Banks, Thomas Beddoes (pioneer of pneumatic medicine), Matthew Boulton and of course James Watt. They also entertained visiting scholars from England and the Continent, and, on a more domestic level, they befriended lonely students, at least at Christmas.

Friends though they were, Hutton and Black had very different temperaments and the disparity delighted their acquaintances. Playfair's well-known comparison is still the best:

> Ardour and even enthusiasm, in the pursuit of science, great rapidity of thought, and much animation, distinguished Dr Hutton on all occasions. Great caution in his reasonings, and a coolness of head that even approached to indifference, were characteristic of Dr Black . . . Dr Black dreaded nothing so much as error and Dr Hutton dreaded nothing so much as ignorance: the one was always afraid of going beyond the truth and the other of not reaching it . . . Dr Black was correct, respecting at all times prejudices and fashions of the world; Dr Hutton was more careless, and was often found in direct collision with both.[12]

As far as we know, Hutton belonged to none of the clubs which were such a conspicuous feature of Edinburgh social life, except the Oyster Club and the Philosophical Society of Edinburgh and its successor, the Royal Society of Edinburgh. The Philosophical Society ('philosophy' at this date meaning 'natural philosophy' or, more broadly, 'science') was founded in 1737 as a forum for learned exchange at home and a point of contact for scholars abroad. In its intermittent periods of greatness it enjoyed the patronage of distinguished patricians, such as Sir John Clerk, and its membership included the most notable scientists, doctors and improvers. About the time Hutton returned to Edinburgh it was rescued from some years of decline 'by the zeal of Lord Kames',[13] and finally, in 1783, was established by Royal Charter under its new title, the Royal Society of Edinburgh. By providing scholars, technologists and the literati with an opportunity to test their views before a scholarly audience, and to publish them afterwards, it had a great influence on the advancement of knowledge in Scotland. Still flourishing today, it is, like the Royal Highland and Agricultural Society, one of the permanent legacies of the Scottish Enlightenment.

Hutton, like Black and Smith, was a member from its inception and he remained very active in its affairs until he took ill in 1793. The number of administrative, as well as scientific, meetings he attended, and the number of offices he held at various times, suggest that he made a substantial contribution to the success of the Society and also that the Society must have played a significant role in his own life. He gave papers on meteorology, chemistry, natural history and geology. More unexpected is a paper he gave on the origin of writing, a subject related to ideas about the origin of speech and the evolution of society, which were being much debated by Monboddo and others. It thus becomes apparent that Hutton's interests extended to the historical and speculative issues of the day and his later work on philosophy is therefore less of a surprise.

Long before the Society was founded – in fact by the time he returned to Edinburgh – Hutton was widely respected as a geologist and frequently consulted on both commercial and theoretical matters, but he had never published anything on the subject. He first made his views public in two lectures delivered on 7 March and 4 April 1785. They were subsequently published in three different versions. Firstly, a brief summary, perhaps written to fulfil the Society's requirement that an abstract of a paper should be read at any meeting assembled to discuss it, appeared in 1785 under the title *Abstract of a Dissertation concerning the System of the Earth, its Duration and Stability*. Three years later, in 1788, the lectures were published in an expanded form in the first volume of the *Transactions of the Royal Society*.

This second version, the 'Theory of the Earth; or an Investigation of the Laws observable in the Composition, Dissolution and Regeneration of Land upon the Globe', occupies 195 quarto pages. The last version, *Theory of the Earth with proofs and illustrations* appeared in 1795 and runs to two substantial volumes. It was written in response to an attack upon his views by Richard Kirwan in *Transactions of the Royal Irish Academy*, volume 5 (1793). It contains the 1788 paper in full with much of the additional material made up of quotations and illustrations from other authorities. Hutton also planned, and wrote part of, a third volume for the 1795 *Theory*. This was still in manuscript when he died in 1797 and suffered a century of neglect before it was eventually published in 1899.

The 1795 *Theory of the Earth* was Hutton's last published work. It was preceded by books on physics, chemistry and philosophy, all written between 1792 and 1794. Since he had previously published very little, this sudden fecundity is probably ex-

plained by his failing health, which now kept him at home. The *Dissertations on Different Subjects in Natural Philosophy* (1792) is divided into three parts. The first, concerned with meteorology, is composed of his published papers on the subject. The second part is a defence of the Phlogiston Theory, based on his papers to the Royal Society. Thirdly, Hutton put forward his theory of matter. He argued that to say a body is composed of tiny particles is only to say that larger bodies are composed of smaller ones, thus giving us no new information about their essential nature. This led him to believe that the elements of a body (which he termed matter) must have no magnitude. He used this concept to explain gravity, volume, hardness and fluidity, heat, light and electricity. His theory resembles that of the Serbo-Croat writer Boscovich (1711–87) but is usually thought to have been arrived at independently.

In 1793 Hutton fell seriously ill and his friends despaired of his life, but he eventually recovered sufficiently to go about the city and to continue writing. In a *Dissertation upon the Philosophy of Heat, Light and Fire* (1794) he discusses the relationships among these three phenomena. His analysis of experimental work done on the Continent led him to conclude that there must be some form of invisible light which has greater powers of heating than any in the visible spectrum. He also thought that light lies dormant within matter as 'fixed light, or a peculiar modification of the solar substance'.[14]

At this period Hutton believed that although science is in itself a profitable subject of study its greatest merit lies in providing the particular facts on which a sound philosophy of life might be based, the highest achievement of mankind being 'the art of human happiness – an art which is only to be attained by education and brought to perfection by philosophy'.[15] This view is expanded and developed, together with a supporting theoretical framework, in *An Investigation of the Principles of Knowledge and of the progress of Reason, from Sense to Science and Philosophy*, 3 vols (1794). Hutton constructed a complete metaphysical system grounded in his study of, and reaction to, Locke, Berkeley and Hume, in which a study of causation played a prominent part. The range of the work is enormous and its results uneven as he shifts his attention from causation to space, time, the origin of society, morality, politics and education. He was an early advocate of better education for women: in his own words 'the culture of the fair sex is necessary for the perfection of the state'.[16]

None of these late works, except the *Theory of the Earth*, have had much influence on their respective

Boulder of conglomerate from Brora, Sutherland. A dramatic example of Hutton's first and most fundamental observation, that rocks "bear the marks of being formed out of materials of more ancient date". Height 10".

disciplines. Prolix, and composed in the main of imperfectly assimilated earlier material, their virtues, though many, are hard to find.

Hutton's last years were sad ones. In the summer of 1794 his former illness recurred, and he never again left the house. He spent two and a half years in increasing pain, writing when he could and seeing his friends when he could. He died on 26 March 1797 and was buried in Greyfriars Churchyard where, on the 150th anniversary of his death, a memorial stone was placed above his unmarked grave.

Geology

OUTLINE AND ORIGIN OF HIS THEORY OF THE EARTH. The *Abstract* (1785), the 'Theory of the Earth' (1788) and the three volumes of the *Theory of the Earth* (1795 and 1899) have the same thesis, despite their marked difference in length. In essence, Hutton declared that the earth processes which are at work today, such as erosion, deposition, uplift, folding and volcanic activity, operated in the same manner in the past and will continue to do so in the future. He believed that their agency alone was sufficient to explain all observed phenomena and declared that, as a result of their operating simultaneously over an immensely long period of time, the surface of the globe had been destroyed and created an indefinite number of times. In consequence, the original surface of the earth had entirely disappeared. There are three particularly significant features of this theory: firstly, Hutton's emphasis on erosion as an agent capable of destroying the entire surface of the earth; secondly, the assumption that the processes which operated in the past are the same as those observed today, and that the average rate of geological change over a long period of time is more or less constant; thirdly, the idea that geological time is virtually unlimited.

What led Hutton to this comprehensive and radical, or – as Playfair put it – this 'new and sublime' conclusion? Fortunately we know at least part of the answer, for while Playfair was writing Hutton's biography he found among his papers 'a few sketches of the Natural History of the Earth'.[17] These were apparently composed at least twenty years before Hutton gave his famous paper to the Royal Society of Edinburgh, and though the essays themselves are long since lost, Playfair's summary of them gives us an insight into the genesis of Hutton's ideas.

As a young farmer he noticed that 'a vast proportion of the present rocks is composed of materials afforded by the destruction of bodies, animal, vegetable and mineral, of more ancient forma-

tion'.[18] (In later life he was to estimate that sedimentary rocks formed nine-tenths, or even ninety-nine-hundredths, of the surface of the earth.) This observation led him to study the various processes by which existing rocks are worn away. Though the thoroughness with which he pursued his enquiries was unusual, there was, of course, nothing new in studying either sedimentary rocks or erosion. Hutton's originality lay in perceiving that there was a necessary connection between them, in other words that the eroded material which is carried away to the sea is somehow consolidated and elevated to form new land.

This imaginative leap was just the first move in Hutton's argument. He went on to claim that as the world we know is built of débris of a former world, and as it is just as vulnerable to erosion as that former world, in the course of time it, too, will be destroyed and refashioned into a future world. He further argued that the cyclical process had been, and would be, repeated an indefinite number of times. He next asked 'what is the space of time necessary for accomplishing this great work?'[19] He concluded that, because land wasted away so slowly and the life span of man (together with the time during which historical records had been kept) are so brief in comparison, man is destined to remain in ignorance both of the origin of this 'succession of worlds' and of its conclusion. In his own most oft quoted dictum, 'the result, therefore, of our present enquiry is that we find no vestige of a beginning – no prospect of an end'.[20]

Eon	Era		Period with duration in millions		Years in millions before the present
Phanerozoic (life on earth)	Cenozoic	Tertiary	Quaternary	2	----- 2 -----
			Neogene	22.6	-----24.6-----
			Paleogene	40.4	----- 65 -----
	Mesozoic		Cretaceous	79	----- 144 -----
			Jurassic	69	----- 213 -----
			Triassic	38	----- 248 -----
	Paleozoic	Upper	Permian	38	----- 286 -----
			Carboniferous	74	----- 360 -----
			Devonian 48 'Old Red Sandstone'		----- 408 -----
		Lower	Silurian	30	----- 438 -----
			Ordovician	67	----- 505 -----
			Cambrian	85	----- 590 -----
PRECAMBRIAN					
Eon					
Proterozoic 2500					-----2500-----
Archean					-----4000-----
Priscoan					-----5000-----

The Geological Succession. 'Dalradian' is a stratigraphic division only applicable in Scotland and Ireland. Roughly speaking, it spans the last 300 million years of the Proterozoic and some of the Cambrian. Table based on W. B. Harland et al., *A Geologic Time Scale* (Cambridge University Press, 1982).

TIME. Hutton was able to pursue his argument to such an extreme, if logical, conclusion because of his views on the nature of time. We do not know whether he developed these by himself or whether he took them from other philosophers, but he certainly held that time is not an independent entity, but merely a way of describing the duration of events. Instead of believing, like most of his contemporaries, that the history of the earth had to be fitted into a certain preconceived period, he considered that time simply continues for as long or short a span as there are events to fill it. 'Time, which measures every thing in our idea, and is often deficient in our schemes, is to nature endless and as nothing; it cannot limit that by which it

alone has existence.'[21] Nearly all Hutton's contemporaries believed that the earth had been created in 4004 BC, the date which Archbishop Ussher had calculated by correlating Middle Eastern and Mediterranean chronologies with Holy Writ. Ussher's chronology was printed in the margins of bibles from 1701 onwards and, since it came to be regarded with the same unquestioning reverence as the Bible itself, was widely cited by opponents of Hutton's views. The age of the earth is now thought to be about 5000 million years and its history during the last 600 million is understood well enough to be divided into different eras and periods.

UNIFORMITARIANISM. Although Hutton declared that the surface of the earth had been recycled many times in the history of the earth, and although he had seen evidence of immense forces at work – for example in steeply folded rocks or igneous intrusions – he denied that these events had been brought about by sudden and major catastrophes such as earthquakes and floods. Instead he believed that the earth processes we observe every day are sufficient to bring them about, given time. 'We are not to suppose, that there is any violent exertion of power, such as is required in order to produce a great event in a little time; in nature we find no deficiency in respect of time, nor any limitation in regard to power'.[22] This view was directly opposed to that of many of his contemporaries who favoured 'catastrophist' explanations.

Hutton then went on to consider the rates at which these processes operate. He pointed out that the life span of man is too short to calculate rates of decay and renovation but he thought them unlikely to be regular: 'we are not to limit nature with the uniformity of an equable progression'. On the other hand he believed they remained closely enough in step to sustain the cycle of destruction and renewal and for 'our computations to proceed upon equalities'[23] since irregularities would even out over a very long time span.

The term 'uniformitarianism', coined by William Whewell in 1832, was applied to this belief in the relative constancy of geological rates and processes, one of Hutton's most fruitful theories. Nowadays the emphasis is on processes rather than rates.

SUBTERRANEAN HEAT. Hutton formulated the outline of his great theory before he left Slighhouses but to make it credible in physical, as well as metaphysical, terms he still had to explain how rocks are consolidated and elevated. At first, according to Playfair, he had 'no physical hypothesis whatever in his mind'.[24] At some point, however, he decided that the clue he was looking for lay in certain rocks and minerals whose appearance suggested that they must once have been fluid. 'Here', he says, 'the science of chemistry must be called particularly to our aid.'[25] Rejecting the prevalent idea that these minerals and rocks must have been precipitated from solutions of sediments, on the grounds that the siliceous and sulphureous compounds which many of them contain are insoluble, Hutton embarked, on his return to Edinburgh, on a long and patient study of heat and fluidity. He concluded that the only agent that could have acted on all substances, and also found its way into them without occupying any space, was heat. He based his claim largely on the appearance of coal, fossil wood, ores, rock salt, septarian nodules, agate and marble, all of which gave evidence of having been heated, and all but coal and fossil wood having crystallised from a melt (rather than a solution). 'All this may be perceived', he added, 'by a man of science in his closet.'[26] Extending his claim to a global scale he concluded that the earth was hot. Today, when the heat of the earth has been common knowledge for generations, it is easy to forget what a great step forward Hutton made.

Equally offensive to the generally accepted view of the world, and equally impossible to investigate, was Hutton's declaration that subterranean heat not only consolidated the sediments on the sea floor but elevated them to form new land. He first considered the less dramatic possibility that the sea level had fallen. In this case sedimentary rocks would be found as they were when they were laid down – unfolded and more or less horizontal – whereas they are in fact often 'broken, twisted and confounded, as might be expected from the operation of subterranean heat and violent expansion'.[27]

As supporting evidence for the existence of subterranean heat Hutton cited the scale and power of all volcanic activity, and the widespread and well documented occurrence of igneous rocks like basalt, which his enlightened contemporaries recognised had formed from lava.

Given Hutton's achievement in concluding that the earth was hot, how accurate were his premises? We know today that he was right about heat and elevation: ultimately, all earth movements are generated by convection currents in the mantle. He was also correct in arguing for the former fluidity of minerals such as agate and jasper. However metamorphic rocks, such as marble or gneiss, formed when existing rocks are subjected to heat and pressure over a long period of time, flow and recrystallise as solids not fluids. Furthermore Hutton placed too much emphasis on heat as the agent of consolidation of sedimentary rocks: consolidation takes place principally by compaction and a complex series of chemical changes.

INFLUENCE ON JOSEPH BLACK. In the early 1750s Black had established that calcium carbonate gives off carbon dioxide when heated. Marble is largely composed of calcium carbonate, so its existence in the crust of the earth seemed to falsify Hutton's theory of subterranean heat. Why has it not decomposed? Or is the earth not hot? Hutton surmised correctly that sufficient pressure would prevent decomposition, and Black agreed with his hypothesis.

Black used to discuss geology in his course of lectures but, judging by student lecture notes, he only made brief commendatory allusions to Hutton's theories – when he mentioned them at all. However, in a private letter to Princess Dashkova, Director of the Imperial Academy of Sciences in St Petersburg, the 'cool and steady Dr Black' (as Adam Smith called him) allowed himself a rare moment of enthusiasm, even of passion:

> In this system of Dr Hutton there is a grandeur and sublimity by which it far surpasses any that has been offered. The boundless preexistence of time and of the operations of Nature, the depth and extent to which his imagination has explored the action of fire in the internal part of the earth strikes us with astonishment . . . The short lived bustle of Mans remotest reach of History or tradition or of the inquisitive antiquarian appear as nothing when compared with an object so great.[28]

PRIMITIVE MOUNTAINS. At the time Hutton was writing there was a common belief, first advanced by Lehman in 1759, that all non-fossiliferous rocks were 'primitive', that is, part of the original surface of the earth. The term embraced rocks that had once been molten (igneous rocks, in modern terminology) and non-fossiliferous rocks formed from sediments. The idea that any part of the earth's surface was immutable was in direct opposition to everything that Hutton believed. It was obvious that no igneous rock would ever contain fossils, so Hutton refuted the idea that all igneous rocks were primitive on quite other grounds (see 'Geological Excursions' below). As regards rocks formed from sediments, he contended that an apparent lack of fossils proved nothing except that they were hard to find and, if they had been much altered, hard to recognise. Before 1785 he had only succeeded in finding one trace of a fossil in mountains designated primitive in spite of more than twenty years of effort and extensive journeys. Nevertheless he was confident

James Hutton, by Raeburn, c.1785. Some of Hutton's geological specimens lie beside him. The quantity of manuscript suggests a prolific output, although by 1785 he had published only one pamphlet.

Section of rocks beneath Castle Street, Edinburgh, by John Clerk. Presumably drawn in 1785, when drains were dug during the construction of the New Town. Sandstone, "schistus" (shale) and limestone are shown with their characteristic texture, jointing, bedding, and faults.

enough of his position to claim it as his very first point in the *Abstract* of 1785:

> We find reason to conclude that the land on which we rest is not simple and original but formed by the operation of second causes.[29]

At last, in 1788 at Lowood on the banks of Lake Windermere, where limestone is found in association with 'primitive' Skiddaw slates, Hutton found the evidence he was seeking, 'a specimen which I have ground and polished and it is evidently full of fragments of entrochi. Here is one specimen which at once overturned all speculations . . . the schistus mountains of Cumberland were as perfect primitive mountains as any on earth before this observation; now they have no claim upon that score.'[30]

The refutation of such a widespread and erroneous belief was one of Hutton's most enduring contributions to geology, and one in which Playfair and a young man named Sir James Hall joined with enthusiasm. Playfair later found many more fossils at Lowood. In 1792 Hall sent Hutton fossils from the Wrae limestone which he found in a quarry situated between Noblehouse and Crook in Peebleshire, in the so-called primitive mountains of the Southern Uplands.

GEOLOGICAL EXCURSIONS. Hutton's theories were based on a lifetime of observations gathered in the course of often arduous journeys. As early as 1770 he claimed to have been through most of England, except Devon and Cornwall, and to this we must add his earlier journeys on the Continent and in Scotland. In 1774 he set out for southwest England and Wales. Travelling with James Watt, who was moving south to join forces with Matthew Boulton in Birmingham, Hutton visited the Cheshire salt mines and stayed some time in Birmingham meeting the intelligensia and attending at least one meeting of the renowned Lunar Society. He then rode southwest as far as Bath and right across Wales. We have few details of his tour but he

climbed the Wrekin, visited the Parys copper mine in Anglesey, and was saddlesore, weary and lonely long before he got home. 'Lord pity the arse that's clagged to a head that will hunt stones' he exclaimed in a letter to George Clerk Maxwell, adding later 'I begin to be tired of speaking to stones and long for a fresh bit of mortality to make sauce to them'.[31]

From the instructions that he sent another friend we know how he conducted his investigations in the field.

> The mineral observations consist both in a history of soil or loose parts and of the solid parts or rocks and beds; the shortest and best way of doing this is to take samples more or less but not to neglect this however small the samples are; these should be carefully marked and packed, and, being brought home, an accurate history may be made from them alongst with drawings of the stratification, veins or other regular appearances; where there is nothing but a confused mass this should be noted; there must be references from the mineral drawing to the sample and vice versa. N.B. a bag of gravel will tell wondrous tales. I need say no more, only, mind, a bag of gravel from a great river should contain samples from a great distance and vice versa and therefore attention should be had to this in marking the sample – thus – gravel from a river – rivulet – hill – plain – shore etc,[32]

He certainly took his own advice about collecting for he 'never failed to return with new materials for geological investigation' and believed that his specimens were more effective advocates for his theories than any number of words.

Glen Tilt, Southwest Scotland and Arran. At the time Hutton gave his 1785 paper he already believed that granite, like basalt, was an igneous rock. Although he had examined many specimens of it he had never seen it in the field, so in the summer of the same year and the three succeeding ones he made a series of excursions to areas where he calculated granite could be found, or where it had actually

John Clerk of Eldin (1728-1812) by James Saxon.

been reported. These journeys are remarkable in that they were carried out to verify, rather than formulate, a theory. They are also remarkable for their success. Hutton's account of them was intended for the third volume of the *Theory of the Earth* but after he died the manuscript was passed from hand to hand and then deposited in the Geological Society of London and forgotten. It was not until 1899 that it was published at the instigation of Archibald Geikie, Director of the Geological Survey, one of the most influential geologists of the nineteenth century and long one of Hutton's admirers.

Hutton's companion and draughtsman on three of these four epic journeys was John Clerk of Eldin, a younger brother of George Clerk Maxwell and once a fellow student with Hutton. Clerk was respected in his own day for his expertise on technical matters, for his etchings of landscapes, and for his treatise on naval tactics. Until recently little was

known of his skills as a geologist except that 'his extensive information made him, to Dr. Hutton, an invaluable friend and coadjutor. . . . Mr. Clerk's pencil was ever at the command of his friend and certainly rendered him most essential service'.[33] In 1968 a large folio of Clerk's geological drawings, mostly made for Hutton, was identified at Penicuik House, Midlothian, home of Sir John Clerk. In the same year, his journal of their travels through southwest Scotland and a brief autobiographical fragment – which describes how his financial involvement in mining triggered his geological studies – came to light.

The first great journey was made to Glen Tilt in Perthshire where Hutton and Clerk had 'an engagement to visit the Duke of Atholl at Blair',[34] probably to make a mineral survey, as they did later on the Duke's estates on the Isle of Man. With the knowledge acquired on previous travels, Hutton believed the glen must be the junction between 'the great mass of granite which runs south-west from Aberdeen' and the metamorphic rocks of the central Highlands (which he termed 'Alpine Strata'). He and Clerk, who were both nearly sixty, resolved to seek it out no matter what hardships it cost them 'among the mountains of this elevated track'. Everything turned out much more comfortably than they expected. They were entertained at the Duke's hunting lodge 'with the utmost hospitality and elegance' and they found the contact they were looking for neatly exposed in the bed of the River Tilt, not two hundred yards away. They saw instantly that the granite had broken the edge of the marble which composes the south side of the valley, and that granite veins had penetrated deeply into it, proving that the intrusive rock must be both igneous and younger than the rock it disturbed. This confirmed Hutton in his opinion that basalt was not the only type of igneous rock and that igneous rocks could in no sense be primitive.

Hutton's delight at finding his theories confirmed knew no bounds 'and as his feelings, on such occasions, were always strongly expressed, the guides who accompanied him were convinced that it must be nothing less than the discovery of a vein of silver or gold, that would call forth such strong marks of joy and exaltation'.[35] Clerk's drawings show that the contact in the River Tilt looked much the same two hundred years ago as it does today (Nat. Grid Ref. 938747; permission to visit it must be obtained from the Duke of Atholl's factor). To demonstrate his discovery to his fellow scientists Hutton despatched to Edinburgh a number of veined marble boulders, one of which weighed 4 cwt.

Contact in the River Tilt, Perthshire, by John Clerk.
This bird's eye view shows the marble interlacing with granite.
The distance between the two branches of the river is about 15 ft.

Boulder from Glen Tilt, by John Clerk.
The boulder shows a contact between granite (speckled) and
marble.

Late the following summer Hutton and Clerk made a three-week tour of southwest Scotland. From Glasgow they went south along the coast to Portpatrick before turning east to seek out the granite of Galloway. 'When we had not gone many miles from Newton Stewart we observed the most unequivocal marks of the vicinity of granite country; this was the abundance of granite rolled in the rivers.'[36] This emphasis on gravel recalls Hutton's letter, quoted earlier, and foreshadows his chapters on rivers and erosion in the *Theory of the Earth*. On the southwest side of Cairnsmore of Fleet, 'a great round granite mountain', and on the shore at Colvend, they found the junction of the granite with the older sedimentary rocks of the Southern Uplands. In both cases the sedimentary rocks had been broken and twisted by the granite, just as they had at Glen Tilt. (Erosion over the past two hundred years has made it impossible to identify either site but a similar outcrop can be seen in an old roadside quarry at NX 923568.)

Arran was Hutton's next object and he visited it in 1787, once again to study 'the nature of granite and the connection of it with the contiguous strata'.[37] Clerk was unable to accompany him, but Clerk's eldest son, John Clerk jnr (later known as Lord Eldin when he was raised to the bench), volun-

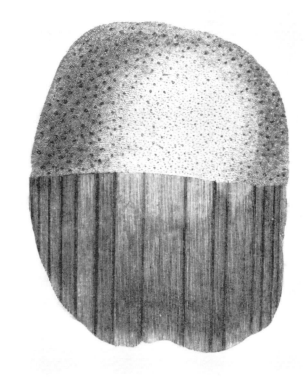

teered to go with him instead. After much travail they found the junction of the granite of the central mountains and the Upper Paleozoic sediments somewhere in Glen Rosa and along the North Sannox River.

Clerk's folio contains watercolours of Arran of amazing accuracy, very much in the style of the other drawings. We do not know whether they were executed by the father, on the basis of his own sketches from an earlier visit in 1763 supplemented by those brought back by his son, or whether they are the work of the son himself, who inherited some of his father's abilities as a draughtsman. The drawings convey all the essentials of the geology of the island. The Tertiary granite to the north, whose highest peak is Goatfell, is seen surrounded by a grey 'skirt' (as Hutton called it) of Dalradian sediments which it had thrust upwards into a steeply inclined position. Outside the Dalradian, and lying at an angle to it, are the strata of the Old Red Sandstone which once lay above it before it was disturbed by the granite. To the south are undisturbed younger sediments and Holy Island (a sill composed of a fine grained igneous rock called felsite) jutting out of Lamlash Bay. The small island of Pladda, just off the south end of the mainland, is correctly represented by whinstone (grey) with sedimentary rocks (red) underneath. Hutton realised it had once been attached to the rest of the island and extended his argument to show how the sea had power to waste away whole continents: 'Pladda is to the island of Arran, what Arran is to the island of Britain and what the island of Britain is to the Continent of Europe'.[38] Taken as a whole,

the drawing shows how thoroughly Hutton must have explored the island, and the knowledge and percipience with which he made his observations.

The unconformities at Jedburgh and Siccar Point. All Hutton's excursions to date had been made with a particular end in view. In the autumn of 1787, not long after he returned from Arran, he made a dramatic discovery quite by chance. On a visit to a friend who lived near Jedburgh, he noticed in the banks of the River Jed an exposure of rock where horizontal strata of sandstone were underlain by vertical strata of greywackes and shales, separated from them by a thin bed of conglomerate derived from the lower rocks. The significant feature of this arrangement was that the strata of upper and lower rocks were not lying parallel to each other but at an angle (a configuration later called an unconformity). Hutton perceived that there could be only one explanation: the sands and muds which formed the greywackes and shales had been deposited at the bottom of the ocean and then compacted, folded and elevated; subsequently erosion had exposed the vertical limbs of the folds while most of the eroded material was carried away; lastly, the land sank, more sediments were deposited and, after consolidation but this time without folding, a second elevation had taken place. Such a sequence of events could only have been enacted over an immense period of time and confirmed Hutton's supposition that the earth is extremely ancient. It is now known that the 'schistus' (i.e. the Silurian greywackes and shales) was laid down over 400 million years ago, and that the interval between its deformation and the deposition of the Old Red

Hutton and Clerk are examining an exposure where the underlying sandstone has been broken by an intrusive sill of teschenite. This contact was later quarried away, and only small exposures are now visible (left).

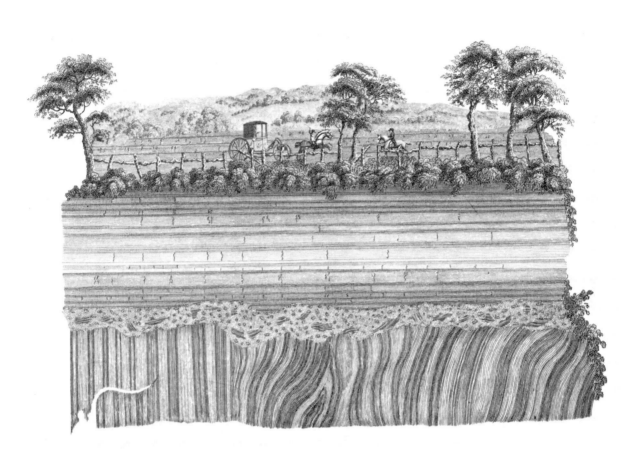

Sandstone was over 100 million years.

The site at Jedburgh is now almost completely obscured by trees and undergrowth. It is half a mile out of town, at NT 652198, and is best seen from the west bank of the river. Clerk, who was either with Hutton at the time or visited the site later at his instigation, made one of his most charming drawings and an engraving of it was published in the *Theory of the Earth*, vol.ii, the only one of Clerk's geological drawings to appear before 1978.

Characteristically searching for yet more evidence, and acting on information that the unconformity he had seen at Jedburgh might also be exposed on the coast 30 miles to the northeast, Hutton set off by boat from Dunglass with Hall and Playfair as companions. They found what they were looking for at Siccar Point, three miles southeast of Cockburnspath, now the most famous unconformity in Scotland and a place of pilgrimage for historians of geology (NT 813710). The discovery, and Hutton's peroration on the occasion, made a lasting impression on his companions:

> The palpable evidence presented to us . . . gave a reality and substance to those theoretical speculations, which, however probable, had never till now been

directly authenticated by the testimony of the senses. . . . We felt ourselves necessarily carried back to the time when the schistus on which we stood was set at the bottom of the sea, and when the sandstone before us was only beginning to be deposited, in the shape of sand and mud, from the waters of a superincumbent ocean. An epoch still more remote presented itself, when even the most ancient of these rocks, instead of standing upright in vertical beds, lay in horizontal planes at the bottom of the sea, and was not as yet disturbed by that immeasurable force which has burst asunder the solid pavement of the globe. Revolutions still more remote appeared in the distance of this extra-ordinary perspective. The mind seemed to grow giddy by looking so far into the abyss of time . . . and we became sensible how much further reason may some-times go than imagination can dare to follow.[39]

Siccar Point was the last of Hutton's great excur-sions. We know nothing of any subsequent travels except the bare fact that he returned to Glen Tilt in 1790.

THEORY OF THE EARTH. During the last years of his life Hutton continued to study the accounts of travellers with close attention. 'I have the satis-faction, almost every day to compare the theory, which I formed from my own proper observation, with the actual state of things in every quarter of the globe.'[40] In the first two volumes of the *Theory of the Earth* Hutton employed much of this accumu-lated material as illustration, principally drawn from continental travellers. To his 1788 paper he added discussions of primitive mountains and un-conformities, and extended his earlier enquiries into subterranean heat and, particularly, erosion. Though he appreciated the extent and power of rivers much better than his contemporaries, since he realised they operated over almost infinitely long periods of time, it was left to the Swiss naturalist Louis Agassiz (1807–73) to establish that successive ice ages, rather than rivers, have sculpted the landscape in northern Europe and America.

The *Theory of the Earth* is often repetitive and difficult to follow. Hutton did not begin work on it until after he was ill, and it gives the impression of having been cobbled together from earlier drafts. Even his most devoted followers lamented the con-trast between the obscurity of his later writings and the clarity of his conversation. Nevertheless the book still has qualities which compel our admira-tion – first and foremost its heroic thesis but also the wealth of evidence that Hutton advances and his ability to travel easily in imagination through space and time.

Ironically, the part of the third volume which deals with Hutton's excursions is the most approachable of all his writings and much the most straightforward. Had it been published as planned, his theories might have been accepted more quickly.

Taking Hutton's work as a whole, it is remarkable for his skill in many disciplines and their practical applications; his powers of observation, exercised over a lifetime; his capacity to predict what evid-ence should be available and to find it; his insist-ence on examining repeated examples of newly

---

CHAPTER I.

THEORY of the EARTH; or an Invefligation of the Laws obfervable in the Compofition, Dif-folution, and Refloration, of Land upon the Globe.

SECTION I.

Profpect of the Subject to be treated of.

WHEN we trace the parts of which this terreftrial fyftem is compofed, and when we view the general connection of thofe feveral parts, the whole prefents a machine of a peculiar conftruction by which it is adapted to a certain end.   We perceive a fabric, erec-ted in wifdom, to obtain a purpofe worthy of the power that is apparent in the production of it.

We know little of the earth's internal parts, or of the materials which compofe it at any confiderable depth below the furface.   But

---

discovered phenomena; and, finally, his gift for interpretation which led Playfair to remark in the concluding pages of his biography: 'None was more skillful in marking the gradations of nature . . . more diligent in the *continuity* of her proceed-ings, or more sagacious in tracing her footsteps, even where they were most lightly impressed'.

RECEPTION OF HIS THEORIES. Both before and after Hutton's death his views were bitterly criti-cised on religious and scientific grounds. His work rings with declarations that a benevolent Deity supervises all the operations of nature and that the surface of the globe is recycled for the sole purpose of producing 'a world beautifully calculated for the growth of plants and nourishment of men and animals'.[41] Nevertheless, because he flouted accepted chronology and denied the Biblical account of the Creation, he was frequently charged with atheism. Even as late as 1810 Professor

Thomas Hope, lecturing at Edinburgh University, found it necessary to reassure his students that a study of Huttonian theory would not corrupt them.

The most prolonged attack on Hutton, however, was made on scientific grounds. Many eighteenth-century theorists, among them Richard Kirwan whose criticisms had prompted Hutton to write the *Theory of the Earth*, believed in the 'primitive' mountains we mentioned earlier, and they further believed that those mountains had been precipitated from a primeval ocean or in the seas created during the Flood. Their leader was Abraham Gottlieb Werner (1750–1817), Professor of Mining and Mineralogy at Freiberg. Nothing could have been further apart than the systems of Werner and Hutton since Werner's rocks were precipitates not subject to erosion while Hutton's rocks were constantly being reduced to sediment and subsequently melted and elevated by heat. The contrast between the two systems, and in particular the differing emphases they place on water and fire, led them to be dubbed 'Neptunist' and 'plutonic' respectively.

In the early years of the nineteenth century the dispute raged most fiercely in Edinburgh where the Neptunists carried much weight because Werner's most energetic advocate, Robert Jameson, was Professor of Natural History. The battle was fought out at scientific meetings, in scientific publications, in the field, in the laboratory, and even in the drawing rooms of the city. Since Hutton had never held a teaching post he had no generation of students to propagate his views but his cause was spearheaded by Playfair and Sir James Hall.

One of the decisive factors in the struggle was Hall's experimental work. In a lengthy series of experiments he showed that igneous rocks could be melted, and that when cooled slowly they returned to their original state. He also proved that limestone, if heated under pressure, fused without loss of carbon dioxide as Hutton had surmised. Playfair, though less original than Hall, was even more influential. In and out of the classroom he never ceased to urge Hutton's point of view and, believing that the obscurity of the *Theory of the Earth* was the chief obstacle to the acceptance of his theories, he recast them in an orderly form, publishing *Illustrations of the Huttonian Theory* in 1802. This lucid exposition did much to gather support and it was through the *Illustrations* rather than Hutton's own writings that his ideas were passed on to the next generation of geologists, notably Charles Lyell.

Modern Scholarship

During the last forty years, Hutton's work, including his work outside geology, has received an increasing amount of attention. His theory of matter has been examined by Patsy Gerstner[42] and his theory of heat by Arthur Donovan[43] while Peter Jones has published a summary and critique of his work on philosophy, paying particular attention to his views on causation and his debt to Locke and Hume.[44] François Ellenberger has investigated the origins of the ideas advanced in his medical dissertation and traced their influence on his later work.[45] Subsequently Arthur Donovan and Joseph Prentiss translated the dissertation into English, adding a lengthy introduction and a facsimile reproduction of the original.[46]

Studies of Hutton's correspondence have thrown new light on his travels, and his early achievements in geology, agriculture and meteorology.[47] His salammoniac business was the subject of an article by A. and N. Clow.[48] His scientific and cultural *milieu* has been discussed by a number of authors, among them D. R. Dean, who published the preface Hutton drafted for the *Theory of the Earth* to defend himself against the charge of atheism and William Robertson's advice not to use it.[47]

In 1947 V. A. Eyles identified the *Abstract*, which had been published anonymously and is very rare. Another notable event, not only for Huttonian studies but for the history of geology as a whole, was the publication of *James Hutton's Theory of the Earth: The Lost Drawings* by G. Y. Craig, C. D. Waterston and D. B. McIntyre (1978). Twenty-seven of Clerk's drawings are reproduced in facsimile, enabling us to see for the first time the detail with which Hutton and Clerk made their observations and their ability to make accurate syntheses on a considerable scale. The accompanying text contains much new information about Hutton's excursions.

Ellenberger has pointed to similarities between Hutton's theories and those of French scholars whose work he might have read during his student days in Paris.[50] D. B. McIntyre and others have discussed possible connections between Hutton and George Toulmin, whose views in *The Antiquity of the World* (1782) are very close to Hutton's and were published first. Since Hutton is known to have formulated the outline of his theory twenty years before, and Toulmin, as Black's pupil, could easily have heard his views, the general opinion is that Toulmin based his theories on Hutton and not vice versa. Hutton has also been accused of plagiarising

Hutton, by John Kay, 1787.
As in the caricature of Joseph Black, the rockface is sculpted into profiles of his friends and contemporaries.

the seventeenth-century scientist Robert Hooke, a charge ably refuted by Giogo Ranalli.[51] Finally, Hutton's influence on geomorphology, much lauded by Archibald Geikie, has been re-assessed and justly diminished by Gordon Herries Davies. At the same time Davies, in agreement with other historians of science, is at pains to stress that Hutton's legacy to geology as a whole was 'brilliant, dramatic and fundamental'.[52]

Notes

1. J. Playfair, 'Life of Dr. Hutton', *Transactions of the Royal Society of Edinburgh*, vol.5, pt.iii (1805), p.74.
2. *idem*, p.40.
3. *idem*, p.41.
4. *The Diary of Sylas Neville*, ed. B. Cozens-Hardy (London, 1950), p.143.
5. 'Elements of Agriculture', p.6.
6. Playfair, p.44.
7. Scottish Record Office, GD 18/5749.
8. 'Elements of Agriculture', p.698.
9. Playfair, p.45.
10. Scottish Record Office, RD 2/223/240/Dal.
11. Playfair, p.95.
12. Playfair, p.95.
13. Playfair, p.50n.
14. *Dissertation upon . . . Light, Heat and Fire* (Edinburgh, 1794), p.229.
15. *idem*, p.6.
16. *An Investigation of the Principles of Knowledge*, vol.iii (1794), p.327.
17. Playfair, p.55.
18. Playfair, p.56.
19. *Abstract concerning the System of the Earth* (Edinburgh, 1785), p.25.
20. 'Theory of the Earth', *Transactions of the Royal Society of Edinburgh*, vol.i, pt.i (1788), p.304.
21. *idem*, p.215.
22. *Theory of the Earth*, vol.i, p.182.
23. 'Theory of the Earth', p.302.
24. Playfair, p.57.
25. 'Theory of the Earth', p.224.
26. 'Theory of the Earth', p.270.
27. *Abstract*, p.17.
28. Quoted in G. Y. Craig, *James Hutton's Theory of the Earth: The Lost Drawings*, p.5.
29. *Abstract*, p.5.
30. *Theory of the Earth*, vol.i (1795), p.331.
31. Scottish Record Office, GD 18/5749.
32. Fitzwilliam Museum, Perceval Bequest, J.11.
33. Playfair, p.97.
34. All the quotations in this paragraph are from 'Observations on Granite', *Transactions of the Royal Society of Edinburgh*, vol.iii, pt.ii (1794), p.79.
35. Playfair, p.68.
36. *Theory of the Earth*, vol.iii (London, 1899), p.43.
37. *idem*, p.193.
38. *idem*, p.262.
39. Playfair, p.72.
40. *Theory of the Earth*, vol.i, p.306.
41. *idem*, vol.iii, p.87.
42. *Isis*, vol.59 (1968), pp.26-31.
43. *Ambix*, vol.25 (1978), pp.176-90.
44. In *Philosophers of the Scottish Enlightenment*, ed. V. Hope (Edinburgh, 1984).
45. *Académie des Sciences*, Series D (1972), pp.93-6.
46. *James Hutton's Medical Dissertation* (Philadelphia, 1980).
47. V. A. and J. M. Eyles in *Annals of Science*, vol.7 (1951, pp.316-39; J. Jones, *Annals of Science*, vol.39 (1982), pp.255-63; vol.40 (1983), pp.81-94; vol.41 (1984), pp.223-44; vol.42 (1985), pp.573-601.
48. *Nature*, vol.159 (1947), pp.425-7.
49. *Annals of Science*, vol.32 (1975), pp.187-93.
50. *Académie des Sciences*, Series D 275 (1972), 69-72; *Annales Guebhard*, 49 (1973), pp.493-533.
51. *Journal of Geology*, vol.90 (1982), pp.319-25.
52. *The Earth in Decay* (New York, 1969), ch.6; *Progress in Physical Geography*, vol.9 (1985), 383-8.

Before Hutton's death in 1797 the mood changed, and Edinburgh began playing soldiers – the Royal Edinburgh Volunteers – as the threat of the French Revolution extinguished the siècle des lumières.

Bibliography

None of Hutton's papers or books was ever reprinted and the originals are hard to find outside major libraries. Recent facsimiles of his geological works have brought them within the reach of many more libraries and of individuals. The best starting point is G. W. White (ed.), *James Hutton's System of the Earth . . .* (New York, 1970). This contains the *Abstract of a Dissertation Concerning the System of the Earth, its Duration and Stability* (Edinburgh, 1785); 'Theory of the Earth', *Transactions of the Royal Society of Edinburgh*, vol.i (1788); 'Observations on Granite', *Transactions of the Royal Society of Edinburgh*, vol.iii (1794); J. Playfair, 'Biographical Account of the late Dr. James Hutton', *Transactions of the Royal Society of Edinburgh*, vol.v (1805). The 1795 *Theory of the Earth* was issued in facsimile in 1972 in the Historiae Naturalis Classica series published in Lehre, West Germany. Unfortunately the third volume is still only available in the edition edited by Archibald Geikie (London, 1899). Playfair's *Illustrations of the Huttonian Theory* (Edinburgh, 1802) appeared in facsimile edited by G. W. White (Urbana, 1956).

The best account of Hutton's life and work is still Playfair's masterly biography, now part of the 1970 facsimile. The most comprehensive modern discussion is V. A. Eyles' excellent article 'James Hutton' in *Dictionary of Scientific Biography*, vol.6 (New York, 1972). The only full length study, E. B. Bailey, *James Hutton: Founder of Modern Geology* (London – Amsterdam – New York, 1967), is useful but uneven. The *Proceedings of the Royal Society of Edinburgh*, Series B, vol.63 (1950) is notable for articles by G. W. Tyrrell, V. A. Eyles and S. I. Tomkeieff. *James Hutton's Theory of the Earth; The Lost Drawings*, ed. G. Y. Craig (Edinburgh, 1978) has been mentioned in the text: besides the description of Hutton's excursions it discusses the textual history of the *Theory of the Earth* and the achievements of Hutton's associates, Clerk of Eldin, Playfair and Hall.

Specialist articles on Hutton were discussed in the section 'Modern Scholarship'.

In autumn 1985, Professor Donald McIntyre of Pomona College, Claremont, California, prepared a most comprehensive bibliography of books and articles on Hutton or containing significant references to him. It has over two hundred entries and will be of the first importance to historians of science.

Scotland and America, 1730–90

ARCHIE TURNBULL

IN THE first chapter, David Daiches notes that the men of the Scottish Enlightenment were much concerned to understand change, including social change, as a *process*, so that they might subsequently put their new knowledge to work for the benefit of Man. This is what is common to the diversity of interests and intellects that comprise the movement, and it is this that gives it its characteristic modernity of outlook. Since the years of the Enlightenment saw radical political changes impending, then happening, on both sides of the Atlantic, largely through the inability of established governments to adapt absolutist principles rapidly enough to changing political realties, it is appropriate to ask whether 'enlightened Scots' took sides in these affairs, or even gave practical expression to their political philosophies.

France has been mentioned several times in this book. Voltaire, Rousseau, Diderot, Quesnay and others have been cited, but as men who influenced, rather than were influenced by, the Scots. Early in the eighteenth century Watteau, painting the plangent dying of the light in his *Fêtes Champêtres*, seems to have guessed at the coming death of the *ancien régime*. But Hume and Smith clearly enjoyed dalliance in the *salons* of the Pompadour era, even though the first, an observant diplomat, sensed the tensions beneath the glitter; while the latter, in his discussions with Turgot and the physiocrats on the sources of wealth, could scarcely have been unaware of the impending bankruptcy of the Court. Daiches and Jones both observed that the spirit of Moderatism had nothing to offer in an age threatened by the French Revolution, but what Lord Cockburn was to call 'a passive devotion to the gentry'. This is a substantial criticism of the political effect, or lack of it, of the Scottish En-

lightenment at home. Ironically, it was in the birth and development of the United States of America that the ideas and ideals of the Enlightenment played a more significant role. The exact nature and extent of this influence has been increasingly studied in recent years.

'Sober, Attentive Men'

By 1790, there were in the United States between 200,000 and 250,000 people of Scots birth or descent. In a population of about four million this represented between 5% and 6%. But the distribution was not uniform. Those Scots emigrants who looked towards the north tended to choose Canada. If they had sufficient capital, in money or skills, to envisage a more prosperous life in the American colonies, they chose to settle south of the Hudson or the Susquehannah. By 1790 the Scots population of the New England states was perhaps 45,000; of the Middle Atlantic states, some 75,000; but in the south, from Maryland to Georgia, about 135,000. In Maryland, Virginia, and North Carolina the Scots element amounted to over 12% of the population.[1] These incomers did not always endear themselves to the older settlers. Indeed, an apt comparison might be the attitude – even into the present century – of the citizens of Glasgow to immigrants from beyond the Highland line. The more remarkable, therefore, that some special attributes of the Scots were quickly recognised by those who would otherwise have preferred to see the back of them.

It would be wrong to infer that all the Scots immigrants to the American colonies during the post-Union decades were apostles of the Enlightenment. The landless men among them who, in return for a free passage, empowered the ships' captains to sell them into five to seven years' slavery

King's College, Aberdeen, the fountainhead of many Scots teachers in the American colonies, much as it would have appeared in Thomas Reid's day.

on the plantations, had not read Hutcheson. Some of them were Highlanders with a traditional culture of their own; but it was not the culture of the Enlightenment, the exclusivity of which is encapsulated in the popular use of the term, the 'literati'. There was a parallel élite among the Scots immigrants, however: not of rank, or of wealth, or even – as in the Calvinist past – of the Elect, but of education.

As the prosperity of the American colonists increased, so too did the demand for schooling and medical care. This demand Scotland (by comparison with England and Ireland) was well fitted to supply. Many men trained in the Scottish universities, in divinity, in arts, and later in medicine, who failed to find work in the Old World or sought the challenge of the New, put their skills to the service of the landed and moneyed classes from Pennsylvania to Georgia. It was on the influence of this relatively small proportion of the Scots immigrants that much was to turn.

The third, fourth, and fifth Presidents of the United States were all native-born Virginians, but this was not the only thing they had in common: they all had a Scottish mentor. Jefferson, in his *Autobiography*, records that his first teacher, William Douglas of Glencairn, was a clergyman from Scotland with 'the rudiments of Latin and Greek languages', who also introduced him to French. Jefferson's use of the term 'rudiments' comes naturally. In eighteenth-century America, as in eighteenth-century Scotland, Latin studies were grounded in Ruddiman's *Rudiments of the Latin Tongue*. Jefferson's successor, James Madison, went to school under Donald Robertson, a Scot who had trained at Aberdeen and Edinburgh Universities. Madison later said of him: 'All that I have been in life I owe largely to that one man'.[2] Robertson's personal library included, in addition to editions of the ancient classics, Montaigne, Montesquieu, Locke, and Smollett's *History*. Finally, James Monroe went to the pretentiously-named 'Campbeltown Academy', a private school in Virginia limited to twenty-five pupils, run by the Reverend Archibald Campbell, another Aberdeen and Edinburgh alumnus.[3] Brock suggests that Campbell may also have taught George Washington, but since that great figure was scarcely conspicuous for educational attainment, the possibility may slumber in a footnote.[4]

Thomas Ruddiman, Rudiments of the Latin Tongue, 1732, title-page.

SCOTLAND AND AMERICA · 139

Is it mere chance that the third, fourth, and fifth Presidents of the United States all received their early education at the hands of Scotch teachers and tutors? Since the Jeffersons, Madisons, and Monroes did not know that their sons would become Presidents of the United States, or even that there would be a United States for them to become Presidents of, these boys cannot have been special cases, singled out by some colonial equivalent of Plato. We know about their education because of what they became later in life. It is fair to assume that it was typical of their time and social class. Scottish schools and Scottish teachers must have been much *à la mode* in Colonial Virginia. What Jefferson believed in 1783 may have been equally true of half a century before:

> I was to enquire for a tutor . . . I concluded, if we might venture to bring a man from his own country, it would be best for me to interest some person in Scotland. . . . From that country we are surest of having sober attentive men.[5]

What Campbell and Robertson, perhaps Douglas also, were teaching was not basic reading, writing, and arithmetic, but something directly and deliberately modelled on the first two years of Arts courses in the Scottish universities, where the average age of first year students was twelve. These courses reflected that peculiarly Scottish belief in a generalist education, based on philosophical exposition of first principles, which George Davie – basing his phrase on an observation by Walter Elliot – has felicitously called 'the democratic intellect'.[6]

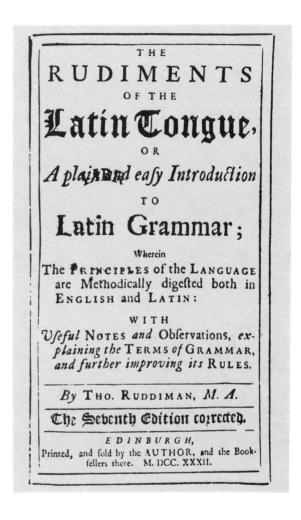

THE
RUDIMENTS
OF THE
Latin Tongue,
OR
A plain and easy Introduction
TO
Latin Grammar;
Wherein
The PRINCIPLES of the LANGUAGE are Methodically digested both in ENGLISH and LATIN:
WITH
Useful NOTES *and* Observations, *explaining the* TERMS *of* GRAMMAR, *and further improving its* RULES.

By THO. RUDDIMAN, *M. A.*
The Seventh Edition corrected.

EDINBURGH,
Printed, and sold by the AUTHOR, and the Booksellers there. M. DCC. XXXII.

From School to University

The origin of the American university system is a century older than the development of Scottish schools in the Southern states. Harvard was founded in 1636, little more than half a century after Edinburgh University itself. Though Scottish immigration into Massachusetts was twice what it was in any other of the New England states, Scots made little direct impact there. The second oldest foundation, in Williamsburg, Virginia, was the College of William and Mary. It opened in 1693, and its first President, the Reverend James Blair, was a Scottish episcopal minister who had trained at Marischal College, Aberdeen. A distinctive feature of the curriculum was a compulsory course in moral philosophy on the Scottish model. Blair stuck stubbornly to his office until his death, fifty-eight years later, and he saw to it that his native country was not forgotten in the choice of placemen. One such appointee to the chair of Mathematics was Dr William Small, another product of

Marischal, where he had studied under William Duncan, professor of Natural Philosophy, and author of *Elements of Logic*. Some have suggested that Duncan's *Logic* can be detected in the drafting of the Declaration of Independence.

If Madison attributed his intellectual and moral strengths to Donald Robertson, Jefferson was all but as generous to Small:

> It was my good fortune, and what possibly fixed the destinies of my life, that Dr William Small of Scotland was then Professor of Mathematics, a man profound in all the usual branches of science, with the happy talent of communication, correct and gentlemanly manners, and an enlarged and liberal mind. He, most happily for me, became so attached to me, and made me his daily companion when not engaged in the school: and from his conversation I got my first views of the expansion of science, and the system of things in which we are placed. Fortunately, the philosophical chair became vacant soon after my arrival at College, and he was appointed to fill it *per interim*; and he was the first who

ever gave, in that college, regular lectures in Ethics, Rhetoric, and Belles Lettres. He returned to Europe in 1772, having previously filled up the measure of his goodness to me, by procuring for me, from his most intimate friend, George Wythe, a reception as a student of law, under his direction, and introduced me to the acquaintance and familiar table of Governor Fauquier, the ablest man who had ever filled that office. With him and at his table, Dr Small and Mr Wythe . . . and myself formed a *partie quarée*, and to the habitual conversations on these occasions I owed much instruction.[7]

It is a startingly recognisable description of the ideals of Edinburgh society (and societies) of the same period. Small himself returned to Britain in 1764 and settled in Birmingham, after Franklin introduced him to Matthew Boulton. He was a founder member of the Lunar Society, a particular friend of James Watt, and was acquainted with Black and Hutton.

Apart from Harvard, and William and Mary, the expansion of colleges of higher education in the American colonies really began in the decades preceding the War of Independence, with Franklin as one moving spirit, and took off in the infancy of the new Republic, with Benjamin Rush as another. It may not be irrelevant that Franklin claimed to have spent the happiest weeks of his life in Edinburgh (in 1759), and that Rush graduated MD of Edinburgh in 1768. At all events, it is in this period – the period both of the Scottish Enlightenment and of the genesis of the Republic – that the Scots advanced from the schools to positions of importance in the rising Colleges.

Francis Alison is a comparatively neglected figure.[8] A pupil of Hutcheson at Glasgow, he came to America in 1735 as tutor to the family of Samuel Dickinson of Maryland. In 1743 he established an 'academy' in New London, Pennsylvania – presumably on the lines of the Glasgow Arts Faculty. His pupils included no fewer than three Signers (signatories of the Declaration of Independence), and – more importantly – Charles Thomson, Secretary to the Continental Congress of 1774, all of whom he 'drilled in Hutcheson's texts'. Alison's academy later moved from Pennsylvania to Delaware and grew into the University of that state. But the key interest of Alison to this enquiry is that, as Vice-Provost, he gave lectures at the newly-established 'College of Philadelphia'; student transcripts of these survive, allowing us insight into what they were taught. As before, what he was teaching was Hutcheson *verbatim*.

The Provost of the College of Philadelphia was another Scot, William Smith, an episcopal divine who was born in Aberdeenshire in 1727, studied at

King's College, Aberdeen, and came to New York in 1751 as tutor to the children of Josiah Martin. During his brief stay in Manhattan he wrote an anonymous pamphlet which, reflecting doubtless his *pietas* for his alma mater, urged the foundation of a King's College there. This came into being in 1754, later changing its name to Columbia University. Meanwhile, in 1752 or thereabouts, influenced by a striking reorganisation of the curriculum in King's (Aberdeen), which reflected the views of Thomas Reid and placed new emphasis on science, Smith set out his own rather similar views on curriculum-planning, in another pamphlet which Brock has called 'the first attempt in America to present systematic analysis of the aims and the methods of higher education'. Notably, in the third and last year, students studied Hutcheson's ethics, astronomy, natural history, chemistry, jurisprudence, economics and theories of government.[9] Smith's pamphlet brought him into communication with Franklin, at whose persuasion he engaged, in 1754, to teach ethics, rhetoric, logic, and natural philosophy at the College of Philadelphia (later the University of Pennsylvania). It was in the following year that he became Provost, and began to organise

John Witherspoon (1722-94), President of the College of New Jersey (courtesy, Princeton University). John Adams called him "as high a son of Liberty as any man in America".

the work of the college along lines familiar to the Scottish university tradition.

Scottish penetration of the system achieved its greatest success in 1768. The trustees of the College of New Jersey (later, Princeton) had, in the twenty years of its existence, suffered grievous calamity. Of its four Presidents:

> Mr Burr . . . was a gentleman of infirm constitution, almost worn out before he came to college. Mr Edwardes died of the pox. Mr Davies . . . being let blood . . . an inflammation seized his arm, which brought on a fever and proved mortal. Dr Finley died of a Schirrous liver and consequent Dropsy.[10]

As Professor Shepperson has written: 'Indeed the trustees needed a tough man!' Their choice fell on the Reverend Dr John Witherspoon, a Presbyterian minister at Paisley, who came from Haddington and had been a student at Edinburgh. He was at first reluctant to accept, and the trustees empowered Rush, who was himself a Princeton alumnus and was then studying medicine at Edinburgh, to persuade him otherwise. John Witherspoon took office as President of Princeton in 1768. Under his aegis Scottish philosophers – especially Hutcheson and Reid – and science were introduced into the curriculum.

This process of transatlantic exchange was not just one way. Many Americans went abroad to study. Respect for Scottish institutions, doubtless imparted by Scottish teachers and doctors to those in their care, is particularly evident in medical training. Taking the year 1770 as a cut-off point for those students who could later have influenced the balance of debate on the Colonists' relationship to the mother country, the number of American-born students studying medicine at Edinburgh before 1770 attests the eminence of its medical school and also reflects the different patterns from state to state.[11]

North Carolina	1
Rhode Island	1
New Hampshire	2
New Jersey	2
Connecticut	3
Massachusetts	7
New York	7
Maryland	5
South Carolina	12
Pennsylvania	15
Virginia	26
	—
Total	81
	—

Of these eighty-odd Americans who studied at Edinburgh in the heyday of the Scottish Enlightenment, many must have carried back to their country something of its spirit. Among them were William Shippen, John Morgan and Benjamin Rush.[12] All graduated MD at Edinburgh – in 1761, 1763 and 1763 respectively. Shippen and Morgan were protégés of Franklin, who wrote to Cullen on their behalf. On their return, they founded the first medical school in America, in Philadelphia. It was opened in 1765, Morgan being appointed Professor of Physics, and Rush, when he joined them in 1769, Professor of Chemistry. Indeed, of the five founding members of the Medical College, four were Edinburgh graduates – all 'Cullen's men'. When Cullen died in 1790, Rush told his colleagues that he had

> filled the capitals, and most of the towns in Great Britain and Ireland with eminent physicians. Many of his pupils arrived at the first honours in their profession in the principal cities of Europe. . . . He taught the different professors in the College of Philadelphia, and in the University of Pennsylvania, the art of teaching others . . . and thereby he conveyed the benefit of his discoveries to every part of the United States'.[13]

No one did more to exemplify 'the art of teaching

Congress Voting Independence, *by Robert Edge Pine,*
c.1788. This painting is considered more accurate than John
Trumbull's more famous rendering of 1818. Jefferson hands the
Declaration to John Hancock, while Franklin, hand on chin, is
seated in the foreground.

others' than Benjamin Rush himself. John Adams
said of him: 'I know of no character alive or dead
who has done more real good for America'.

The New York medical school at King's College
was founded in 1768 by Samuel Bard, in association
with two other Americans who had also trained in
Edinburgh, and a Scotsman, Peter Middleton. With
the medical school at Philadelphia, it remained one
of the most enduring results of Scottish influence.

The advances in pure and applied science made in
Scotland during the Enlightenment were reflected,
as we have mentioned, in the establishment of
scientific studies as an integral part of the university curriculum, and on both sides of the Atlantic
the usefulness of science to society was emphasised. The influence of individual scientists was less
important. [14]

In sum, then, by 1770 Scottish-born and Scottish-

trained scholars had established a Scottish model
of education in William and Mary, in Philadelphia,
in Princeton, in smaller colleges like Alison's Academy and, later, in Dickinson College. This model
the Americans adopted and developed. The Scots
had also advanced to some of the commanding
heights of American academe. Edgar Smith, a later
Provost of the University of Pennsylvania, and to
that extent partial, claimed in 1912 that

> There is not the slightest doubt that the Scottish im-
> print upon American collegiate training is the only
> imprint worth talking about. If Cambridge or Oxford
> had influenced Harvard very profoundly, it is not likely
> that Harvard, William and Mary, Yale, Princeton and
> Columbia would have accepted the Plan that William
> Smith put into operation here. [15]

The Declaration of Independence

Given the influence of the Scottish Enlightenment on education, an even more interesting question is whether this Scottish bias influenced the climate of opinion that led to *The Declaration of Independence* in 1776. The intellectual and philosophical sources of the 'self-evident' truths and 'unalienable rights' of the Declaration of Independence are to be found in theories of natural law and natural rights. To cite works like Harrington's *The Commonwealth of Oceana* (1656), Locke's *Second Treatise on Government* (1689), Montesquieu's *De l'Esprit des lois* (1748) or those of the Scottish philosophers as of paramount importance is to denigrate the native convictions of the Americans. However it is possible to argue that the spirit that infuses many of the central doctrines of Congress, from 1774 to 1787, is in peculiar harmony with the legal, philosophical and moral teachings of Hutcheson, Reid and Kames; whose views in turn reflect the historical and constitutional inheritance of Scotland itself. Directly through their books, and as mediated by their disciples in the American colleges, the ideas of these three men were familiar to all the most eminent statesmen, Franklin, John Adams, Dickinson and Jefferson among them.

Pride of place must go to Hutcheson. His *Inquiry into the Original of Our Ideas of Beauty and Virtue* (though Witherspoon did not like its moral laxity), the *Essay on the Nature and Conduct of the Passions*, the *Short Introduction to Moral Philosophy* (first in its original Latin text) and the two-volume *System of Moral Philosophy*, were all widely read in the American colonies. John Adams had read the *Short Introduction* before 1756 and Franklin, Dickinson and Jefferson no doubt studied Hutcheson under the tutelage of Small at William and Mary. Since Hutcheson postulated the ideal of 'the greatest happiness for the greatest number', he may well be a source of 'the pursuit of happiness' as an 'unalienable right'. Further, Hutcheson (unlike Locke) did not include the right to property among his list of 'unalienable rights' and in this Jefferson followed him.[16] Reid's *An Enquiry into the Human Mind on the Principles of Common Sense* (1764) was well known. 'The dictates of common sense', along with 'reverence for our Great Creator' and 'principles of humanity' are cited in the 1775 'Declaration of the Causes and Necessity of Taking up Arms' which Jefferson drafted for Congress, as proof that Government 'was instituted to promote the welfare of Mankind'. However, the common-sense reference may more likely have its source in Tom Paine, though his revolutionary pamphlet of that title was not published until January 1766. Likewise, Kames' *Essays on the Principles of Morality and Natural Religion* (1751) and his *Essays upon Several Subjects* (1747) were popular in America. Kames himself gave John Adams a copy of his *Historical Law-Tracts*. Jefferson owned a copy; and Madison was familiar with Kames' writings, probably because Witherspoon, a keen student of Kames, was lecturing on his legal philosophy at Princeton when Madison studied Ethics under him, for a postgraduate year.

The Declaration of Independence states that, to secure their unalienable rights, 'Governments are instituted among men, deriving their just powers from the consent of the governed, that whenever any form of government becomes destructive of these ends, *it is the right of the people to alter or to abolish it, and to institute new government . . .*' [my italics]. To those who upheld the Divine Right of Kings this might seem heretical; but it would not have seemed so to any Scot. Long before the American Declaration the Scots had said much the same in the famous *Letter of the Barons of Scotland to Pope John XXII* drawn up at Arbroath in 1320. Writing of King Robert the Bruce, it is said:

> Him, too, divine providence, his right of Succession according to our laws and customs . . . and the due consent and assent of us all, have made our King. To

him . . . we are bound both by law and by his merits, that our freedom may be still maintained. . . . Yet if he should give up what he has begun, and agree to make us or our kingdom subject to the King of England . . . *We should exert ourselves to drive him out as our enemy and a subverter of his own rights and ours, and make some other man . . . our King* [my italics] for, so long as but a hundred of us remain alive, never will we on any conditions be brought under English rule. It is in truth not for glory, nor riches, nor honours that we are fighting, but for freedom – for that alone, which no good man gives up but with his life.[17]

Here, four hundred and fifty years before that day in Philadelphia, is an explicit statement about life, liberty, and the rights of a people to choose who will govern them. I am not suggesting that the *Declaration of Arbroath*, the noblest statement in the constitutional history of Scotland, was in any direct sense a source of the 1776 Declaration. We are dealing not with the letter but with the spirit. What matters is the conviction of the Scots that, in the end of the day, theirs was an elective monarchy, the choice of 'the community of the realm of Scotland' to use the traditional phrase. This democratic conviction was later restated in 1579 by the Scots humanist, George Buchanan, in his *De iure regni apud Scotos* (on the constitutional law of the Kingdom of the Scots). An English translation was published in 1680 (on the very eve of the publication of Stair's *Institutions*), and the Latin text was republished by Ruddiman in 1715.

The belief of Buchanan, and Stair, in government as the expression and will of the people carried over into eighteenth-century Scotland. Kames dismissed the Divine Right of Kings with characteristic incisiveness when he wrote that there was nothing in Man's nature 'to subject him to the power of any, his Creator and his Parents excepted'.[18] Again, 'Kings have no other commission from God, but what every magistrate has, supreme and subordinate, who is legally elected *according to the standing laws* [my italics] of the Society to which he belongs'.[19] Hutcheson, in turn, wrote pointedly on the rights of subjects:

If the mother country attempts anything oppressive toward a colony, and the colony be able to subsist as a sovereign state by itself . . . the colony is not bound to remain subject any longer; 'tis enough that it remains in a friendly state.[20]

Again:

Large numbers of men cannot be bound to sacrifice their own and posterity's *liberty and happiness* [my italics] to the ambitious views of the mother country . . . there is something unnatural in supposing a large society, sufficient for all the good purposes of an independent political union, remaining subject to the

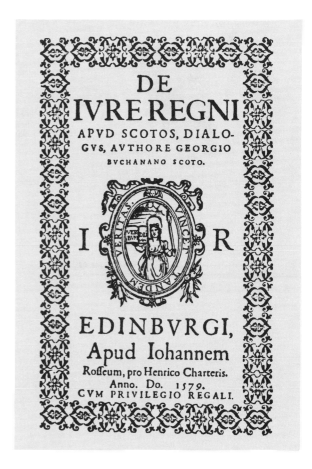

direction of a distant body of men who know not sufficiently the circumstances and exigencies of this society.[21]

Since Hutcheson died in 1746, it is unlikely that he had the American colonies in the forefront of his thought. The more impressive, then, must such statements have appeared to the students of Small, Alison, Smith and Witherspoon.

What evidence is there that Scottish teachers in American colleges, in the critical decade of the 1770s, saw contemporary events through the spectacles of this Scottish tradition of a people's government? A colleague of Witherspoon's, during the 1777 Congress, remarked:

He can't bear anything which reflects on Scotland. The Dr says that Scotland has manifested the greatest spirit for liberty as a nation, in that their history is full of their calling Kings to account and dethroning them when arbitrary and tyrannical.[22]

The passage suggests that the inspiration of what Hume called 'the historical age' may well have coloured philosophical and political teaching of the time. In Witherspoon's case, it was more than

teaching, since he was active in the counsels of the 'rising people'. A member of New Jersey's Somerset County Committee of Correspondence, he served in Congress for almost the entire Revolutionary War, 'commuting on horseback', as Shepperson puts it 'between Princeton and Philadelphia'.[23] In a sermon on 17 May 1776 Witherspoon spoke of the 'ambition of mistaken princes, the cunning and cruelty of oppressive and corrupt ministers'. He also said:

> I willingly embrace the opportunity of declaring my opinion without any hesitation that the cause in which America is now in arms is the cause of justice and liberty.[24]

On 4 July the President of the College of New Jersey signed the Declaration of Independence, the only Christian minister to do so.

In some ways Witherspoon's views ran contrary to the mainstream of Enlightenment thought. His confidence in the will of God and the rights of the people made him, like the High Flyers, at once more radical in his politics but more rigid in his philosophical views than the Moderate faction.

Since America, herself, split on the issue of Independence, resorting at times to local coercion of factions, we should not look for unanimity at home, unless it were in rejection of Witherspoon. The older and conservative Moderate divines –

Ferguson, Robertson, Blair, Carlyle and John Hume – while admitting blunders on the part of the British administration, agreed that the colonists needed to be brought to heel by a short sharp shock of cold steel. 'We are past the hour of lenitives', Robertson wrote in 1775, aggrieved that he could not conclude his *History of America* with a paean in praise of British colonisation. Ferguson remained more moderate, joining the Earl of Carlisle's Peace Commission of 1778, in the hope of talking the colonists into submission. But when Washington refused to treat with him, he, too, on his return home, became a hard-liner, arguing that 'proper measures' would soon reduce the influence of the 'Johnny Witherspoons . . . to Franklin, Adams and two or three more of the most Abandon'd villains in the world'.[25] Hume and Smith, however, broke ranks. This may appear the more surprising, in that they·supported the Treaty of Union and the House of Hanover.

Smith's views were complex and sometimes ambiguous. Emotionally he sided with the colonists, believing them to have been treated 'with savage injustice', but he argued that British pride would never permit the voluntary separation that he held the circumstances warranted. Instead, he advocated colonial representation at Westminster as a first step to an imperial union. At the same time, he

A Map of the United States of N. America, 1786.

The surrender of Earl Cornwallis at Yorktown, Virginia, in October 1781.

noted that: 'They [the American revolutionaries] are become statesmen and legislators, and are employed in contriving a new form of government for an extensive empire, which, they flatter themselves, will become, and which, indeed, seems very likely to become, one of the greatest and most formidable that ever was in the world'.[26]

From the start of the quarrel, Hume took the side of the colonists. He welcomed the repeal of the Stamp Act and, as early as 1768, anticipated America 'totally and finally' in revolt.[27] He saw Revolution as inevitable, just as he saw revolution in France as inevitable, and stressed the impossibility of a small country controlling a much larger one, three thousand miles away. 'I am an American in my principles', he wrote in 1775, 'and wish we would let them alone to govern or misgovern themselves as they think proper'.[28] One should not dismiss out of hand the possibility that Hume's response to the American question reflected both his knowledge of Scottish constitutional history and his increasing sensitivity to anti-Scottish feeling in London in the 1760s.

Witherspoon was not the only Edinburgh Univer-

Cullen, First Lines of the Practice of Physic, Philadelphia, 1781. Rush had this work by his revered teacher published in America during the war: "Sir, you have had a hand in the Revolution by contributing indirectly to save the lives of officers and soldiers of the American army."

Rush, An Oration . . . 1786. This pamphlet set out the philosophical principles by which the new nation could advance, spiritually and materially.

sity graduate 'Signer'; another was Benjamin Rush, who had pledged in the *sponsio academica*:

> I will to my latest breath abide steadfastly in all due loyalty to the University of Edinburgh. Further, I will practise the art of medicine with care, with purity of conduct and with uprightness, and so far in me lies, will faithfully attend to everything conducive to the welfare of the sick.

Although Rush's signing of the Declaration was perhaps the only overtly political act in his whole life, his influence on the early years of the new Republic was decisive. The revolution, he asserted, did not cease with the end of the war. It gave, he wrote 'a spring to the mind in objects of philosophical and moral enquiry'. In the 1780s Rush encouraged in the United States almost precisely those attitudes which, Daiches has argued, typified the Scottish Enlightenment. Believing that men and societies could be improved if the material reasons for their shortcomings were eradicated, he called on his fellow citizens to finish the work of the Revolution. 'Learning', Rush wrote, 'is favourable to liberty. A free government can only exist in an equal diffusion of literature . . . and where learning is confined to a *few* people, we always find monarchy, aristocracy, or slavery'.[29] In the field of medicine, he urged his fellows to study 'specifically American diseases, identify American drugs, and the effect of American conditions on human beings'.[30] The Society for the Attainment of Useful Knowledge set out 'to investigate the means of promoting the happiness of mankind' and 'to strengthen those benevolent ties which bond us together'. Rush advocated the gradual abolition of slavery, prison reform, and, most of all, the reform and expansion of university education, accommodated to 'the many national duties and objects of knowledge that have been imposed on us by the American Revolution'.[31]

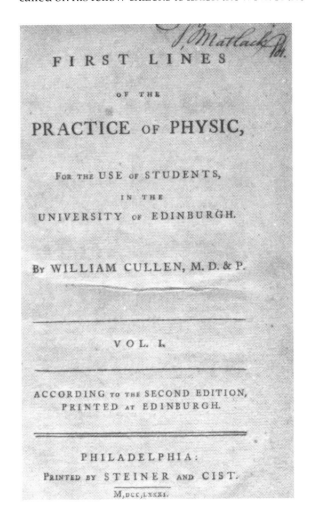

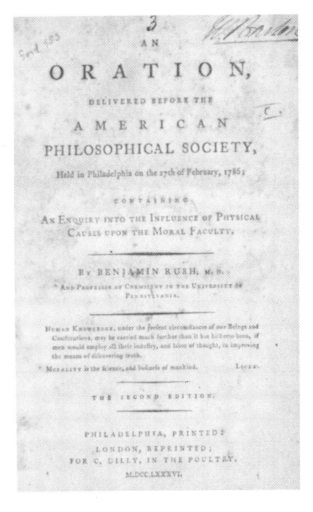

James Wilson, engraving by Albert Rosenthal. Bryce called Wilson "one of the deepest thinkers and most exact reasoners" in the Constitutional Convention.

The Federal Constitution

Hume's political essays were widely read, and as thought turned towards the framing of a constitution his views proved influential. He had addressed the problem of how to sustain freedom and avoid faction over very large geographical areas; in his essay of 1752, 'Idea of a Perfect Commonwealth', he proposed that areas be divided into communities of such a size that electors and representatives remained mutually aware of each other's needs and responses. Adapting this view to the American States, Madison argued that their very size must therefore be a guarantee of stability under a properly drafted new constitution.

Madison and James Wilson, the second of the two native-born Scots to sign the Declaration, were the principal authors of the Federal Constitution of 1787. Wilson, enigmatic, aloof, greedy for power and for land, none too scrupulous in the means to attain his end, ultimately failed in both his ambitions: to be Chief Justice of the Supreme Court and a great landowner. Because his career ended in failure, and with a suspicion of peculation, he has been denied his rightful place as a statesman alongside Franklin, Adams, Jefferson and Madison. Yet Rush said of him: 'His mind, when he spoke, was one blaze of *light*'. Another contemporary wrote: 'Government seems to have been his peculiar study; all the political institutions of the world he knows in detail, and can trace the causes and effects of every revolution from the earliest stages of the Grecian Commonwealth down to the present time'.

Born in Fife in 1747, eldest son of a smallholder, Wilson attended Cupar Grammar School, and then an Arts course in St Andrews. From there he went on to the divinity school, but his father's death ended his training for the Church, and like so many others of his kind, he became a tutor. He emigrated to America in 1765, and the following year he was appointed to teach Latin at the College of Philadelphia. Already ambitious, he began to study law under John Dickinson, the influential Pennsylvania political philosopher, whose *Letters from a Farmer in Pennsylvania to the Inhabitants of the British Colonies* (1768) set the tone of protest in the pre-Revolutionary era. Wilson soon established his own legal practice and by 1774 he was active in the political life of Pennsylvania. In 1776, in the Continental Congress, he was a member of a committee appointed to draft an *Address to the Colonists*, of which he said: 'It was meant to lead the public mind into the idea of Independence'. Wilson in fact took over the drafting, and the final sentence, in

his hand, reads:

> That the Colonies may continue connected, as they have been with Britain, is our second wish: our first is – *that America be free.*

Later that year Wilson – though apparently with no great zeal – signed the Declaration.

The basic legal and philosophical doctrines that helped Wilson to shape the Constitution eleven years later certainly reflect the teaching of Hutcheson, Reid and Kames, whose ideas were already familiar in the Scottish style universities and at large among the new American generation. He was an advocate of the Philosophy of Common Sense, whose leading exponent was Reid.

> This philosophy will teach us that first principles are in themselves apparent; that to make nothing self-evident is to take away all possibility of knowing anything; that without first principles there can be neither reason nor reasoning . . . Consequently, all sound reasoning must rest ultimately on the principles of common sense.[32]

Edinburgh. A corner of Parliament Square, seat of the Scottish Parliament until 1707, and thereafter of the College of Justice.

Wilson also argued that man was a social, benevolent animal. 'It followed', Geoffrey Seed writes, 'that the political judgement of the people could be relied on, and that only good could come of the wide diffusion of political influence.'[33] Here we have both Hutcheson and – more to the issue – Kames, who wrote:

> A man is made to purchase the means of life by the help of others in Society. Why? Because for the constitution of his body and his mind, he cannot live comfortably but in society.[34]

In the debates, in the Federal Convention, on the tripartite basis of the Constitution – legislative, executive, and judicial – Wilson argued repeatedly that governments derived their authority from the consent of the governed. Even the law was based on the consent of the people whose obedience it requires. Wilson fought with clarity and brilliance for the principle that representation, in both Houses, should be proportionate to the population of each state; gaining this right in the case of the House of Representatives, but losing it in that of the Senate (to the regret of some sober minds of the present day). He argued strongly for the authority of the Executive *vis-à-vis* the legislature, on the grounds that the President, also, represented the will of the people. As to the authority of the judiciary, his basic intention was to ensure that the government should be – to quote Seed again – 'amenable to the judicial process'.[35] To the judicial branch should be conferred 'the power of declaring and enforcing the superior power of the Constitution, the Supreme law of the land'. Lord Cameron, among the wisest and most eminent Scottish judges of the twentieth century, is prepared to speculate that the Scottish concept of the status of the law may have influenced this aspect of the Constitution. In an address in Washington in 1985, which is unpublished, he drew attention to the fact that, at least until the Union of 1707, the interpretation of the legal system of Scotland rested with the Supreme Courts of Scotland. As Stair pointed out: 'In this we differ from the English, whose statutes of parliament of whatsoever antiquity, remain ever in force until they be repealed'. Lord Cameron noted:

> Under Scots law even Statute law passed by the Scottish Parliament could be set aside by the Courts, if it had fallen into desuetude.

In the same address he traced the philosophical approach to legal exposition from Stair through the thought of his eighteenth-century successors – especially Kames – and thus to 'some of the most eminent and distinguished minds of the American Revolution and of the makers of the Constitution', concluding:

> I think it can be fairly said that the legacy of the Scottish Enlightenment and of the studies made, philosophical and practical, of the Scottish legal system, have not been wholly insignificant in the development of the Jurisprudence of the Republic . . . When one contemplates the majestic jurisdiction of the Supreme Court, I sometimes wonder if one can discern a legacy from the Scottish Constitution, in the supremacy of interpretation of the law, be it customary or statutory, of the Supreme Courts of Scotland . . . As the guardian of the Constitution the Supreme Court is charged not only with the tremendous function of interpretation, but with the interpretation and development of the spirit.

It would appear that the medium by which these ideas entered the Constitution was the thought of James Wilson, of whom James Bryce has written:

> Whoever gives to a nation . . . just principles for the conduct of its government, principles which are in harmony with its character and are capable of progressive expansion as it expands, is a true benefactor to that nation, and deserves to be held in everlasting memory. Such a one was James Wilson.[36]

Wilson's political importance (he later became a justice of the Supreme Court) did not end with the adoption of the Federal Constitution by the Convention, on 17 September 1787. This still required ratification by the States, and Wilson was eager that Pennsylvania should give a lead. In the Pennsylvania ratification convention Wilson, with Benjamin Rush and Thomas McKean (who had studied under Alison at New London), faced strong anti-Federalist opposition. Wilson argued eloquently that, when one took 'an extensive view of the streams of power that appear through this great and comprehensive plan . . . we shall be able to trace them to one great and noble source, the PEOPLE'. A quickly-published text of this speech, of 24 November, rallied public support, and Pennsylvania ratified the Constitution on 12 December (a week after Delaware, the first State to do so). By the following June it was evident that there would be the required majority of States in favour of the Constitution, and Pennsylvania decided to mark the occasion by holding, on 4 July 1788, a 'Grand Federal Procession'. Seventeen thousand citizens paraded, behind triumphal floats each drawn by ten horses, and as many others were onlookers. This large and happy assembly was then addressed, on the banks of the Schuylkill river, by Wilson, in words that may fittingly close this study of Scotland's contribution to the birth of the nation:
'A people free and enlightened . . .'

THE SUBSTANCE

OF A

SPEECH

DELIVERED By

James Wilſon, Eſq.

Explanatory of the general Principles of the propoſed

Fœderal Conſtitution;

Upon a Motion made by the

Honorable *Thomas M⁽Kean,*

In the CONVENTION of the

STATE OF PENNSYLVANIA.

On Saturday the 24th of November, 1787.

PHILADELPHIA:

Printed and Sold by THOMAS BRADFORD, in *Front-Street,* four Doors below the *Coffee-Houſe,* M,DCC,LXXXVII.

Notes

1. The information in this paragraph is largely drawn from W. R. Brock, *Scotus Americanus* (Edinburgh, 1982).
2. Cited by I. Brant, *James Madison*, vol.i (Indianapolis, 1941), p.60.
3. H. Ammon, *James Monroe* (New York, 1971), p.3.
4. Brock, *op. cit.*, p.254, n.4.
5. J. P. Boyd, *Papers of Thomas Jefferson*, vol.6 (Princeton, 1952), p.433.
6. G. E. Davie, *The Democratic Intellect* (Edinburgh, 1961), p.75.
7. Thomas Jefferson, *Autobiography* (reprinted in many collections).
8. Information from *Dictionary of American Biography*, vol.i (London, 1928); Brock, *op. cit.*, pp.92 and 93; and D. Sloan, *The Scottish Enlightenment and the American College Ideal* (New York, 1971).
9. Brock, *op. cit.*, p.112.
10. Cited by G. A. Shepperson, 'Theology and Politics: John Witherspoon', *New College Bulletin*, no.14 (Edinburgh, 1983), p.10.
11. C. H. Brock in W. R. Brock, *op. cit.*, p.118.
12. *Idem*, p.118-26; James Gray, *History of the Royal Medical Society* (Edinburgh, 1952), pp.45ff.
13. B. Rush, *An Eulogium on William Cullen delivered before the College of Physicians* (Philadelphia, 1790).
14. A. Donovan in *Scotland, Europe and the American Revolution*, eds O. D. Edwards and G. A. Shepperson (Edinburgh, 1976).
15. Brock, *op. cit.*, p.91.
16. Garry Wills, *Inventing America* (London, 1978), p.176.
17. Sir J. Ferguson (trans.), *The Declaration of Arbroath* (Edinburgh, 1970).
18. Kames, Appendix to 'Succession or Descent' in *Essays upon Several Subjects* (1747).
19. *Ibid.*
20. F. Hutcheson, *A Short Introduction to Moral Philosophy*, bk.iii, ch.7 (Glasgow, 1747).
21. Hutcheson, *A System of Moral Philosophy*, vol.ii (London, 1755), bk.iii, ch.8.
22. V. L. Collins, *President Witherspoon*, vol.ii (Princeton, 1925), p.188.
23. Shepperson, *op. cit.*, p.10.
24. *Idem*, p.12, citing Witherspoon, *The Dominion of Providence over the Passions of Men* (Philadelphia, 1776).
25. Cited in R. B. Sher, *Church and Universities in the Scottish Enlightenment* (Edinburgh, 1985), p.274.
26. Adam Smith, *Wealth of Nations*, bk.vii, ch.3.
27. David Hume, *Letters*, ed. J. Y. T. Greig, vol.ii (London, 1932), p.184.
28. *Idem*, p.303.
29. B. Rush, *Plan for the Establishment of Public Schoools* (Philadelphia, 1786), reprinted in F. Rudolph, *Essays on Education in the early Republic* (Cambridge, Mass., 1965).
30. Cited in *A Rising People: The Founding of the United States*, compiled by the American Philosophical Society and others (Philadelphia, 1976), p.198.
31. Rush, *Notes on Education, 1789.* (ms The Library Company of Philadelphia).
32. Cited in R. J. McCluskey, *The Works of James Wilson* (Cambridge, Mass., 1967), vol.i, p.213.
33. G. Seed, *James Wilson* (New York, 1978), p.17.
34. *Essays on the Principles of Morality and Natural Religion* (Edinburgh, 1751).
35. Seed, *op. cit.*, p.72.
36. J. Bryce, 'James Wilson; An Appreciation', *Penn. Mag. Hist. and Biog.*, lx (1936), p.361.

Bibliography

The most up-to-date and comprehensive information is listed in R. B. Sher's *Church and University in the Scottish Enlightenment* (Princeton and Edinburgh, 1985), pp.373–4. The following are among the more accessible secondary sources: W. R. Brock, *Scotus Americanus* (Edinburgh, 1982); O. D. Edwards and G. A. Shepperson, *Scotland and America: a study of cultural relations* (Glasgow, 1975); D. Sloan, *The Scottish Enlightenment and the American College Ideal* (New York, 1981); M. White, *Philosophy of the American Revolution* (New York, 1978); G. Wills, *Inventing America: Jefferson's Declaration of Independence* (New York, 1978).

A full list of secondary sources dealing with James Wilson is included in Geoffrey Seed's *James Wilson* (New York, 1975), pp.219–20. The standard biography of John Witherspoon is V. L. Collins' *President Witherspoon*, 2 vols (Princeton, 1925). Other studies include R. J. Fechner, *The Moral Philosophy of John Witherspoon and the Scottish-American Enlightenment* (phd Diss., Univ. of Iowa, 1974); J. L. McAllister, Jr., 'Francis Alison and John Witherspoon: Political Philosophers and Revolutionaries', *J. Presbyterian Historical Soc.* (Philadelphia), 54 (1976), 1, 38; G. A. Shepperson, 'Theology and Politics: John Witherspoon', *New College Bull.* (Edin.), 14 (1983), 9–15; M. L. L. Stahlman, *John Witherspoon. Parson, Politician, Patriot* (Philadelphia, 1976).

Robert Adam: Landscape with castle.
Towards the end of his life Robert Adam, high priest of the
Neoclassical style, turned to an eclectic, picturesque mode
which foreshadowed the Romantic movement.

Conclusion

PETER JONES

NO TWO GROUPS of scholars agree how to define the nature and limits of a cultural movement, how to establish its causes and effects, how to trace its origins and demise. No single date marks the beginning or end of the Scottish Enlightenment, no single tenet united its most distinguished figures, no single view typified their approach, although, like the overlapping strands of a rope, enough links existed to ensure harmony of effort for more than half a century.

Attempts to understand the nature of man and society fostered enquiry into social and political arrangements, and encouraged systematic study of change and an awareness of history; the goals of much scientific work were explicitly practical, and the notion of improvement was everywhere apparent. Hume remarked that 'the only immediate utility of all sciences is to teach us how to control and regulate future events by their causes', and in an essay of 1752 he declared: 'the spirit of the age affects all the arts, and the minds of men being once roused from their lethargy, and put into a fermentation, turn themselves on all sides, and carry improvement into every art and science'.

But the Scottish Enlightenment, it is generally held, did not survive the death of its great men. The urge for rapid political change, evident in the American War of Independence, the French Revolution and the Romantic movement, was inimical to the moderation they had counselled. Moreover, the cult of the individual and his emotions was the antithesis of the disinterested judgment which they canvassed as the only sure means to social sympathy and harmony. Moderation may well be a recipe for stability, but it is unlikely to appeal to those already engaged in the passionate pursuit of their ideals, or to fanatics of any kind; moreover, Hume's advocacy of calm judgment sat uneasily with his belief that man is primarily motivated by his passions, not by reason. Inner tensions of this kind do not help to secure the impetus of a movement.

Another factor, one foreseen by Smith and Ferguson, was the fragmentation of knowledge which follows increasingly specialised inquiry. Specialisation usually needs funding beyond the means of individuals and small institutions, and scientific research, especially, requires a long training which puts it beyond the comprehension of outsiders. Though the boundaries between disciplines are largely a matter of convenience, the limitations on human time and energy prevent more and more people from crossing them. It is no longer possible to be at the forefront of several disciplines as men were in the Enlightenment.

The authors of this book have traced some of the plans and accidents which combined to enable men who came from different directions to work in parallel for a time, and to pursue recognisably similar goals. The value of ideas lies in the use to which they can be put, and the extent to which they can be developed in new contexts. Special effort is often needed, however, to discern the authorship and early life of those ideas, and to recognise the true achievement of our ancestors. It is part of our cultural duty, nevertheless, constantly to re-assess the debts we owe to them, for we cannot tell in advance what we might be able to learn from them. The ideas of Hume and Smith, Black and Hutton, which have been absorbed into our present ways of thinking will continue to need re-interpretation as our understanding of man and nature changes.

The Poker Club; Minute Book, 1776.
Members include Joseph Black, 'Jupiter' Carlyle, John Clerk of
Eldin, Henry Dundas, Adam Ferguson, John Home, David
Hume, William Robertson, John Robison, and Adam Smith –
among the 'men of genius and learning' with which this book
began.

List of the Poker Club
26th Jany 1776

1 Lord Elibank D.+
2 Dr Carlyle
3 Professor Ferguson
4 Mr. Fordyce
5 Mr John Home
6 Mr George Dempster
7 Mr James Ferguson
8 Mr Andrew Crosbie
9 Mr William Pulteney
10. Mr William Nairne
11 Mr David Hume D.+
12 Mr James Edgar
13 Mr John Adam
14 Dr Robertson
15 Mr Andrew Stewart
16 Mr Adam Smith
17 Sr John Dalrymple
18 Dr Blair
19 Sr Adam Ferguson
20 Sr John Whitefoord

21 Mr Baron Mure D.+
22 Mr David Ross
23 Dr Black
24 Lord Elliock
25 Mr Baron Grant D.+
26 Mr Ilay Campbell
27 Mr James Dundas D.+
28 Mr John Clerk
29 Colonel Fletcher
30 Sr James Stewart D.+
31 Mr Hume of Ninewells
32 Mr Andrew Grant D.+
33 Colonel Campbell
34 Mansfield Cardonnel
35 Mr Dr Ferguson
36 Mr Robert Chalmers
37 Mr Robert Cullen
38 Mr George Brown
39 Professor Robison
40 Mr William Gordon D.+
41 Mr George Home
42 Lord Advocate H. Dundas
43 Capt Elliot

About the Authors

DAVID DAICHES, a graduate and honorary graduate of the University of Edinburgh, received his doctorate at Oxford, where he was Fellow of Balliol College. Subsequently he went to the United States where he was Professor, first at the University of Chicago, and then at Cornell. He returned to Britain to teach at Cambridge, where he was a Fellow of Jesus College, and in 1961 he became Professor of English at the University of Sussex, of which he was one of the founding fathers and is now Emeritus Professor. He returned to Edinburgh in 1977 and was Director of the Institute for Advanced Studies in the Humanities at the University of Edinburgh from 1980–86.

His many books include a study of the development of the Authorised Version of the Bible, critical studies of the modern novel and of modern poetry, a Critical History of English Literature, critical and biographical works on Milton, Burns, Boswell, Scott and Stevenson, and his 1983 Gifford Lectures, *God and The Poets*. In 1991 he was awarded the CBE for Services to Literature.

PETER JONES is a professor of Philosophy and, since 1986, Director of the Institute for Advanced Studies in the Humanities, in the University of Edinburgh. A graduate of Cambridge, he has held many posts as Visiting Professor in the United States, Canada, Australia and Malta. He is the author of numerous works on aesthetics and the history of philosophy, including *Hume's Sentiments* (Edinburgh, 1982). He delivered the Gifford Lectures in Aberdeen in 1995 under the title "Science & Religion before and after Hume".

D. D. RAPHAEL was born in 1916 at Liverpool and was educated at the University of Oxford. After World War II service in the Army and then the Civil Service, he held professorial appointments in New Zealand, Glasgow, Reading, and London, retiring in 1983. He has also held Visiting Professorships in the USA. His publications have been mainly in Moral and Political Philosophy, including *The Moral Sense* (1947), *Moral Judgement* (1955), *The Paradox of Tragedy* (1960), *Political Theory and the Rights of Man* (1967), *British Moralists 1650–1800* (1969), *Problems of Political Philosophy* (1970), *Hobbes: Morals and Politics* (1977), *Justice and Liberty* (1980), *Moral Philosophy* (1981), *Adam Smith* (1985). He was much involved in the Glasgow Edition of the Works of Adam Smith, acting as the main editor of *The Theory of Moral Sentiments* and as one of the editors of the *Lectures on Jurisprudence* and the *Essays on Philosophical Subjects*.

R. G. W. ANDERSON is Director of the British Museum. After receiving his doctorate from Oxford he joined the Royal Scottish Museum in Edinburgh where he studied the collections associated with the early chemistry professors, including Joseph Black. Moving to the Science Museum in London he worked in the Wellcome Museum of the History of Medicine, afterwards becoming Keeper of the Department of Chemistry. In 1984 he returned to Edinburgh as Director of the Royal Museum of Scotland and subsequently of the National Museums of Scotland.

He has written on the history of chemistry, notably *The Playfair Collection and the Teaching of Chemistry at the University of Edinburgh* (1978) and (with J.G. Fyffe) *Joseph Black: A Bibliography* (1992); on early scientific instrumentation; and on the history of museums. From 1988 to 1990 he was President of the British Society for the History of Science.

JEAN JONES was born and bred on a farm near Kelso, Roxburghshire. After she left Oxford University she worked as a free-lance editor and historian of science. Her publications include 6 articles on James Hutton in *Annals of Science*, and G.Y. Craig and E.J. Jones (eds.), *A Geological Miscellany* (2nd ed. Princeton, 1985). In 1986 she organised the 'Hotbed of Genius' exhibition which was the occasion for this book; in 1989 she organised the exhibition 'Revolutions in Science; 1789–1989', which traced scientific developments since the Scottish Enlightenment, and in 1990, 'Morals, Motives & Markets', an exhibition to commemorate the bicentenary of Adam Smith's death.

ARCHIE TURNBULL became Secretary to the Edinburgh University Press in 1953 and retired in 1987. A graduate and honorary graduate of Edinburgh, and Fellow of the Royal Society of Edinburgh, he has taken a keen interest in the social and cultural history of post-Union Scotland. Books on the subject published by the Edinburgh University Press include *After the '45* (A. J. Youngston) *Scotland in the Age of Improvement* (R. Mitchison and N. T. Phillipson), *The Making of Classical Edinburgh* (A.J. Youngson), *Philosophical Chemistry in the Scottish Enlightenment* (A. Donovan), *Scotus Americanus* (W. R. Brock), *The Democratic Intellect* (G. E. Davie), *Experience and Enlightenment* (C. Camic) and, most recently, *Church and University in the Scottish Enlightenment* (R. Sher).

Index

Illustrations are in italics after the main entry.

Some Saltire Publications

J D McClure	*Why Scots Matters*	0 85411 039 9	£2.95
Geoffrey Barrow	*Robert the Bruce and the Scottish Identity*	0 85411 027 5	£1.00
I B Cowan	*Mary Queen of Scots*	0 85411 037 2	£2.50
David Stevenson	*The Covenanters*	0 85411 042 9	£2.95
Kenneth MacKinnon	*Gaelic: a Past and Future Prospect*	0 85411 047 X	£7.95
Meston, Sellers and Cooper	*The Scottish Legal Tradition (New Ed.)*	0 85411 045 3	£5.99
Rosalind Mitchison (ed.)	*Why Scottish History Matters*	0 85411 048 8	£5.99

(contributions from Geoffrey Barrow, AAM Duncan, Alexander Grant, Michael Lynch, David Stevenson, Bruce P Lenman, TM Devine, RH Campbell, Christopher Harvie)

William Neil	*Tales frae the Odyssey o Homer owreset intil Scots*	0 85411 049 6	£7.95
William Ferguson	*Scotland's Relations with England: a Survey to 1707*	0 85411 058 5	£12.99
Paul Scott	*Andrew Fletcher and The Treaty of Union*	0 85411 057 7	£12.99
Paul Scott	*Walter Scott and Scotland*	0 85411 056 9	£7.99
David Stevenson	*Highland Warrior: Alasdair MacColla and the Civil Wars*	0 85411 059 3	£12.99
David Daiches	*Robert Burns, the Poet*	0 85411 060 7	£12.99

Saltire New Poetry
| Raymond Vettese | *A Keen New Air* | 0 85411 063 1 | £6.99 |

Forthcoming Editions (Autumn 1995/Spring 1996):
| John Sibbald Gibson | *Edinburgh in the '45: Bonnie Prince Charlie at Holyroodhouse* | 0 85411 067 4 | £7.99 |
| Thorbjörn Campbell | *Standing Witnesses: an Illustrated Guide to the Scottish Covenanters* | 0 85411 061 5 | £15.99 |

Complete list (and details of Saltire Society membership etc.) available from the Saltire Society, 9 Fountain Close, 22 High Street, Edinburgh EH1 1TF